New Directions in Social Theory

New Directions in Social Theory

Race, Gender and the Canon

Kate Reed

SAGE Publications
Los Angeles • London • New Delhi • Singapore
www.sagepublications.com

First published 2006

Reprinted 2007

 SAGE Publications Ltd
1 Oliver's Yard
55 City Road
London EC1Y 1SP

SAGE Publications Inc.
2455 Teller Road
Thousand Oaks, California 91320

SAGE Publications India Pvt Ltd
B 1/I1 Mohan Cooperative Industrial Area
Mathura Road, New Delhi 110 044
India

SAGE Publications Asia-Pacific Pte Ltd
33 Pekin Street #02-01
Far East Square
Singapore 048763

British Library Cataloguing in Publication data

A catalogue record for this book is available from the
British Library

C 978-0-7619-4270-2
P 978-0-7619-4271-9

Library of Congress Control Number: 2005928701

Typeset by Newgen Imaging Systems Pvt Ltd, Chennai
Printed in Great Britain by TJI Digital, Padstow, Cornwall
Printed on paper from sustainable resources

This book is not intended to be a political or historical chronicle, only a series of recollections, which always are selective and tinted by one's own experience and ideology.

Isabel Allende, *My Invented Country: A Memoir*

Social theory is what we do when we find ourselves able to put into words what nobody seems to want to talk about. When we find those words, and say them, we begin to survive. For some, learning to survive leads to uncommon and exhilarating pleasures. For others, perhaps the greater numbers of us, it leads at least to the common pleasure a pleasure rubbed raw with what is: the simple but necessary power of knowing that one knows what is there because one can say it.

This, whatever else, is what makes social theory worth reading.

Charles Lemert, *Social Theory*

For Mary Evans

Contents

Contents

Part Two: Modern Sociology

Part Three: Contemporary Sociology

Biographical Note

Kate Reed is a lecturer in Sociology at the University of Sheffield. She has published broadly in areas such as social theory, gender, race and ethnicity, and the sociology of health, illness and medicine. She is the author of *Worlds of Health* (Praeger 2003).

Acknowledgements

The book has taken just over two years to write. The idea for the book, however, was conceived several years ago during my time teaching social theory to undergraduates as a PhD student at the University of Southampton. The book was written during my time as a lecturer at the University of Kent and completed at the University of Sheffield. As a result, there are numerous people I would like to thank from a variety of institutions. Thanks, first, to the editorial staff at Sage for their help and support. Thanks to those who commented on the initial proposal, including Wendy Bottero, Larry Ray and John Solomos. My participation in a British Sociological Association round-table discussion in 2004 on sociological theory and its audiences, along with Graham Crow, John Holmwood, Gregor McLennan and Larry Ray, also helped me to develop the book's argument. Informal conversations with others on social theory have also helped immensely with the development of the book. In particular, thanks to John Jervis for social theory discussions over cake and hot chocolate during the writing process, and to Les Back for conversations on C. Wright Mills and others. Also thanks to Richard Jenkins and Bridgette Wessels for discussions in and around social theory. Special thanks to Claire Alexander for making me think hard about my overall arguments and for her insightful comments regarding race and ethnicity. Thanks to Graham Crow for his encyclopaedic knowledge of sociology. Thanks also to colleagues at the Department of Sociological Studies at the University of Sheffield for giving me the space to finish the book on arrival there.

Finally, thanks to close friends, in particular Mel Semple and my family – my mum Ann, my dad Lewis, siblings Sarah, Nick, and especially my fabulous and entertaining younger brother Dominic. Finally, I would like to extend special thanks to my partner Leo, who has been essential to the production of the book. He has helped me to develop ideas, read the manuscript and has personally made me very happy.

1

Introduction

As sociology students, or academics of sociology, many of us have read a variety of books about the origins and development of sociological theory. We are taught through these books and through standard curricula design various 'facts' about the development of the subject. According to Parker, 'producing great social science is a gift credited to great men of history and relayed to students through the imagery of a patriarchal lineage' (1997: 124). As a sociology student myself (many years ago), I studied the work of the founding fathers and their contemporaries. I was taught to examine the work of each theorist by turn but never really to question why these theorists were canonical or classical, taking for granted the story that I was being told about sociology's past, present and future. I thought that this was a 'true' story of the development of the canon. It was not until I was a PhD student some years later, teaching on an undergraduate social theory course myself, that I began to think about the authenticity of the sociological canon as told through the textbooks. I began to ask, why is the history of the discipline taught in this way? Can we take for granted that these were the discipline's founders?

In core courses and textbooks on sociological theory, social theorists often appear to be dropped into the curriculum and presumed important. For example, when the origins of sociological theory are taught, canonical writers such as Marx, Weber and Durkheim are often unquestionably presented as the founders of the discipline. These authors are presumed to make up a coherent 'canon' of theorists. According to Stones (1998), the question of whether a discipline such as sociology should have a discernible and recognizable canon of works or thinkers that in some sense provide a core of that discipline is a vexed one. Nevertheless, in literature and curricula on the development of the sociological canon, a canon of thinkers has been presumed to exist. Furthermore, this canon of sociology is presumed to be male, and Jewish or white. Students are seldom taught about the racialized and gendered nature of the origins of the canon. If the gendered and racialized nature of the canon is acknowledged, this is only explored at the end of core courses or textbooks rather than integrated into the discipline's history.

There are, of course, many theorists who do situate the classical canon and the work of the founders of the canon in a political context, in the

context of the Enlightenment, drawing on the various political and philosophical influences on sociological theorists' work (e.g. Callinicos 1999; Ray
1999). However, most accounts of the history of sociology never question the
validity of theorists and the history of the discipline. There seems, then, to be
a presumption that the founding fathers and Comte, who coined the term
'sociology', were the only ones who mattered in accounting for sociology's
origins. As Parker argues, there is a breathtaking failure on sociology's part
to apply the social constructionist perspective to itself. According to him, this
is something of a paradox because the discipline, which

> debunks everything else by socializing whatever it studies, deifies and
> reifies a tiny number of individuals at the expense of an understanding
> of their historical and institutional conditions of emergence. The
> orthodox narrative is enshrined in teaching practices by a move from
> founders to classics, a mapping of persons to texts, short circuiting
> historicization and inventing a canonical tradition of quasi-sacred
> writings, most of which were written between 1840 and 1920. (1997: 124)

In light of Parker's claims, I began to study various social and political
writers and activists who have written 'sociologically', but who have, throughout the development of the discipline, remained ghosts or shadows on the
fringes of, or outside, sociological theory. These are theorists who have written social theories just as worthy of our attention as those identified as canonical. These are theorists who are female and/or black who have been
excluded from the boundaries of social theory because of their gender or
race and because they often wrote social theories that include an analysis of
gendered and racial inequality.

Historically, a range of social theorists have written beyond the boundaries of sociological theory. For example, W.E.B. DuBois, Harriet Martineau
and Anna Julia Cooper were all writing their social theories during the
period of European classical theory but remained outside its boundaries.
This also occurred in the case of the dominant paradigm of American social
theory of the 1950s and 1960s. This was a time when theorists such as Hannah
Arendt, Frantz Fanon and Simone de Beauvoir were also writing theories of
sociological interest, yet they remained outside the canon. Such a process of
exclusion has at times been performed by outsiders themselves, who have
chosen to remain outside the discipline, or by sociological theorists working
within dominant social theoretical paradigms. However, perhaps more
frequently it has resulted from the countless sociological reconstructions of
those paradigms that we find in contemporary accounts of social theory.

Contemporary social theorists writing about the history and development
of sociological theory have tended to internalize the conservative views of
gender and race often held by early sociological theorists, rather than
looking beyond these. They have subsequently failed to explore the deeply
gendered and racialized nature of the origins and development of sociological

theory. Furthermore, those writing general accounts of the history of socio-logical theory have tended to be white men who view sociology's past as a past largely about white or, in the case of classical theory, mostly Jewish men.[1] Therefore, accounts have come to reflect this.

It is these contemporary accounts, however, that have drawn boundaries around who and what constitutes sociological theory. They have shaped mainstream perceptions of sociological theory, providing us with what Parker (2001) argues is a somewhat selective history of social thought. Within these accounts certain theorists (namely, white and/or Jewish men) are seen to up-hold the sociological tradition, whereas others are simply missed out. Such a selective presentation of the history of sociological theory applies not only to its origins but also to its development throughout the twentieth century.

It is only now – after the gendered and racial challenge to social theory occurring from the late 1960s onwards and after disciplinary shifts towards postmodernism – that such views are beginning to be questioned and previ-ous exclusions redressed. The deconstruction of sociological theory and opening up of the canon have meant that those outside authors of the past have now become an important part of social theory's present and future. This has significant implications for the status of sociological theory as a dis-cipline. If the canon has been opened up to include 'outsiders' does this mean that sociological theory has lost its specificity?

The aim of this book is to explore the ways in which, as sociological theory has developed, certain theorists have come to be seen as sociological insiders whereas others have stayed on the peripheries or outside the discipline. The book explores the ways in which insiders often may not see themselves as in-siders. For example, the classical theorists hardly saw themselves as socio-logists, yet they are viewed as founding fathers of the discipline. Why is this so? Although I recognize that there are many reasons why theorists are included or excluded from social theory, the particular aim of this book is to explore why some theorists have been excluded from the canon because they are black or female (or both) and because their social theories included an analysis of race and gender.[2] From the outset, the exclusion from the canon of those writing from the position of the racial and gendered 'other' and those writing social theories around issues of race and gender are explored. Although accounts of the development of sociological theory have been con-cerned with inequality and power, this has been mostly in relation to social class, not race or gender. Consequently, many authors have been excluded from the sociological canon.

It is important to be clear here about what is meant by race and gender. Put crudely, gender refers to the social relations between the biological sexes. To put it another way, to study gender is to study the socially structured differentiation of the sexes. In terms of race and ethnicity, these are both contentious concepts and ideas that refer to social and political distinctions made between people and groups of people (Knowles 2003). They are not natural or fixed categories. However, these ideas and concepts are used discursively to make social distinctions between people, which subsequently often have material consequences (Bulmer and Solomos 1999). Throughout the book, I explore the ways in which the unequal construction of social relations between the sexes, and between racial categories, has led to the exclusion of black and female social theorists from social theory. In doing so, I also focus on the ways in which an exploration of inequality in terms of gender and race has been excluded from the centre of social theory.

The book moves on to explore the ways in which this exclusion has changed over time. As the canon has opened up, class analysis has declined and once-peripheral topics such as race and gender have become more central. It asks, has social theory now included those seen previously as outsiders? If so, what does this mean for the future of social theory? In exploring the history and development of social theory in this way, I hope not only to provide an exploration of the process of inclusion and exclusion but also to showcase the work of some of the most fascinating social theorists who have, until recently, written their social theories from beyond the boundaries of social theory.

Before these issues are explored, the remainder of this introduction gives some background information to the book. First, it provides some brief examples of the diversity of social theories and theorists and how they have changed over time. This section aims to give background information on the history of sociological theory. Second, changes in key concepts and substantive concerns in sociology are explored. This provides a background to arguments developed later on in the book about the gendered and racialized nature of the history and development of sociological theory. Moving on, the reasons behind changes in sociological theory and theorists are explored. Accounts of social theory in particular tend to focus on the relationship of social change to social theory. They also tend to explore the ways in which theorists and theories change as paradigms of theory and theorists are challenged and overthrown. However, within this introduction, the importance of the process of selection and exclusion of sociological theorists based on race and gender are also explored. This issue, as already suggested, underpins the main argument of the book. The final sections of the introduction concentrate on the aims, structure and outline of the book.

Sociological Theory Past and Present

As presented in core courses and textbooks on the history and development of sociological theory, the discipline has gone through radical changes over the past century or so, from the classical theories concerned with revolution and industrialization, to the focus of many contemporary theories on issues of deconstruction and *difference*. Each theory and school of thought in the development of sociological theory has developed in varied and often competing ways in order to explain the social world of the time. Social theories have thus varied dramatically according to time and place. Within this introduction (and in the book more generally), I am not aiming to write (or rewrite) an extensive history of social theories past. (There are plenty of books that attempt this already). However, if we take a few examples of theorists and theories written over time, we can see the enormity of the diversity and change that have been part of the history of sociological theory. We can see the ways in which theorists develop theories in response to other theories, competing to best explain and explore the societies of their times.

Comte, for example, developed scientific 'positivist' views of sociology to combat what he felt to be the destructive philosophy of the Enlightenment (Ritzer and Goodman 2004a). Marx was a founder of revolutionary communism and, in sociology, historical materialism. He wrote extensively on the alienating effects of capitalism and, along with Engels, wrote the *Manifesto* on the eve of the 1848 revolutions. The members of the Chicago School wrote of urbanization and social change, too, but developed an empirical focus in their theories to explore issues happening in their own city during the early part of the twentieth century. Talcott Parsons, writing in the 1950s, developed grand functionalist optimistic theories that reflected the economic boom in the United States. During the 1960s such authors as Goffman in the United States provided a challenge to grand theories through the development of micro approaches aimed at studying the minutiae of social life. During the 1970s, while the United States was still at war with communism, Gouldner called for a more reflexive approach in sociology. During the 1980s and 1990s, within European sociological theory, such sociological theorists as Giddens and Bourdieu attempted to deal with issues of structure and agency. In contemporary theory there has been a shift from sociological theory to social theory and a move in emphasis from economics to culture. Many theorists are attempting to deal with these after-effects of postmodernism. Throughout its emergence and development, then, sociological theory has produced diverse and often conflicting theories in response to one another and to the society in which they inhabit.

According to Elliott and Ray (2003), over the past 20 years social theory has undergone significant change. There has been a broad sense of disillusionment with classical forms of social theory and a significant diversification of new conceptual approaches. According to them, this diversification has ranged from re-examination and revitalization of older forms of thought, such as the resurgence of Marxist cultural theory, to the development of new positions, including cultural studies, postfeminism and queer theory (ibid. xii). Traditions of thought previously ignored or marginalized have been rediscovered and reinterpreted, creating new approaches in the process. The rise in postmodernism has also had a profound effect on the social theory canon. With its emphasis on decentred subjectivity, difference, otherness, undesirability and ambivalence, the coherent and cohesive canon of a century before has been blown apart.

Along with these various changes in sociological theory, there has also been a change in theorists and their popularity. Theorists have, of course, changed over time as sociology as a discipline has developed and schools of thought have changed. Some theorists, including the founding fathers Marx, Weber and Durkheim, have maintained an enduring presence in social theory well after their death. Other theorists, however, have been popular only during the time they were writing and shortly after (e.g. Spencer). Spencer was influential during the nineteenth century – the time he was writing – and both European and American theorists adapted his theories shortly after his death. However, Spencer soon fell from favour. As Parsons remarked in the introduction to *The Structure of Social Action* (1949), 'who now reads Spencer?' Furthermore, there are theorists who remained on the peripheries of the canon at the time of their writings only to be instated at a later date. For example, Simmel sat on the peripheries of the classical canon at the time he was writing during the late nineteenth and early twentieth centuries but has now been inserted into social theory. Some even claim he is postmodern (Weinstein and Weinstein 1993).

We can see that the history and development of sociological theory have been presented as a varied and diverse field of study that has changed enormously over time. As presented in histories of the discipline, social theorists seen to make up the social theoretical canon have been a diverse and changing group.

Changing Concepts: Class, Gender and Race

Shifts in theoretical models and theorists have been accompanied by continual change in the types of theories developed and by changes in the dominant concepts and substantive areas in sociology. For a long time social class has been a central element in the development of the discipline. Sociologists have long identified social class as one of the key types of social stratification. Class and socioeconomic patterns of inequality are central themes in sociological theory from the founding fathers onwards. Class was central to the work of Marx and Weber, who focused on the newly emerging class structure of industrial capitalism in the nineteenth century. The centrality of the concept of social class within sociology continued throughout the twentieth century in Britain through the work of such authors as Goldthorpe *et al.* (1968) and in the United States in the work of such people as E.O. Wright (1976). There has, however, over more recent years been a retreat from class analysis in the discipline. According to Skeggs (1997), the retreat from class has occurred across a range of academic areas. Those retreating from class either ignore it or argue that class is becoming redundant. Furthermore, a great deal of postmodernist theorizing dismisses class as a relic from the past. The concept of difference has come to stand in for inequality in many cases (ibid.).

The same cannot be said for the concepts of race and gender. In her recent book *Gender and Social Theory*, Evans (2003) entitles one chapter 'Now you see it, now you don't' when talking about the relationship of gender to social theory. Historically, both women as theorists and gender as a subject of study have long been invisible within sociological theory. Oakley (1974) traces this back to the era of classical sociology, an era in which women were most oppressed. According to Oakley, the early sociologists writing during the classical era established a number of traditions that have subsequently shaped the place of women in sociology. These include a biological reductionism applied to gender roles, a presumption that women belong in the private sphere and a 'functionalist' analysis of the family that puts women naturally within the home. This was a view that was held for a long time by many sociological theorists working within the field.

Similar points can be made regarding the relationship of sociological theory to race. According to Parker (2001), in interpretations of the origins of sociological theory there is often a failure to explore the relationship between modernity, slavery and imperial domination. There is also a failure to explore race and ethnicity in the work of the classical theorists or to explore the connection between the early eugenics movements and social science journals. Thus, from the outset the concept of race as an aspect of stratification central to the study of sociological theory has been bypassed. As we see within this book, while sociological theories were developed on race and gender during the early part of the twentieth century, it was not until later that gender and race as concepts and substantive concerns became more central to the discipline.

During the 1970s, women attacked sociology for its refusal to admit women both institutionally and theoretically (Evans 2003). There were further attacks on sociology from homosexuals and people of colour, who voiced their dissatisfaction. Sociology was accused of refusing to acknowledge or study the worlds of people who were not white or male. It was accepted that sociology had always included the working class in its remit, but this was a remit that had defined social exclusion or social disadvantage mostly in terms of discrimination in the labour market. A new agenda began to challenge existing sociology (ibid.). Since that time, both race and gender have become increasingly important theoretical and substantive areas within sociology. As an area of sociology, race has grown to become an increasingly popular subject of study. Gender has also become a core element of contemporary sociology courses. This has, of course, affected social theory. According to Elliott and Ray (2003), contemporary social theory has come to underpin academic output in fields as diverse as gender studies, cultural studies, film studies, psychoanalytic studies, communications and media studies, postcolonialism and queer theory.

Throughout the development of sociological theory, certain concepts and substantive concerns have dominated the discipline, although these have changed over time. As shown here, although class has dominated the discipline historically as both a key concept of analysis and a substantive concern, gender and race have now become more central as analyses of stratification and have grown to be significant substantive areas of study within the discipline. More specifically, as Skeggs (1997) highlights, with the advent of postmodernism *difference* has actually now come to stand in for different analyses of stratification.

Reasons behind Changes in Sociological Theory

When we study sociological theory and the development of sociology more generally, we can see that there have been many changes in theories, in theorists and in concepts and substantive areas. Some examples of these have been given in the sections above. This diversity and change are reflected in core courses on sociology and in core textbooks. But why have there been these changes in sociological theory, concepts and theorists? There are numerous reasons. In textbooks and courses on sociological theory these are often related to two issues in particular, social change and paradigmatic revolutions. These are outlined below.

Social Change

First, the most prominent reason given for changes in theory, theorists and concerns relates to social change. Changes in social theory reflect changes in society and the explanations used to explore these changes. The theories of the classics reflect a response to revolution and crisis across Europe. The grand theories of Parsons were a response to the economic buoyancy of the golden era. The inclusion of feminist writings and writings on race into sociology relate to the women's movement and the civil rights movement. In terms of more recent theory, Elliott and Ray (2003) argue that the rapid expansion in competing versions of social theory can be seen as resulting from broad-ranging changes in social relations in modern institutions. For example, they argue that the analysis of postmodernism or cosmopolitan culture as a core concern of social theory is an effect of the complex process of globalization, transnational finance and capital movements, as well as global civil society (ibid. xi). Indeed, according to them, an array of social developments and political transformations – including new information technologies, the hyper-technologization of war and the proliferation of globalized risk – have been crucial to both disciplinary specialization and interdisciplinary studies within the academic humanities and social sciences (ibid. xi–xii). Therefore, change in social theory and sociology more generally will always reflect changes in society.

Paradigm Shifts

Second, the sociological canon is often presented as changing over time depending in part on whether the discipline is engaged in the practice of 'normal' or 'revolutionary' science (Kuhn 1970). According to Holmwood (1996), the idea that a major transformation of categories and concepts is part and parcel of a progressive development within any rigorously pursued undertaking has been reinforced by Kuhn's account of the natural sciences as a process of dramatic change. According to Kuhn (1970), during periods of 'normal science', the primary task of scientists is to bring the accepted theory and fact into closer agreement. As a consequence, scientists tend to ignore the research findings that might threaten the existing paradigm and provoke the development of a new and competing paradigm. Kuhn argued that a scientific revolution is a non-corroborative developmental event whereby an older scientific paradigm is replaced at least in part by an incompatible new one. Social theory has been subject to this kind of influence on change. In moments of revolutionary science, new theoretical paradigms have replaced the old. Also at such times of revolutionary science, the discipline of sociology has frequently reached out to incorporate new or forgotten figures, for example Parsons' reintroduction of Weber in the 1930s (Ritzer and Goodman 2004a). Paradigm shifts, therefore, are outlined as another reason why there are changes in theories, theorists and concepts over time.

These accounts of the ways in which theorists, concepts and sociological theory have changed over time and their subsequent explanations are important. However, there is a third explanation for such changes that is only ever glossed over in most existing accounts of sociological theory. This relates to the ways in which the history and development of sociological theory have been based on selection and exclusion.

Selection and Exclusion

Whenever we look back on the development of social theory, we are also constantly reinterpreting and rewriting it. As social theorists we are engaged in an ongoing process of construction. Sometimes we simply forget theorists and theories and then remember them at a later date. Canons often change through such selective amnesia, as Ray (1999) argues with regard to the classical canon. The canon is subject to both forgetting and remembering. Theorists come in and out of fashion as they are forgotten and then rediscovered (e.g. Simmel). At other times, however, theorists and theories appear to be actively excluded either by their contemporaries or in accounts written about the history and development of sociological theory. This process of selection and exclusion, whether part of a conscious attempt to exclude or relating to the fashions and fads social theory is heir to, plays a large part in constructing the history and development of sociological theory.

Within this book I want to explore the issue of social theoretical exclusion in the context of gender and race. I want to ask why throughout the development of sociological theory certain theorists and topics have been excluded from accounts of social theory whereas others have been venerated. How does this relate to theorists' gender or race and to their social theoretical focus on aspects of inequality such as class, gender and race? Contemporary accounts of the history and development of social theory tend to presume the importance of some theorists and topics without challenging this presumed importance. They often fail to explore the gendered and racialized nature of the emergence and development of sociological theory. It is the aim of this book to challenge existing accounts of social theory. In doing so, the book exposes some interesting social theories that have been written from outside the discipline.

This Book: Themes, Aims and Arguments

As mentioned earlier, this book aims to explore how, why and by whom social theorists are ascribed their roles as insiders or outsiders with respect to the sociological canon. In particular, two issues are highlighted here. First, those viewed historically as sociological insiders are on the whole presented as being white and/or Jewish men. Second, female and black social theorists are mostly cast in the role of sociological outsiders. As the book shows, through the selection of white, male theorists as insiders and black and female theorists as peripheral figures or outsiders, the discipline's history as told in accounts of sociological theory is a partial one. It is partial because it excludes some excellent sociological theory written from the fringes or beyond the boundaries of sociological theory. Nevertheless, the white, male vision of the history of the discipline has become fixed in our memories of what sociological theory is and is seen to represent the truth about the discipline's past and present.

The book explores the ways in which theorists are ascribed their positions through a process of self-selection. In this sense social theorists may decide to identify themselves as sociological insiders or outsiders. Historically, sociological theorists may also have acted as disciplinary gatekeepers, deciding who was included and who was not. Finally, and perhaps most importantly, contemporary social theorists writing accounts of the history and development of sociological theory often decide who are deemed to be sociological insiders and who are not. Thus, some theorists are written into sociological theory's history whereas others are simply left out or excluded. The book takes three key points in the development of sociological theory to explore these issues of selection and exclusion: classical theory, theories of the golden age and contemporary and future social theory. It looks at the ways in which the position of outsiders and peripheral figures has been transformed through these different eras, focusing on the rigid insider/outsider constructions of the classical tradition, on the half-hearted attempts of sociological theory to include outsiders in the politicized canon of the 1960s and on a marginal acceptance of outsiders through the deconstruction of the contemporary canon. In the final chapter of the book, possible ways forward for a more inclusive social theory are developed, along with an exploration of the implications of this for the future of social theory.

In Parts One and Two, the chapters of the book take a similar format. The first chapter of each of these two parts is designed to provide an overview of sociological theory and an exploration of those deemed insiders and those deemed marginal figures, including an exploration as to why this was the case. The second chapter in each part also explores the work of those viewed as sociological outsiders, focusing on why they were outside and how their position in relation to contemporary social theory may have changed. This format changes in Part Three as it is argued that in contemporary social theory (with the advent of postmodernism) there has been a further inclusion of past outsiders. Chapter 6 focuses on exploring this inclusion, highlighting in particular the ways in which the work of a range of social theorists (white, male, black, female) can now be found in contemporary profiles of social theory. However, as I show, although women and black theorists are included in accounts of contemporary social theory, they are still ultimately sidelined in relation to white men. Thus Chapter 7 focuses on developing ways forward for a more inclusive social theory.

In order to illustrate the ways in which selective constructions of the discipline have been produced, the book needs to take part in a process of selection itself. The book selects a number of canonical insiders and outsiders in order to support its overall argument. The insiders chosen are those who have most often been seen as canonical or dominant figures within sociological theory, both in Europe and in America. In this analysis I have also included a number of marginal figures. The figures chosen here were peripheral figures at the time of their writings because their theories did not fit in with social theoretical trends of the time. These are theorists who have recently been rewritten into sociology's past and future as their theories have become more fashionable (e.g. Simmel).

As noted previously, in terms of outsiders, those chosen are black or female authors whose sociological theories have often included a racial or gendered dimension. This is because many sociological theorists working outside the canon during the nineteenth and twentieth centuries remained excluded because of issues of race and gender. By exploring the work of these gendered and racial outsiders, the book explores the changing relationship of the fields of race and ethnicity and of gender studies to the social theoretical canon.

It is important to be clear here that I am not making the claim that black and female theorists can theorize only about issues of race and gender (as becomes apparent in Chapter 7). Nor am I saying that we need to include people of colour and women into social theory in order to make the study of race or gender possible (white men are, after all, not beyond gender or race). However, when we look at the discipline of sociological theory, the inclusion of women and black people into social theory is often aligned with the position of the subject areas of race and gender within social theory. This does not suggest a causal link between the two but rather highlights a more complex connection that has been based on a relationship of mutual influence.

Although this book focuses on sociological exclusion in relation to issues of gender and race, in more recent times arguments about exclusion and outsider status have been made in terms of disability and sexuality and so on. The book could have included a whole range of other theorists who have been seen as canonical, peripheral or outsiders. However, it is not meant to be an exhaustive list of sociological theorists working both inside and outside the canon. Neither is it designed to be an exhaustive introductory textbook to the development of sociological theory. Its aim is rather to provide a critical account of the emergence and development of the discipline, looking at the ways in which (and also why) we construct selective histories of the canon and, in particular, exploring those selective histories in the context of gender and race. It is unnecessary to provide an exhaustive list of sociologists to do that.

Chapter Outline

Chapter 2 explores the origins of sociological theory. The aim of this chapter is to look at the origins of the discipline, focusing on its institutionalization and in particular the work of the founding fathers. Despite the fluid nature of constructions of classical theory, Marx, Weber, Durkheim and Simmel are presented as the key founders of the discipline. The chapter outlines the work of the classical theorists (in brief) and explores the reasons these theorists are seen as enduringly classical and canonical. In particular, two issues are highlighted in exploring the nature of the classical canon. First, those seen to make up this enduring classical canon are mostly Jewish and white men. Second, the work of these men is focused on socioeconomic issues; their views on gender and race are mostly conservative in nature and form subsidiary themes in their works. These attitudes are replicated in contemporary accounts of classical theory that fail to go beyond existing accounts of classical theory to explore the gendered and racialized nature of early sociology. As I show, this blinkered view of the classical era means that those female and black authors writing sociologically on gendered and racial inequality during this time have been cast out beyond the boundaries of sociological theory.

Chapter 3 focuses on those writers and activists writing 'beyond the boundaries of sociological theory'. These were contemporaries of the classical theorists who remained outside constructions of the classical canon. They were all authors who were 'thinking sociologically' and who provided insightful social and political comment. The chapter outlines the theories of the three chosen canonical outsiders, Harriet Martineau, W.E.B. DuBois and Anna Julia Cooper, exploring their relationship to the canon and their outsider status. The chapter moves on to explore one of the next phases in the development of sociological theory, focusing on the work of the Chicago School, which included work on race (although not black theorists). However, despite its affiliations with the Women's Chicago School and the work of Jane Addams, the Chicago School continued to exclude women from the core of the canon.

Chapter 4 moves on to focus on the golden age of sociological theory. The golden age or 'golden moment' (Lemert 1999: pt 3) refers to a time during the 1950s and 1960s when capitalism was booming after the Second World War. Constructions of sociological theory during the golden age present a fragmented picture, identifying a diverse range of sociologists within or on the margins of the canon. This chapter focuses on some of the dominant and marginal American and Europe-based sociological theorists of the time. It explores the ways in which whereas some theorists, such as Talcott Parsons, writing during this time worked within bounded sociological paradigms, others, including C. Wright Mills, Alvin Gouldner and the Frankfurt School, provoked by the growth in social movements, felt the need to move towards a more inclusionary canon. However, as is argued, although some sociologists working during the 1950s and 1960s began to turn towards the social and political issues of the time, most focused on the socioeconomic situation. Despite the civil rights and women's movements, sociological theorists appeared closed off to ideas from those theorists writing about inequalities of race and gender. Any attempts at the inclusion into the canon of authors writing about these issues were at best partial.

The aim of Chapter 5 is to explore the work of some of the social and political writers writing during the mid-twentieth century whose general social theories included an analysis of gender and racial inequality but who remained outside the sociological canon. It focuses on Hannah Arendt, Frantz Fanon and Simone de Beauvoir. Again, all of these writers were developing sociological theories and unearthing social inequalities of sociological interest, yet all remained outside the sociological canon. They were theorists who were kept out of the golden age canon by sociologists writing at the time and also by contemporary constructions of that canon. They have since become key figures in social and political thought. The chapter moves on to look at developments in feminist sociological theory and the sociology of race relations in the 1960s and 1970s.

Chapter 6 explores the position of the contemporary canon. It has been argued by many that postmodernism has led to a deconstruction of the sociological canon. The deconstruction of the discipline has meant an emphasis on interdisciplinarity and a shift in focus for sociology from traditional forms of inequality to an emphasis on *difference* and diversity. Such a shift has led to the opening up of sociological theory to include those previously classed as outsiders. The aim of this chapter is to explore the status of contemporary social theory, paying particular attention to the repercussions of deconstruction for so-called sociological outsiders. The chapter is split into three sections. First, it looks at the deconstruction of the canon, exploring the impact of postmodernism on the discipline. Second, it looks at the ways in which this opening up of the canon has meant that disciplinary insiders, marginal figures and outsiders are now found in textbooks on social theory. Third, it looks at the position occupied by outsiders in the canon. It highlights the ways in which social theory, although now more inclusive, still keeps 'outsiders' in positions of inequality.

The concluding chapter draws the book to a close and explores some of the possibilities for rewriting a non-exclusionary social theoretical past and developing a non-exclusionary social theoretical future. The chapter focuses, first, on the canon of the past and outlines the ways in which the canon must be opened up to explore the multiplicity of possible sociological histories. It advocates the incorporation of accounts and theorists of race and gender into existing accounts of the history of sociological theory. The chapter moves on to explore contemporary social theory and its future. Within this section suggestions are put forward for developing a more inclusionary social theory. These include a further centralization of issues of gender and race, a move to encourage outside social theorists to become public social theorists and, finally, a need for a more substantive and empirically linked social theory, which both conceptualizes and makes empirically operable social theories. Although I recognize the limitations to social theoretical change, the chapter explores the impact of these proposed changes on the future of social theory. For example, does the incorporation of outsiders mean an end to social theory? Does it lead to a more complex and less sociological social theory, as authors such as Mouzelis (1991, 1994) have suggested? The chapter explores these issues and concludes with an overview of the book and conclusion.

Notes

1. The racial categorization of Jews remains a contested issue that cannot be fully discussed here. According to Brodkin (1998), in her exploration of the history of Jewish identity in America, Jews came to be equated with the category 'white' after the Second World War. Jewish intellectuals were primarily responsible for this 'whitening' process. However, before this Jewish people were considered to be outside the boundaries of 'whiteness' and its privileges. This categorization of

Jews and the changing process of identification from non-white to white is acknowledged throughout this book.

2. The term 'black' was a tactical position developed in the United States and United Kingdom during the 1960s and 1970s, which both reflected and challenged the social inequalities of the racial landscape (Knowles 2003: 30). In more recent years such blunt forms of categorization have been challenged for failing to recognize diversity in identity and experience. As Knowles points out, there is much more to identity than situating whiteness opposite blackness. However, I use the terms 'black' and 'people of colour' in this context (particularly in earlier chapters of the book) in order to make clear the starkness of the racial landscape in the history of social theory. There is a clear distinction made between the categories of black and white that relates directly to those theorists included in the canon and those excluded. The theorists I discuss under the category black include African Americans, British West Indians and people from a range of other former European colonies. I want to make it clear that I am not trying to generalize people's experience here; however, what is apparent is that many people have been excluded from the social theoretical canon because they were viewed as 'black', whether African American or French African.

PART ONE

Classical Sociology

2

The Classical Tradition

This chapter explores the origins of sociology, focusing on its institutionalization and in particular the work of the founding fathers. In evaluating the classical canon, Ray (1999) asks the key question: What is the classical tradition? In part, he argues, it is derived from the works that have shown the strongest staying power, notably those of Marx, Weber, Durkheim and latterly Simmel. However, like other traditions, it is in part a contemporary construction, and the way we view sociology's past is closely linked to our present concerns. As such, he argues that the classical corpus is not fixed but subject to both forgetting and remembering. Within this chapter, however, what I make clear is that despite the fluid nature of constructions of classical theory, Marx, Weber, Durkheim and Simmel are still presented as the key founders of the discipline. The aim of the chapter is to outline the work of the classical theorists and to explore the reasons why these theorists are seen as enduringly classical and canonical.

In particular, two issues are highlighted in exploring the nature of the classical canon. First, those seen to make up this enduring classical canon are Jewish or European white men. Second, the work of these men is focused on socioeconomic issues; their views on gender and race are mostly conservative in nature and form subsidiary themes in their work. As shown within this chapter, the views of the classical theorists towards issues of race and gender reflect the position of women and ethnic minorities within society during the time they were writing.[1] However, these views have been perpetuated in contemporary accounts of classical theory. These contemporary accounts have also tended to internalize rather than challenge or explore such views. In doing so, they have taken social class as the only aspect of inequality worthy of attention during the classical era, thus failing to explore the gendered and racialized nature of early sociological theory. Furthermore, this blinkered view of the classical era means that those female and black authors writing sociologically on gendered and racial inequality during this time have been cast out beyond the boundaries of sociological theory.

The chapter begins with a brief outline of the development of the discipline, focusing on the discipline's institutionalization and the emergence of the classical tradition. The chapter moves on to introduce the classical tradition, sketching out the work of Marx, Weber and Durkheim and exploring their social theories and methods. In particular, their focus on the socio-economic situation of the time is emphasized. The chapter also includes the work of Simmel in the context of classical sociology. His focus on fragmentation and culture made him more of a peripheral figure in relation to the holy trinity. His more inclusive attitude towards women is also explored here as a contrast to the work of the other three theorists.

Finally, the chapter explores the positions of these classical theorists. It is argued that although these theorists may not have been identified as canonical all the time, in accounts of the history of sociological theory these Jewish and white men have come to be seen as the founding fathers. They are seen as the classics, the standard markers from whom sociological theory developed. What is highlighted in this final section is that whereas these three have come to be seen as classics and founders, women and black theorists have been excluded from classical sociological theory, as have issues of race and gender more generally. Thus, I conclude that sociological theory has historically been presented as a discipline written by white or Jewish men about white or Jewish men. Gender and race as theoretical areas of concern and female and black theorists are seldom featured in visions of classical sociological theory. This in turn has set the parameters on which subsequent developments in sociological theory have been based.

The Emergence of Sociology

The roots of sociology are often traced back to Greece from France and Germany, with possible excursions to Italy and the United States (Parker 1997). As argued in the introduction, the production of social science is accredited to great men of history, which is taught through imaginary and patriarchal lineage (ibid.). Reconstructions of the history of sociology normally begin with the search for laws of society and the work of Auguste Comte (1798–1857). It was Auguste Comte who coined the term 'sociology' after the French Revolution in the eighteenth century. Comte is conventionally understood to be the first 'proper' sociologist. Along with Henry Saint-Simon, he set about devising a science of society. These theorists were, however, somewhat constrained by the conservatism of post-revolutionary France. Saint-Simon (1760–1825) was influential in his development of both conservative and radical Marxist theory (Ritzer and Goodman 2004c: 14). Saint-Simon wanted to preserve society as it was, although he did not want to return to life as it had been in the middle ages. He was also a positivist who believed that the study of social phenomena should utilize the same scientific techniques as those used in the natural sciences.

As mentioned previously, in discussing sociology's origins Comte is the one accredited with coining the concept 'sociology'. Comte believed that the study of sociology should be scientific. He was greatly troubled by the anarchy that pervaded French society and was critical of thinkers whose writing had contributed to the Enlightenment and revolution (ibid. 15). He developed his scientific 'positivist' view to combat what he felt to be these destructive philosophies. He developed 'social physics', or what in 1839 he called 'sociology' (Pickering, cited ibid. 16). This new science, which in Comte's view would ultimately become the key science, was to be focused on social statics (existing social structures) and social dynamics (social change) (ibid.). This involved the search for laws of social life. Comte did not push for revolutionary change; he felt that society would evolve naturally for the better. He thought that social reforms would help with this process. Overall, Comte felt that sociology would become the key scientific force in the world because of its capacity to discover and understand laws in society and its ability to develop reforms aimed at addressing social problems.

Comte's attempts to establish sociology as a scientific discipline spread throughout Europe. The period from the 1880s to the 1920s was one in which sociology began to be established as a scientific discipline in universities in Europe and North America. During this time, more professors began to call themselves sociologists or to take the ideas of sociology seriously (Fulcher and Scott 2003: 32). Thus sociology started to be institutionalized and identified as a discipline in its own right. The process of institutionalization was uneven and gradual. It began in France, largely through the work of Durkheim, then spread to Germany through the work of Weber. It is with these two theorists, alongside Marx, that the classical tradition of sociological theory has been identified. Marx, Durkheim and Weber may or may not have classified themselves as sociologists; Marx and, to a lesser extent, Weber did not nominate themselves as sociologists. They became sociologists after they died. Durkheim, of course, was a formidable advocate for the emergent discipline, yet he could not be said to have founded sociology alone (Parker 1997). These three theorists are, however, known in accounts of the discipline's development as pioneers of the sociological canon. Their identities and work helped demarcate the boundaries of classical sociology. According to Sharrock *et al.* (2003a), despite a succession of theoretical fashions in sociology, the ideas of these thinkers continue to exert a powerful influence on the discipline that, if anything, has increased over the years since they first wrote.

Race, Gender and the Classical Agenda

Although these three theorists use different frameworks and methods in their analyses, they all produced social theories that reflected the times in which they lived. According to Lemert (1995: 201–2), classical social theories arose when Europe was most disrupted by the uncertain progress of the modern world. Marx and Engels wrote their *Manifesto* just before the 1848 revolutions. Marx wrote *Capital* during the economic confusion of the two subsequent decades. Durkheim developed his social theories during the *bouleversement* that arose as a result of France's attempts, during the Third Republic, to conclude its century-long revolution by founding a modern social order. Weber and Simmel wrote during the time of social conflicts in Germany caused by its transition from a traditional society to a world industrial power. Each of these men, in their personal lives as in their published social theories, reflected the tensions of their times (ibid.).

In terms of the politics of gender, these classical social theorists worked during an era when women were highly oppressed. The late nineteenth century saw the development of the women's suffrage movement and feminist activism. However institutionally during this time women were deprived of most individual freedoms, rights and responsibilities, and ideologically they appeared as little more than chattels, slaves or decorative ornaments (Oakley 1974: 21). This era also saw the development of scientific racism. Attempts were made at this time to classify humans based on 'race' and language; notions of racial otherness were pervasive in western society, as were the notions of orientalism and exoticism (Pieterse 2002). Darwinian evolutionary theories were also popular at this time (Solomos and Back 1996). Furthermore, the development of the capitalist system itself was endowed with a racist ideology that condemned all 'coloured' peoples to racial and cultural inferiority (Sivanandan 2001). The social theories of the founding fathers to varying degrees reflected rather than challenged these attitudes towards women and the issue of race. As we see later in this chapter, this in part set a precedent for the history of exclusion of race and gender from the core of sociological theory.

It is important, of course, to note here the position of Jews during the time the classicists were writing. Marx, Durkheim and Simmel were all Jewish by origin. The emergence of hostility towards Jewish people is traced back to Christian and medieval times, even to pre-Christian times by some. However, many scholars argue that the real hatred towards Jews came only with the development of scientific racism in the mid-nineteenth century and the beginning of an organized political movement against Jewish power in Germany from the 1870s (Kushner 2002: 68). This was, of course, precisely the time Marx was writing. However, according to Kushner, Jews were not viewed as being necessarily inferior by race thinkers during that time, nor were they automatically deemed racially unsuitable to be allowed entry into the nation-state. In fact, during the early part of the twentieth century (when most of the classical theorists were writing) in certain parts of Europe (particularly Germany) there was some evidence of social advancement and greater tolerance towards Jews. This remained the case until the Great Depression and Hitler's rise to power in 1933. After this time the attitude towards Jews became one based on persecution.

An exploration of the oppression of Jews did not appear directly in the work of the classics with the exception of Marx. He wrote briefly on Jews in his essay 'On *The Jewish Question*' (1844), an article written initially as a response to claims made by another German Jewish thinker, Bruno Bauer. Bauer claimed that Jews could never be emancipated and granted full rights as citizens because their commitment to Judaism was not compatible with the universalism of human emancipation. Marx attacked this argument in his essay by stating that religion is not incompatible with the development of the state and that the demand for civil rights should not be made on the basis of religion. Furthermore, human emancipation for Marx was not about religion but about political emancipation. Marx has been criticized for being anti-Semitic. As Draper (1977) argues, there is a wealth of literature alleging that Marx's essay was anti-Semitic because of its association of Jews with money-making, self-interest and the commercialism of the bourgeoisie. As I note throughout this chapter, the attitudes of Marx, Durkheim and Simmel towards the oppression of Jews and to their own Jewish identity were characterized on the whole by ambivalence. Furthermore, it is argued that the Jewish identity of these classics does not seem to have impeded their incorporation into the sociological canon or hindered their recognition as founders of the discipline.

Overall, the classics undoubtedly reflected the tensions of their time. However, the tensions on which these theorists focused were mostly socio-economic. Socioeconomic patterns of inequality and social change are central themes in the sociological theory of the founding fathers and onwards. They were fundamental to the work of Marx and Weber, who focused on the newly emerging class structure of industrial capitalism in the nineteenth century. This focus on capital and, in particular, class set a precedent for the development of sociology during the twentieth century, as these became principal issues of concern. When it comes to issues of race and gender, however, the classics have little to say.

Details of the work of the classical theorists are explored in the following section. The main thrust of their general social theories, methods and attitudes towards race and gender are explored. It is important to emphasize here that the theories of these sociologists are outlined only in brief. This is because the purpose of this book is not to provide an in-depth analysis of their work but rather to look at why they came to be seen as classical theorists, to analyse and put into context the origins of gendered and racial exclusion. Key readings are provided at the end of the chapter for those who want more in-depth information on these authors.

Karl Marx and the Theory of Capitalism

Karl Marx (1818–83) was a German social theorist who, along with Frederick Engels, developed one of the most important social theories of the nineteenth century, which was situated in the nineteenth-century genre of grand evolutionary theorizing (Ray 1999). He was the founder of Marxist social thought and had an enduring impact on sociology. However, during the time he was writing, Marx refused to regard himself as a sociologist. His theories were too broad to be encompassed by the term 'sociology' (Ritzer and Goodman 2004a: 22). It was not until later, during the twentieth century, that Marx's ideas began to receive attention within sociology.

Marx was a founder of revolutionary communism and historical material- ism. He shared with other social theorists writing during the mid-nineteenth century a concept of progressive social evolution set against a perceived crisis in European society. This would be resolved through a combination of scientific knowledge and social agency (Ray 1999). Marx saw history as a succession of modes of production, from primitive communism through cap- italism to communism. Each mode of production for Marx marked an in- crease in the level and scale of production and defined a dynamic class conflict, which is the driving force of historical change. Throughout these transitions capitalism is marked out as a mode of production whereby the products of labour generally take the form of commodities that are then brought and sold in the marketplace. The market price of commodities is based on their value, on the necessary labour time required to produce them. In this capitalist system, labour power is also a commodity (Callinicos 1999: 87).

Marx wrote extensively on the alienating effects of industrial capitalism in the 1860s, when the system was developing. He offered a theory of capitalist society based on his own image of the basic nature of human beings (Ritzer and Goodman 2004c: 23). He believed that people are basically productive. In order to survive, people need to work in and with nature; by doing so, they produce the food, clothing, tools, shelter and necessities that enable them to live (ibid. 23–4). According to Marx, capitalism is a structure (or series of structures) that erects barriers between an individual and the production process and other people. Ultimately, it even divides the individual himself or herself (ibid. 24). This is what Marx meant by the concept of 'alienation'. Alienation is the breakdown of the connection among people and between people and what they produce. Alienation occurs because capitalism has evolved into a two-class system in which a few capitalists own the production process, the products and the labour time of those who work for them (ibid.). Under capitalism, this was how Marx came to define a two-tiered class system, divided between those who owned property and those who were property- less–those who owned the means of production and those who laboured for this production. According to Marx, in a capitalist society instead of naturally producing for themselves, people produce unnaturally for a small group of capitalists.

At the heart of Marx's social theory was revolution and the transforma- tion from capitalist to communist society. Marx felt that the contradictions and conflicts within capitalism would lead dialectically to its ultimate collapse (Ritzer and Goodman 2004a). According to Marx, contradictions gradually develop in each form of production; capitalism in particular is subject to cyclical crises that arise because market conditions change more rapidly than investment and production processes. This has three consequences: immiseration and exploitation of the proletariat, technological change and a breakdown in capitalism (Ray 1999). This results in class conflict and revolution, leading to greater freedom for the dominated classes.

According to Callinicos (1999), Marx does not simply imply that capitalism is likely to break down purely because of its economic contradictions. Marx's own expectations of the downfall of capitalism depended on the key development of a working class capable of taking control of society. Socialist revolution is indeed necessarily a process of *self*-emancipation (ibid. 94). Although Marx talked about the means for social change, he said very little about what a socialist or communist society would look like. Deeply critical of utopian socialists' attempts to anticipate the course of history by developing detailed comments about a postcapitalist society, Marx said very little about communism (ibid.). In one of his last key texts, 'Critique of the Gotha Programme' (1875) he suggested that distribution in the 'higher phase of communist society' will be regulated 'from each according to his abilities to each according to his needs'.

In Marx's theory of capitalism and social change, social class as a form of stratification and mobilization for change took centre stage. Marx was not interested in gender as a form of inequality or as a catalyst for social change. He focused primarily on issues that arose in a masculine public sphere and rarely concentrated on the position of women in capitalist (or socialist) society (Ray 1999). This was reflected in his own personal life and his relationship with his wife. His marriage to Jenny was based on a traditional division of labour. The year that Marx died, Engels published the classic Marxist analysis of patriarchy; 'Origins of family, private property and the state' (1884). This was a text that did include a focus on women – albeit in a secondary form of analysis. Here women's oppression was seen to have an economic basis in property relationships. Gender inequality, it was argued, was established in capitalist society through the emergence of the state and private property. As men became dominant in the division of labour, women became concubines, slaves and prostitutes and were subsequently excluded from the public realm. Through socialism and the eradication of private property women would be freed (Ray 1999). This inclusion of women's position was an advance from Marx's earlier theories; however, it was still superficial as women were still viewed by Engels and other Marxists as secondary to men.

Marx's theories on the development and eradication of capitalism did pay more attention, perhaps, to the issue of race and ethnicity. In 1844, Marx reviewed two studies on the Jewish question written by Bruno Bauer, another young Hegelian. Here (as noted earlier) Marx explored the issue of Jewish emancipation in the context of overall political emancipation from capitalist society. He also provided a systematic interpretation of colonialism. This he did in essays such as 'On imperialism in India' (1853), in which Marx turned his critique of bourgeois civilization against its colonial system (Lemert 1999).

Colonialism was significant for Marx because of its contribution to the development of capitalist societies. Colonialism was an extension of capitalism and could be analysed in terms of the proletariat and the bourgeoisie, but translated onto a world stage. Despite this work, Marx can still be viewed as Eurocentric as his work is written from a European perspective. Furthermore, as we have seen, according to Draper (1977), his work on the Jewish question has often been deemed anti-Semitic, relying on social stereotypes. Overall the same conclusions can be drawn from his work on both race and gender – that is, that the emancipation of women or black or Jewish people was not his central concern; the emancipation of the proletariat was. Furthermore, for Marx, the emancipation of women, black people and Jews would not occur because of their own mobilization; rather, it would be a welcome consequence of social change brought about by class agitation.

Although Marx may not have placed either gender or race at the centre of his key social theories, his work has nonetheless been integrated into contemporary feminist and race theories. According to Delamont (2003), there is a relatively large literature in feminist sociology that starts from Marx. For example, Hamilton (1978) used Marx as the key theorist for understanding how women experienced the passage from feudalism to capitalism in Europe. Dorothy Smith (1987) combined elements of Marxism and ethnomethodology in her feminist theories. Other feminists have used a Marxian analysis to explore issues of sexuality (e.g. Barrett 1988). These are only some of the ways in which Marx has been used in feminist analysis.

Furthermore, Marx's theory of capitalism (and Marxism more generally) has been taken up by numerous contemporary theorists in the study of race and ethnicity and in postcolonial studies. For example, as Chapter 5 explores further, during the early 1960s Frantz Fanon drew heavily on Marxism and placed Marx's theory of capitalism onto a global stage. During the 1980s such authors as Robert Miles incorporated the study of racism into mainstream social theory (Solomos and Back 1996). These are but two of the race theorists who have drawn on a Marxist analysis.

In conclusion, Marx has been identified as one of the most significant social theorists of his time. There are, of course, many problems with his social theories. For example, Marx's communist vision does not seem to have worked. State socialist societies were extremely authoritarian. Since 1991 almost all such formerly socialist economies have become capitalist. Furthermore, the proletariat, whom Marx saw at the forefront of revolution and change to a communist society, is often the most opposed to communism. Marx's work is also gender blind and based on western, Eurocentric conceptions of progress. However, despite these problems, Marx is a canonical figure who is viewed as central to the development of sociology. His social theories were broad and wide ranging, making Marx an enduring member of the sociological canon even if he did not see himself as a sociologist.

Emile Durkheim and the Study of Social Facts

Emile Durkheim (1858–1917) was born in Lorraine, in rural eastern France. His father and forefathers for generations were rabbis. Though Durkheim abandoned these roots in a provincial religious community, he devoted his intellectual life to studying, teaching and advancing the sociology of moral life (Lemert 1999: 69). Unlike Marx, Durkheim has been perceived as aggressively sociological, despite the fact that he drew heavily on the discipline of psychology in his social theories. His central concern was the problem of order. He aimed to move away from earlier speculative sociology to establish the sociological method as 'scientific'. He also wanted to establish sociology as a discipline in its own right, distinct from the disciplines of philosophy, psychology and economics. He wanted to show that sociology was a practical discipline, that it was relevant to social reform.

As Hadden (1997) notes, one of Durkheim's major contributions was to help define and establish the field of sociology as an academic discipline. Durkheim distinguished sociology from philosophy, psychology, economics and other social science disciplines as he argued that sociologists should study particular features of collective life. He saw sociology as the study of social facts, things that are external to, and coercive of, individuals. In *The Rules of the Sociological Method* (1895) we see an outline of his positivist position – 'seeing social facts as things'. According to Durkheim, a social fact is any way of acting, fixed or not, that is capable of exerting an external constraint on the individual. Society is viewed as a moral order with observable regularities. For Durkheim, social facts are features of the group. They cannot be studied apart from the collective or be obtained from the study of individuals. Some examples of social facts are suicide, religion, urban structures, legal systems and moral values such as 'family values'. Durkheim argued that these are features of collective existence that cannot be not reduced to the individuals who constitute it (Hadden 1997). Durkheim set about studying these social facts in a variety of social settings. One of the most famous of his studies is *Suicide* (1897). This study has been considered by many to be the first work of empirical sociology. Its aim was not only to provide an account of suicide but also to illustrate how his methodology could be applied to even the most individual acts. The book was intended to serve as a model of sociological explanation (Fulcher and Scott 2003: 37).

Durkheim wrote extensively about social change as well as about the scientific study of social facts. He held an evolutionary view of social change. He believed that social evolution starts from simple and undifferentiated and moves to complex and differentiated forms of organization. Durkheim drew a distinction here between the physical and moral division of labour in which the latter is determinant. Durkheim's evolutionary theory is structured around the major change from mechanic to organic forms of the division of labour, which described a transition from simple segmented to complex, functionally integrated societies (Ray 1999).

An exploration of this transformation forms the centrepiece of *The Division of Labour in Society* (1893), his first major work. Central to the book are two types of solidarity identified by Durkheim, mechanic and organic solidarity. These are different forms of moral order with distinct collective conscience/consciousness. According to Durkheim, as societies became industrialized and urbanized, they become much more complex. Accompanying these changes is an increasingly sophisticated division of labour. This destroys mechanical solidarity and moral integration. As a result social order becomes problematic. Durkheim believed that a new form of social order would arise in modern advanced society. This would be based on organic solidarity. Organic solidarity, as distinct from mechanical solidarity, consists of the interdependence of economic ties arising out of differentiation and specialization within the modern economy. From this there emerges a new network of occupational associations that link individuals to the state.

The exploration of differences between premodern and modern societies continued through many aspects of Durkheim's work, as did his emphasis on social facts, moral order and the relationship between the individual and the collective. For example, all these are present in his later work on religion.[2] Durkheim's emphasis on social facts can also be extended to his views on race and ethnicity. According to Stone (1977: 67), several of his works contain discussions of the problem of defining race and its irrelevance for the explanation of social facts. In his study *Suicide*, he insisted that Germans committed suicide more than other peoples not because of their blood but because of the civilization in which they were reared. According to Stone (ibid.), Durkheim rejected racial–innate in favour of cultural explanations of variations in suicide rates. He was sceptical of the claims that races were concrete factors in historical development.

Durkheim's views on social order, evolution and the division of labour can also be extended to his views on gender. Like Marx, Durkheim held very traditional views on gender. According to Oakley (1974), the perspective he held on women was shaped by biological doctrine. In his eyes women belonged 'naturally' in the family. Durkheim's analysis of the structure of the modern conjugal family was explored entirely from a male point of view. He regarded it as essential that men were committed to their work through the formation of professional/occupational groups, because for men an involvement in the family did not provide a solid moral basis for their continued existence (ibid. 22). According to Delamont (2003), the majority of feminist sociologists have not been able to draw analytic concepts from Durkheim as they have from Marx and Weber; liberal sociologists have, however, used Durkheim's approach to official statistics. Yet there are no feminists drawing on his concepts of 'anomie' or 'conscious collective', as there are feminists using ideology or patriarchy (ibid. 101).

Durkheim is one of the most frequently cited classical social theorists. He was a key founding father who set out to establish sociology as a scientific discipline. He developed a sociologically scientific method that focused on the study of social facts. He conducted perhaps the first empirical study in sociology on suicide. His work, however, has been critiqued for a variety of reasons. He is most often criticized for his study on suicide, which is based on official statistics. These depended on coroners' decisions on the ways in which deaths were classified as suicides, and it has been shown that their practices varied (Douglas 1966). Durkheim can also be criticized for slipping into a 'functional analysis' – assuming that societies as a whole have needs and that social structures automatically emerge to respond to these needs (Ritzer and Goodman 2004c). Like Marx's, his theories were also gender blind, and his vision for social change involved the sequestration of women within the private realm. Despite these problems, Durkheim is also a canonical figure. His work invariably forms an essential part in the telling of the story of sociology's development.

Max Weber and the Science of Interpretation

Max Weber (1864–1920) was the ideal-typical university scholar. Master of several fields, Weber wrote on music, economic and legal history, religion and sociology. He was a founder of German academic sociology even though a debilitating breakdown ultimately forced him to abandon his own professorship (Lemert 1999: 99). Weber is often seen as the founder of modern sociology because he provided a systematic statement of the conceptual framework of the sociological perspective. He developed a clear philosophy of the social sciences. In a number of substantive areas he grasped the basic characteristics of modern civilization. Through these empirical studies he identified key issues that became central to the discipline. Weber's legacy can often be seen as his sense of pessimism, his emphasis on the importance of ideas and his stand against overgeneralization. It could be said that his work represents one of the most systematic and comprehensive attempts to develop a comparative methodology, through which he wanted to highlight the specific rationalism of western culture (Ray 1999).

Weber saw sociology as 'a science concerning itself with the interpretative understanding of social action and thereby the casual explanation of its course and consequences' (1913: 4). His Sociology emphasizes *Verstehen*, or subjective meaning and understanding. His approach is often referred to as 'methodological individualism'. His theories, however, also convey a heavy sense of rationalization. Weber's methodological contribution to the formation of sociology was immense (Ray 1999). In his early commentaries on developing a methodology appropriate to sociology, Weber did not believe that sociology could establish laws of human behaviour comparable to those of the natural sciences. He did not believe that sociology could confirm evolutionary progress in human societies or develop collective concepts (such as the family) unless they could be situated in terms of individual action. Weber argued that sociology needed to develop an understanding of the meaning of actions; he developed this idea using the concept of *Verstehen*. On the basis of this, sociology would be able to work towards formal models or ideal types of action that could in turn be conducted on a comparative basis. Sociology in this sense, according to Weber, was not purely a subjective interpretation of action. Sociologists were also guided by certain norms. The findings of sociologists were open to scrutiny and criticism within the academy.

Within Weber's work, as in the work of Marx, the possession of economic resources is crucial for the achievement of ends. Weber was also prepared to characterize the extent to which people are unequally placed with respect to economic resources as their 'class position' (Sharrock *et al.* 2003a). However, Weber differed from Marx in his conceptualization of class. First, Weber's analysis of class emphasized market position, rather than property, as the form of criterion. Weber also felt that any resulting conflict would not polarize society in the way Marx had expected. According to Weber, there is a tendency towards increasing complexity of social structure, the multiplication of hierarchies rather than the polarization of society between two hostile camps (Ray 1999). Furthermore, class for Weber was only one aspect of stratification. He also identified status as a form of stratification. For Weber, status groups were usually communities that are kept together through shared consumption patterns and lifestyles of social esteem, rather that market or property position (ibid.). Weber also saw power or position in organizational groups as a form of stratification.

Weber did not believe in the possibility of developmental laws in sociology; rather, he presented rationalization as the most important trend of western capitalist society. Whereas Marx offered a theory of capitalism, Weber's work was basically a theory of rationalization (Brubaker 1984). In particular, he was interested in the issue of why institutions in the western world had become increasingly more rational while powerful barriers seemed to prevent similar development in other parts of the world (Ritzer and Goodman 2004c). Weber identified rationalization as the process whereby every area of human relationships is subject to calculation and administration. He saw rationalization as the growing calculation of action plus disenchantment with the world. He argued that rationalization pervaded all social spheres – politics, religion, economic organization, university administration, scientific laboratories and so on – and ultimately led to a life in a meaningless 'iron cage'.

Weber's social theory – certainly his theory of rationalization and theory of stratification – did not specifically include an analysis of gender. He was, however, married to a feminist activist named Marianne Weber, and some of his social theories have been influential within contemporary feminist theory. For example, his methodological emphasis on *Verstehen* can be seen as a precursor to subsequent feminist writings on standpoint epistemologies (discussed in Chapters 6 and 7). Furthermore, according to Delamont (2003), feminist sociology owes a large debt to Weber, for, according to her, it was Weber who brought into sociology the concept of patriarchy or, to be more precise, patriarchal authority. He differentiated three types of authority – charismatic, bureaucratic and patriarchal – as part of his attempt to theorize nineteenth-century European societies. Although second- and third-wave feminist theorists have not always located the roots of this term with Weber, they have nonetheless found it a useful label for male domination (ibid. 100).

In his theory of social stratification, Weber did include an analysis of race and ethnicity. He acknowledged the theoretical implications of recognizing nationalism, ethnicity and race as elements in the stratification systems of diverse societies. Several sections of *Economy and Society* are devoted to these issues (Stone 1977: 67). Weber regularly visited the United States and in fact was also one of the teachers of W.E.B. DuBois, one of the greatest writers on race and social theory (explored in Chapter 3). His visits to the United States and his subsequent engagements with American race relations made him more aware of the significance of these factors and their relationship to his general theories of social stratification (ibid.). He witnessed firsthand the ethnic heterogeneity of urban contexts such as New York and Chicago. Weber contrasted the position of the Negroes in America with the position of Native Americans. He identified the differential reaction of whites to these two subordinate groups as a consequence of slavery (ibid.).

However, it is on the issue of nationalism that Weber's work in this regard is best known. Indeed, although he included a focus on race and ethnicity in his social theories, he mostly concentrated on issues of nationalism rather than on racial inequality. He recognized that nationalism varied among different strata of society in relation to sentiments of prestige. Weber's approach to race fits in with his overall conception of sociology as the science that aims at the interpretive understanding of social action. His emphasis here, as with his other social theories, was on subjective definitions. For Weber this emphasis explains why it is that once qualities are defined as 'racial', whether they are innate or culturally created becomes irrelevant as far as the social behaviour is concerned (ibid. 68).

To summarize, Weber, like Marx and Durkheim, has come to be seen as fundamental figure in the development of sociology. As in the case of these other theorists, however, a number of criticisms have been levelled at his work. There has been criticism of Weber's method of *Verstehen*. This method could be seen as falling between two schools, subjectivity and objectivity, and fitting wholly in neither. Weber declared that his method should be located between these two choices, but he never fully explained how. There is often a contradiction between individualism in his method and his focus on large-scale social structures and world historical norms. This prevents him from fully developing macro sociology. Weber's sociology is also critiqued for being very pessimistic, with no room for social change in the iron cage. He provided us with no alternative visions of society and no opportunities for progressive social change. However, despite these problems, Weber's social theories earned him a place in the social theoretical canon and, along with Marx and Durkheim, he is a central figure in the development of sociology.

Evaluating the Holy Trinity

So far, we have explored the work of the holy trinity – Marx, Durkheim and Weber. These three theorists, as shown within this section, had differing relationships to sociology. Although Durkheim and, to a large extent, Weber both identified themselves as sociologists, Marx did not. He has become constructed as a founding father through accounts of the origins of the discipline from the 1970s onwards. Nevertheless, all three are seen as key founding fathers in sociology's history. Although they had diverse theories and methods, they were all working within the grand narrative of progress, and their theories all reflected the tensions of the times. Ultimately, their social theories were focused on socioeconomic issues. Although they did include analyses of race and gender to varying degrees in their explorations of forms of stratification, their views on these issues were often conservative, compatible with the norms of the time.

Peripheral Visions

Marx, Weber and Durkheim are ubiquitously regarded as the founding fathers. There have been other theorists who are much more marginal figures in the development of the discipline. A case in point is Simmel, a subsidiary figure in relation to the classical canon. Simmel's peripheral status to the canon can be explained partly by his own self-selected outsiderness, and it also relates to his alternative visions of society. Marx, Durkheim and Weber developed diverse theoretical frameworks. However, they were all working within a grand narrative and their theories were also weighted towards a socioeconomic focus. Unlike the other founding fathers, Simmel emphasized fragmentation, ephemerality and culture. The next section examines the work of Simmel. In particular, his more inclusive attitude towards women is noted here as a contrast to the work of the holy trinity.

Georg Simmel and the Fragmentation of Society

Georg Simmel (1858–1917) never held a significant position in a university. However, he was a founder (with Weber and Toennies) of the German

Sociological Society. In many ways Simmel lived the life of an independent bourgeois intellectual, which earned him the respect denied by the university establishment (Lemert 1999). He has often been regarded as a 'perennial outsider' to sociology and is considered to be the most neglected of the founding fathers (although this is perhaps more so in Britain than in the United States). It is difficult to give an overview of his work as it was so broad and fragmented and he was himself opposed to attempts to systematize or summarize his work. His style and approach differ from that of the other classical sociologists because of their fragmentary and ephemeral nature.

Simmel wrote short essays exploring segments of social life. These were rich in texture but unsystematic and often incomplete. His range of explorations is broad and varied: studies of art and culture, religions, money, capitalism, gender, social groups, urbanism and morality (Marshall 1998). Even love and prostitution are among the many topics he studied. Details rather than grand generalizations are the focus of Simmel's work. In contrast to the other founding fathers, he argued that although it is not possible to understand the whole of the totality itself, any fragment of study might lead one to grasp the whole. Until recently he was 'a stranger in the academy' (Coser 1991). Recently, however, he has been brought back into the canon as one of the key founders of symbolic interactionism, and more recently he has been seen as the key classical sociologist to establish debates on modernity and postmodernity (Weinstein and Weinstein 1993).

Simmel's sociology was not entirely intuitive and unsystematic (Ray 1999). He also developed a 'formal sociology'. His formal sociology was to study the forms of association that made generalized and routinized social interactions possible (ibid.). According to Levine,

> His method is to select some bounded, finite phenomenon from the world of flux; to examine the multiplicity of elements which compose it; and to ascertain the cause of their coherence by disclosing its form. Secondarily, he investigates the origins of this form and its structural implications. (1971: xli)

Simmel suggested that one can isolate the form of interactions from their content, so that apparently different interactions (with different contents) could be shown to have the same form (Abercrombie *et al.* 1988). Simmel believed it possible to separate form and content analytically in (relative) abstraction, if the rules for their identification are followed (Ray 1999).

One of Simmel's key studies was *The Philosophy of Money* (1900). Here Simmel was concerned particularly with the emergence in the modern world of a money economy that becomes separate from the individual and predominant (Ritzer and Goodman 2004c: 31). In *The Philosophy of Money*, Simmel argues that the development of money is a key element of a profound cultural trend. Simmel analysed money, the ultimate symbol of materialism, precisely as a symbol and stressed its cultural meanings. Money is indifferent to all specific purposes; the elevation of money stands for the dominance of means over ends in society. According to Simmel, the money economy creates a paradoxical kind of freedom; impersonal relations foster individuality, yet the decline of old social obligations promotes an atomization of social life (Ray 1999).

This theme forms part of a broader and more pervasive theme in Simmel's work – the domination of culture over the individual. Simmel felt that the modern world enabled wider social culture and all its various components (including the money economy) to expand. As culture expands, the importance of the individual decreases (Ritzer and Goodman 2004c). For example, as the industrial technology associated with a modern economy grows in complexity and sophistication, the skills and abilities of the individual worker grow less important. Eventually workers are confronted with an industrial machine over which they have little or no control. This amounts to what Simmel describes as 'the tragedy of culture' (ibid.).

Simmel included an analysis of gender in his social theory generally, and in these discussions of the tragedy of culture in particular. According to Ray (1999), Simmel was aware that the transformation of gender relationships is one of the core elements of social modernization. He went further than the others by regarding the very process of the formation of objective culture as gendered (ibid.). When he talked about objective culture he associated it with the male characteristics, which became dominant. Capitalism, according to Simmel, intensifies the dominance of male culture as money creates a division of labour between the domestic (unpaid) work of women and the external (paid) work of men (ibid.). As a consequence, a woman's economic value loses substance and she seems to be supported by her husband. Simmel also acknowledged the ways in which proletarian women had been chased from the home while bourgeois women were confined within it. As a result, economic autonomy was a curse for one woman and a blessing for another. According to Ray (ibid.), Simmel's analysis appears to resonate with some contemporary feminist theory. However, he ultimately fell back on essentialist notions of gender when he focused on female culture. This reflects the view, which we find too in Comte and Durkheim, that women are closer than men to nature (ibid.).

Simmel's discussion of the gendered differentiation of modern culture did not extend to an exploration of differences constructed along the lines of race and ethnicity. On these issues Simmel was relatively silent. However, his work on the stranger can be seen to explore issues of otherness (1950: 402–8). For Simmel the stranger is a wanderer who comes today but may go tomorrow. The stranger is someone who is different, someone who does not belong. Being a stranger is a form of interaction in itself, a way of relating to wider society. The behaviour of the stranger is marked out by independence from the rest of society. In talking about the stranger, Simmel alludes to the position of Jews in Europe and the merchant. This can in turn be related to notions of racial otherness, as the view of the stranger is one of both an outsider and a participant in a society.

As is the case with the other theorists discussed here, Simmel's work has been subject to numerous critiques. For example, according to Ray (1999), his formal sociology risked becoming a completely descriptive set of cases with no ability to actually explain anything. His work could also be contradictory. Within his social theories, on the one hand he views social structures as a form of interaction. On the other hand he sees them as coercive and independent of interactions (Ritzer and Goodman 2004c). Furthermore, he does not suggest a way out of the tragedy of culture. He sees alienation as an unavoidable part of the human condition. Marx, in contrast, was more positive and anticipated that alienation would be driven away by socialism. According to Ritzer and Goodman (ibid.), the most common criticism of Simmel's work is perhaps that it is fragmented, ephemeral and piecemeal. However, in comparison with the other theorists discussed so far, he does provide the most thorough focus on gender, recognizing the gendered nature of modernity despite appearing to fall back somewhat on naturalist explanations. Overall, although Simmel was a social theorist marginalized during the time he was writing, in recent years he has been rewritten into the sociological canon and has come to be viewed as an important figure in the development of the discipline.

The Endurance of the Classics

In this chapter, we have explored a selection of the works of the classics, outlining some of their theories in brief. The theorists discussed in this chapter – namely Marx, Weber and Durkheim, and more recently Simmel – have come to be seen as the founders of the classical canon of sociology. As argued, they have not always been seen as canonical and classical. For example, it was not until 1937, with the publication of Parsons' *The Structure of Social Action*, that Durkheim and Weber became firmly established among scholars in the English-speaking world. It was not until the 1960s and 1970s that Marx became identified as a founding father. Furthermore, Georg Simmel was invisible during the time he was writing but has attracted great attention in recent years. Despite the fact that these theorists have not been seen as canonical all the time, they have all nonetheless played a crucial part in the development of modern sociological thought. In accounts of the history and development of the discipline of sociology, the work of these theorists, and in particular that of Marx, Weber and Durkheim, has come to define the parameters of classical sociology.

If one picks up a textbook on classical sociological theory or attends an introductory module on the discipline, the theorists discussed here are always portrayed as the founding fathers. But why? What makes these theorists canonical or classical? Tiryakian (1994) outlines three criteria for judging a sociological work as a classic. First, it is a necessary reading for beginners because it demonstrates, captures and highlights the sociological imagination. Second, it has contemporary relevance and can be used by contemporary social theorists and researchers. Third, it offers enough depth and complexity that it is worth rereading at a later point in a sociologist's career. The works of the holy trinity, and latterly of Simmel, seem to fit all three of these requirements. They are required reading for sociology undergraduates, they are still used within contemporary theory, and sociologists continue to read and reread them. According to Sharrock *et al.* (2003a), the sheer extent of the influence exerted by Marx, Weber and Durkheim makes them essential reading for anyone who wishes to understand the nature of modern sociology. Furthermore, they argue that the works of these classicists provide us with a way of understanding important theoretical and methodological issues within sociology, as well as a means of appreciating the intellectual concerns that mark out sociology as a discipline.

The classical theorists are also widely regarded as being of key importance for contemporary social theory. According to Camic (1997), classical sociological theories are important not only historically but also because they are living documents with relevance to modern theorists and the contemporary social world. According to Parker (1997), new ways of legitimating the sociological classics have been emerging, with a growing interest in the *fin-de-siècle* precursors of postmodernity; authors ranging from Weber, Marx and Durkheim to Simmel and even Parsons are said to have anticipated recent conceptual developments. Furthermore, there are a variety of ways in which the classics have been used to illuminate recent phenomena. For example, J. Alexander (1988) has used some of Durkheim's ideas on culture and religion to analyse the Watergate scandal. Weinstein and Weinstein (1993) have presented a postmodernized version of Simmel's theories. Ritzer has drawn on Weber's theories of rationalization in his McDonaldization thesis (Ritzer 2000). Furthermore, Braverman (1974) has used Marx's social theories in his work on the labour process and monopoly capitalism.

The classics are widely influential and have come to be identified as the founders of the discipline. It must be noted here, though, that while these theorists are constructed as classics in accounts of the history of social theory, there is also recognition that other theorists played a part in the development of the discipline. For example, authors including Sharrock et al. (2003a) highlight the importance of scholars such as Herbert Spencer (1820–1903) in the development of sociological theory. Spencer was an early evolutionary theorist writing during the nineteenth century. Although perhaps not allocated the key role that the other founding fathers have had in the history of sociology, he has nonetheless had his followers and advocates in modern sociology. However, although the fluidity and diversity of the canon are recognized in the telling of sociology's history, there are theorists who have been excluded from accounts of classical social theory. These are female and black theorists whose social theories focus on gender and racial inequalities. They are excluded because they are black and/or female theorists, not white men, and because their social theories take not social class as their central focus but rather race and gender.

The Emergence of Sociological Exclusion

This chapter has shown how the work of the classical theorists was focused centrally on issues of socioeconomic inequality and change. According to Parker (1997), early sociology's engagement with inequality, power and the meaning of human life in a period of extraordinary upheaval was of key importance. However, dimensions of power and inequality in texts on classical theory are mostly associated with class analysis. The classical theorists wrote to varying degrees on other issues such as gender and race. For example, Simmel wrote extensively on the position of women. Weber had much to say about race and nationalism. However, the classical focus on race was often Eurocentric and fell back on essentialist visions of a 'natural' gendered division of labour. The issues of gender and race were peripheral to these theorists' other interests. Subsequently, gender and race have often been rendered invisible and sidelined in accounts of classical theory. Thus, with the emergence of a classical canon, there began a protracted period of racial and gendered exclusion in social theory. Furthermore, this sidelining and conservatism with regard to race, gender and classical theory is something that has been internalized in contemporary accounts of classical theory. Rather than exploring the gendered and racialized nature of the origins of sociological theory, highlighting the ways in which the classical theorists were implicated in this,[3] contemporary reconstructions of the classical era often fail to look beyond existing interpretations of classical theory. They take the focus on socioeconomic issues within the works of the classics for granted, thus reproducing, rather than looking beyond, classical social theory, perpetuating the dominance of social class and the exclusion of gender and race in social theory.

This in turn impacts on who is seen as classical and canonical and who is not. The acceptance of conservative views held about women and people of colour during the classical era, and the emphasis on socioeconomic issues in classical theory, have led to the exclusion of women and black social theorists from accounts of classical theory. During the classical era, there were a number of women social theorists and theorists of colour who have been excluded from accounts of social theory. According to Parker (2001), this exclusion is misguided. He argues that in studying the origins of sociology, it is equally important to explore the nineteenth-century and early-twentieth-century treatments of gendered and racialized inequalities in the work of authors such as Harriet Martineau, W.E.B. DuBois and Anna Julia Cooper. These are people who wrote acutely perceptive social theories from the position of gendered and racial exclusion during the time that the existing classics were written. They have, however, been omitted from most contemporary reconstructions of the origins of sociology. As noted before, if classics are seen as classical because of their enduring relevance for sociology, then why not theorists such as DuBois and Martineau? Their studies of racial and gendered inequalities are relevant to understanding both past and present society, but until very recently they have remained firmly outside the classical canon.

It could be argued, of course, that Marx, Durkheim and Simmel were Jewish and thus would have suffered as much racial prejudice as black theorists such as DuBois. Their Jewishness, however, has not stopped them being viewed as central to the foundations of social theory. In light of this, it would perhaps seem that race does not affect inclusion and exclusion from the sociological canon. If Marx, Durkheim and Simmel were Jewish but were included in the canon despite their Jewishness, then surely black theorists such as DuBois cannot have been excluded because they were black? As argued in the previous section, the inclusion of the classics into the canon, then, surely rests on the quality and endurance of their work, not on issues of race? This is not necessarily the case. Not only was the classical era a time of greater tolerance towards Jews in many parts of Europe (as noted previously), but these theorists did not really identify as Jewish and, in fact, held a somewhat ambivalent relationship to their Jewish identity. For example, Durkheim turned his back on his religious background and Marx has often been critiqued as being anti-Semitic. Furthermore, these theorists never really explored social inequality with regard to their own position as Jews or challenged racial inequality in general. Rather, these theorists (perhaps unwittingly) were directly caught up in a project of modernity whose backdrop was slavery and imperial domination. It was only half-heartedly that Marx and Weber tried to challenge this, placing race on the sidelines of their work on social stratification. Ultimately their theories did not directly challenge or threaten the thinking about race held at the time. In contrast, African American theorists such as DuBois and Anna Julia Cooper directly challenged racial inequality from their own experiences as 'black' African American social theorists. This challenge came at a time when 'racial otherness' was being inescapably associated with the being black. As Chapter 3 argues, such a direct challenge to racial inequality can be seen in part as a reason for the exclusion of these theorists.

The next chapter explores the work of theorists excluded from the sociological canon on the grounds of race and gender. These theorists wrote social theories that were just as relevant as those of Marx, Weber, Durkheim and Simmel. They have, however, remained outside the canon until recently.

The following chapter explores the work of these theorists, their exclusion and the reasons behind it.

Conclusion

This chapter has focused on an exploration of the origins and development of the classical canon. While it has recognized the diversity of the canon, what is clear is that Marx, Weber and Durkheim and latterly Simmel have been constructed as core sections of the classical canon. They are seen as classics because of the endurance of their works, many of which are still most relevant to analyses of contemporary society. They have influenced countless generations of sociological theorists and empiricists and have spurred many reinterpretations and reconfigurations of their own original theories. Marx, Weber, Durkheim and Simmel were theorists who aimed to explain the differences between traditional and modern societies. According to Lemert (1999), each of these men, in his personal life as in his published theories, reflected the tensions of his times.

As highlighted above, the classical theorists were mostly interested in socioeconomic patterns of inequality and social change. On the other hand, classical coverage of the issues of race and gender (as argued throughout the chapter) in varying degrees reflected the society of the time. With regard to gender in Simmel's work, this involved a battle between recognizing women's rights and succumbing to notions of biological reductionism. It involved an emerging interest in race as a scientific field of study by theorists such as Weber, along with a penchant for Eurocentrism (Marx). This in part set a precedent for a history of exclusion of the subjects of gender and race – and theorists of gender and race – from the core of sociological theory. As the classicists came to be seen as canonical, there were many other contemporaries of the classical theorists (public intellectuals and activists, all of whom were writing sociologically) who remained outside the core of classical sociology. The voices of people such as DuBois, Cooper and Martineau have been muffled by prejudice. In the next chapter we explore these voices.

Chapter Summary

- The aim of this chapter has been to explore the origins and institutionalization of sociological theory.
- In particular, the chapter has focused on the work of the founding fathers – Marx, Weber, Durkheim and latterly Simmel.
- These are European white and Jewish male theorists who have come to be seen as the founding fathers of sociology.

- They wrote their social theories during the late nineteenth and early twentieth centuries on the cusp of revolution and great social change.
- Their theories focus on socioeconomic issues but neglect, or provide conservative approaches, to gender and race.
- This focus on socioeconomic issues and neglect of gender and race has been internalized by contemporary accounts of classical theory.
- Furthermore, contemporaries of the classical theorists who were women or theorists of colour who wrote on gender and racial inequalities have been excluded from the boundaries of social theory.
- Thus began a history of gendered and racial exclusion, an exclusion that has been perpetuated in contemporary accounts of classical theory.

Further Reading

G. Ritzer and D. Goodman, *Sociological Theory* (McGraw-Hill, 2004), gives a good overall account of both classical and modern social theory. It also includes women authors and black authors. L. Ray, *Theorizing Classical Sociology* (Open University Press, 1999), provides good coverage of classical theory, also taking into account the gendered nature of the origins of sociological theory. For feminist accounts, see S. Delamont, *Feminist Sociology* (Sage, 2003). For accounts that include a focus on race, see C. Lemert, *Social Theory: The Multicultural and Classical Readings* (Westview Press, 1999). For more general accounts of classical theory, see I. Craib, *Classical Social Theory* (Harvester Wheatsheaf, 1992) and W.A. Sharrock, J.A. Hughes and P.J. Martin, *Understanding Classical Sociology* (Sage, 2003).

Notes

1. 'Ethnic minority' is widely understood in Britain to denote a category of people whose origins lie in countries of the new commonwealth and Pakistan; in other words, in former British colonies (Mason 2000: 15). Immigration took place from these places to the United Kingdom from the 1950s onwards. The term 'ethnic minority' often denotes homogeneity; however, diversity must be recognized between and within such categories.
2. In *The Elementary Forms of the Religious Life* (1912) Durkheim suggested that primitive religions embodied the idea of society. He argued that sacred objects were sacred because they symbolized the community. Religious culture held collective values and religious ceremonies in particular served to reinforce collective values. They also reaffirm community among individuals. This was easily identifiable in primitive societies but was less so in modern ones. In modern societies, it was difficult to find sacred objects and collective rituals. Overall, in his study of religion Durkheim was interested in understanding the universal functions of religious systems for the continuity of society as a whole.

3. Many textbook accounts of classical social theory fail to explore the gendered and racialized nature of early sociology; see Parker (1997) for an account of this. Many feminist authors have, however, explored the gendered nature of early sociology (see Delamont 2003; Evans 2003). Very few authors have explored the connections between race and classical theory (see Stone 1977).

3

Race, Gender and Hidden Classics

In the previous chapter we focused on an exploration of the origins and development of the classical canon. Although the diversity of the canon was recognized, what became clear through the analysis was that Marx, Weber and Durkheim, and latterly Simmel, have been constructed as constituting the classical canon. Although these theorists remain important in exploring the origins of sociology, there are many other contemporaries of the classical theorists (public intellectuals and activists, all of whom were writing sociologically) who have remained outside the corpus of classical sociology as a result of their gender and/or race and their social theoretical focus on gender and racial inequalities. The aim of this chapter is to explore the work of some of these black and female social and political writers whose general social theories included an analysis of gender and racial inequality.

The chapter focuses on the work of Harriet Martineau, W.E.B. DuBois and Anna Julia Cooper. All were developing sociological theories and unearthing social inequalities of sociological interest, yet all remained outside the classical sociological canon. They are theorists who have been kept out of the classical canon through reconstructions of classical sociological theory. This has changed somewhat, as I argue later on in the book, because shifts to postmodernism in the sociological canon have meant that it has been opened up and some past and present outsiders have now been inserted into it through reconstructions of social theory. However, until very recently, most accounts written on classical sociological theory have provided a very white or Jewish male portrayal of the canon, one that fails to include these other theorists in their accounts of classical sociological theory.

This chapter focuses on several issues. It first outlines the theories of the three chosen canonical outsiders, Harriet Martineau, W.E.B. DuBois and Anna Julia Cooper. It explores their relationship to sociological theory and their outsider status. The chapter asks why these theorists were kept outside interpretations of the classical canon. In doing so, the chapter explores the gender- and race-blind nature of sociological theory. It also explores the changing nature of these theorists' relationship to social theory through a focus on their relationship to contemporary social theory, gender and ethnic and racial studies. The chapter moves on to explore one of the next phases in the development of sociological theory, focusing on the work of the

Chicago School, which developed at the end of the nineteenth century and overlapped in time with classical theory. It reached its peak in America later, however, during the 1920s and 1930s. The Chicago School was renowned for its empirical studies of urban life concerned with the problems of social change and upheaval, and with the possibilities for social reform and the establishment of an ordered community. One of the reasons for exploring the school within this context is because of its relationship to race and gender. The Chicago School became known for its work on race, particularly in the work of Robert Park. There was also an equivalent Women's Chicago School, most prominently led by Jane Addams. The chapter therefore asks whether, with the emergence and growth in dominance of the Chicago School, sociology has started to include issues of race and gender. Furthermore, did this mean an inclusion of black and female social theorists into interpretations of sociological theory?

Race, Gender and Sociological Exclusion

As argued in the previous chapter, visions of the sociological tradition are severely foreshortened in their focus on the holy trinity (and Simmel) and on socioeconomic issues such as class; they are, according to Parker (2001), ultimately conservative as a result, and in studying the origins of sociology it is equally important to explore the nineteenth-century and early-twentieth-century treatments of gendered and racialized inequalities in the work of authors such as Harriet Martineau, W.E.B. DuBois and Anna Julia Cooper. These theorists are curiously omitted from most accounts of the origins of sociology. The first section of the chapter outlines the work of these canonical outsiders.

Harriet Martineau (1802–1876)

Harriet Martineau was born into an upper-middle-class English family. She was an early-nineteenth-century novelist, journalist, social reformer, educator, social scientist and feminist. She published more than 50 books and almost 2,000 articles and newspaper columns. Alice Rossi (1973) even celebrates Harriet Martineau as the first woman sociologist.

Throughout her lifetime, Martineau's influence spanned North America and Europe. She was a theorist who, through her translations of the work of Comte, bought positivism to America. Some have even said that her theories of political economy paved the way for Marx. Martineau based her ideas around the social sources of morality and the significance of both biology and society for determining human behaviour, along with an emphasis on the universality of cause and effect. According to Hutcheon (1996), most of Martineau's insights (although not recognized) survived to become the foundation stones of sociology and in particular Marxist social thought. She had a passion for social justice and a commitment to radical social change. According to Hutcheon (ibid.), Martineau sought a way of dispersing, rather than centralizing, economic and political power. The cultural and social transformation that she envisioned was to be slower and deeper than a mere surface disruption to the ownership of the means of production put forward by Marx. According to Hutcheon (ibid.), hers was a revolution not only in the values and attitudes that determine our expectations about gender and work roles but in the very way we view reality in general.

Martineau had a broad range of sociological interests aside from those already listed. She had a comparative sociological focus. She also wrote about religion, crime and punishment, poverty, labour conflicts, colonialism, war, and health and illness. Her sociological perspective – which was anchored in her gendered position – produced not only a sociology of gender but also a general sociology with theoretical relevance for all aspects of social life (Ritzer and Goodman 2004a: 277). There have been a number of biographies of Harriet Martineau, ranging from those by her contemporaries to commentaries written more recently. A number of these have come from feminist sociologists. However, Harriet Martineau's work has largely remained outside general interpretations of classical theory.

A Founding Mother?

Martineau undoubtedly belongs in that founding generation of sociologists usually represented by Comte, Spencer and Marx (Ritzer and Goodman 2004a). She and thinkers like her wanted to undertake the grand task of systematically and scientifically studying human society. The subject matter of sociology for Martineau was social life in society. She was interested in its patterns, causes, consequences and problems (ibid.). Like both Comte and Spencer, she understood society as roughly equivalent to a nation-state or politico-cultural entity. She believed that any society is influenced to some degree by general social laws. These include the principle of progress, the emergence of science as the most advanced product of human intellectual endeavour and the significance of population dynamics and the natural physical environment (ibid. 274). But for Martineau, the most important law of social life was that of general human happiness.

However, she differed from Comte and Spencer in that in her sociology she was much less interested in developing an ideal-type theoretical model, a generalized social system. Nor did she want to develop an abstract typology of societies, identifying their development in terms of stages. Rather, she aimed to study the organization of society through the actual patterns of human relationships and activities in historically developed societies – England, Ireland, the United States and the countries of the Middle East (ibid. 275).

Illustrations of Political Economy

One key area of interest for Martineau was political economy. Between 1832 and 1834 she published 25 instructive novels in a series called *Illustrations of Political Economy*, intended to teach the key facets of a new science of society to a general middle-class and working-class readership through stories (Ritzer and Goodman 2004a). The realism and working-class concerns of these stories ran counter to the fashionable 'silver-fork novels' of aristocratic life and manners produced by such authors as Disraeli, although Logan (2002) points out that in the *Illustrations* Martineau too joined the 'silver fork' with working-class concerns and clarified the 'economic interdependence' of the two groups. She concluded each volume with a summary of the principles of the new science that shaped her plot. These fables paved the way for other novels about the condition of England, for example Dickens' *Oliver Twist*. They also established her as a woman writer brave enough to write on social and political issues that were normally only the domain of men.

Furthermore, according to Ritzer and Goodman (2004a), the premises she held about political economy underpinned her move into sociology:

> The people then must become practically acquainted with the principles of political economy. . . . Viewing this science as we do, – as involving the laws of social duty and social happiness, – we hold it as a positive obligation on every member of society . . . to inform himself of its leading principles. . . . We think this study partakes much more of the nature of a moral than a mathematical science, and are quite certain that it modifies, or ought to modify, our moral philosophy. (Martineau 1836: 275–7; cited in Ritzer and Goodman 2004a: 273)

As mentioned earlier, Martineau wanted justice, and for her this would come through social change. Martineau did not think that this would happen by centralizing economic and political power but rather, she felt, through dispersing it. In this sense she sought political transformation that would be slower and deeper than that put forward by Marx's disruption to the ownership of the means of production (Hutcheon 1996).

Feminism and the Sociology of Women

Martineau is well known for her work on gender, and her work has influenced contemporary feminism. Logan (2002) emphasizes how critics have made various claims for her feminism, her anti-feminism, her masculinity, her femininity and her identification with and resistance to male literary hegemony. A synthesis of these tensions in her work gave it a certain sort of energy. We see her feminist approach to social analysis evident in *Society in America* (1836/7), where she investigates the conditions of women's lives. She makes the relational facts of marriage in the United States a key index of the moral condition of that society. The enslavement of the African American population is her second key index. Within this book, she recognizes the interplay of gender and race (Ritzer and Goodman 2004a: 277). Martineau controversially claimed that women were treated like slaves. According to her, both women and slaves were given indulgence rather than real justice. Through her feminist perspective she went onto argue for advancement in women's education so that marriage was not the only option available to women.

In her writing and research after the study of US society, Martineau continued to place women at the centre of her sociology with investigations of women's education, family, marriage and the law, violence against women, fashion, women's position in Arab harems and the injustice of the treatment of prostitutes in Britain. Furthermore, in study after study she explored the nature of women's paid work in terms of its heavy physical demands and low wages (ibid.). Overall, Martineau can be seen as an inspiration for contemporary feminism. Rossi's inclusion of Martineau's chapter on women from *Society in America* in her selection of classic feminist statements, *The Feminist Papers* (1973), indicates the relevance of her work to contemporary feminist thought.

Sociological Research

In *How to Observe Morals and Manners* (1838), Martineau focuses on the research work of the social scientist and develops the first methods text in the history of sociology (Ritzer and Goodman 2004a). In the book, Martineau gives an outline for the appropriate attitudes of sociologists towards the research experience, in terms of problems of sampling and the identification of social indicators for research. Martineau suggests that sociologists should try to develop empathy in their approach to research, a sympathetic understanding as a way to uncover the meanings of actors' actions and activities. Furthermore, in order to move away from problems of sampling, Martineau felt sociologists must look for aspects of social life that represent the collectivity.

In the book, Martineau presents a view that is not dissimilar to Durkheim's much later exploration of social facts (*The Rules of the Sociological Method*, 1895). Martineau talks about the social study of facts, which for her can be collected from a variety of sources, including architectural remains, epitaphs, civic registers, national music and 'any other of the thousand manifestations of the common mind which may be found among every people' (1838: 63). She moves on to develop strategies for 'doing' fieldwork. This includes the use of diaries, journals and notebooks that contain the sociologist's views, observations and recording of events. In 1853 she famously published an extensively edited English translation of Comte's *Positive Philosophy*. Comte wholeheartedly approved of this and thus substituted it, translated back into French, for his original edition. It is only in this relationship to Comte that, until recently, Martineau's name survived in the record of sociology's history (Ritzer and Goodman 2004a).

Critiques

Martineau's work has been subject to numerous critiques from her contemporaries and more recent theorists. Here is a selection of critiques of her work.

- Martineau has been criticized for not being an original thinker. Rather, she was often seen as someone who summarized and communicated the ideas of others.
- Some of her feminist ideas were critiqued by male social and political commentators of the time who saw her as 'unladylike'.
- She was criticized in her autobiographical work for attacking her own family, especially her mother and her contemporaries.
- Her views have also often been seen as contradictory and confusing, frequently resulting in her being seen as all things to all people.

Summary

Overall, then, we can see that Martineau could be classed as a founding mother of sociology. Like Marx, she wrote theories on political economy. Before Durkheim's study of social facts, Martineau focused her own research methods on the study of social facts. She successfully translated *The Positive Philosophy of Auguste Comte*. Furthermore, gender permeated the heart of her social theories, and she wrote her social theories from her own position of gendered exclusion. She has, however, been cast out of the canon by those writing on the history of sociological theory.

W.E.B. DuBois (1868–1963)

W.E.B. DuBois was born and grew up in Great Barrington, Massachusetts, where, according to Lemert, he experienced racial discrimination only obliquely, yet he came to be one of the greatest American social theorists of race (1999: 162). DuBois wrote about the interaction of race and class inequality. He also unearthed the links between social theory, social science and eugenics in the late nineteenth century. However, until very recently, he remained outside constructions of the classical canon.

Within his social theory, DuBois emphasized the importance of social class and social structure as the determinants of social behaviour, social action and conflict. *The Philadelphia Negro* (1899) can be seen as the first significant work of American empirical sociology. According to Monteiro (1995), his most important works have been paradigmatic; that is, they have set the broad philosophical and conceptual outlines of disciplinary research. Thus DuBois' work in both sociology and history established an alternative research programme to the dominant ones in the US academy.

According to Monteiro (ibid.), what his scholarship and research did was to verify the interactive relationship among race, class and the multilevel configurations of the social structure of modern society. Furthermore, DuBois saw race in a global context; hence he connected the problem of race to the colonial system and world economic system. DuBois wrote numerous books, including biographical works. His work was even much admired by Weber, who offered to take care of the German translation of the book *The Souls of Black Folk* (1903). He was a poet, a race man, an intellectual and political organizer (Lemert 2002). However, despite all this, until recently DuBois had largely been ignored within sociological theory.

The Philadelphia Negro

In 1899 DuBois wrote *The Philadelphia Negro*. This book has been declared a masterpiece of sociological fieldwork and is still cited for its insights into the life of urban blacks. It did not, however, become his best-known book, partly because professional sociologists were slow to read it and partly because, according to Lemert (1995), it was soon eclipsed by an even greater book, *The Souls of Black Folks* (of which more in the next section). Although often ignored by scholars in the field, it is a key model in urban sociology. Much subsequent urban sociology literature owes an enormous debt to DuBois (Monteiro 1995).

In *The Philadelphia Negro*, DuBois studied Philadelphia's African American community. Within the book, he challenged the widespread belief that black people were inferior to white people. DuBois considered the position of black people to be a disgrace and attributed the problems of African Americans to white prejudice. He explored issues that many existing sociologists had previously failed to study, arguing that ghettoization and poverty are not created by the poor themselves but are the consequence of economic, social and political processes far removed from those in the ghetto. According to DuBois, poverty, ghettoization and crime were the symptoms of institutional and structural racism (Monteiro 1995). These links made by DuBois (as is argued later in this chapter) became central to the work of the Chicago School of Sociology, which became the dominant school of thought from the First World War to the mid-1930s.

Within *The Philadelphia Negro*, DuBois was not only critical of white people but also extended his criticism to black people who had been successful. He criticized them for being so eager to win white acceptance that they gave up all ties with the black community, which needed their help (Macionis 2001). The study itself demonstrated the use of a variety of research methods, such as historiography, survey research, ethnography, urban mapping, urban ecology, geography, criminology and demography. Overall, DuBois' study can be seen as part of the social reform movement of the late nineteenth century. Furthermore, his work on poverty, class and race became crucial in the reform movement against poverty and racism in the United States.

The Souls of Black Folk

DuBois' *The Souls of Black Folk* was published in 1903, the year before Weber wrote the first of the studies that became *The Protestant Ethic*. Though Henry James considered this work the only great southern literature of the time, the book was recognized and widely read mostly by blacks around the world (Lemert 1995). According to Ritzer and Goodman (2004a), *The Souls of Black Folk* allowed DuBois to develop interesting theoretical ideas in the context of his own life. In the foreword to the book, DuBois sketches out his aims: 'I have sought here to sketch, in vague, uncertain outline, the spiritual world in which ten thousand Americans live and strive.'

The book can be seen as an effort to address the problem of race and the failure of American pragmatism to provide a philosophical framework for a social science of race (Monteiro 1995). DuBois used poetry, autobiography and history to make theoretical points. DuBois' literary method reflected his theory, for example in his practice of composing epitaphs that situated the classic literature of the west and unmarked bars of music from the American black tradition side by side (Lemert 1999: 163).

DuBois took as his starting point the difficult reality of being black in America and asserted that 'the problem of the twentieth century is the problem of the color line'. For DuBois the colour line is the stark exterior of the American Negro's experience (Lemert 2002). He argues that the colour line is an analytical tool, a category serving to divide, classify and segregate on the basis of race (ibid.). According to Ritzer and Goodman (2004a), one of DuBois' best-known concepts in *The Souls of Black Folk* is the veil. The veil is a barrier, a cause of separation between African Americans and whites. The image here is not of a wall, but of a thin material through which each race can see each other race, but which nonetheless separates them. DuBois returned again and again to the concepts of the colour line and the veil, but he never allowed them to relax into analytic calm (Lemert 2002: 172). In discussing both the colour line and the veil, DuBois identifies the American Negro as exhibiting a 'double consciousness'. By this he means

> It is a peculiar sensation, this double-consciousness, the sense of always looking at one's self through the eyes of others, of measuring one's soul by the tape of a world that looks on in amused contempt and pity. One ever feels this twoness, – an American, a Negro; two souls, two thoughts, two un-reconciled strivings: two warring ideals in one dark body, whose dogged strength alone keeps it from being torn asunder. (DuBois 1903: 2–3)

For DuBois, the American Negro is caught in a double bind; he is two at once, always looking at 'himself' through the eyes of a world that looks on in contempt and pity (Lemert 2002). However, it is this struggle with this twoness of being that gives the black man his strength. For DuBois, it is what makes the American Negro gifted with a second sight.

Black Reconstruction

During the years after its publication in 1903, *The Souls of Black Folk* brought DuBois' name into the homes of black people across the world. He passed quickly beyond mere fame, and for many he became an icon of racial possibility (Lemert 2002). In later years, well after the First World War, he became more of a Marxist. This was consolidated in 1935, when he wrote a Marxist interpretation of the reconstruction era called *Black Reconstruction*. To some *Black Reconstruction* might appear to be an exercise in class analysis. However, according to Lemert (ibid.), it was more than that. Lemert argues that it endures because no other work of its day, and not many since, examines the facts of economic history in terms of the relations of racial production; *Black Reconstruction* was to be DuBois' last great work of science.

In later years, Africa also began to feature more prominently in the work of DuBois. Within *The Souls of Black Folk*, race and nation were prominent. According to Lemert (ibid. 184), beginning with his memoir of 1920, *Darkwater*, Africa became clear in DuBois' picture of the racial situation as his American nationalism came to fade. Twenty years later, in *Dusk of Dawn* (1940), his thinking had changed, and he saw America as an object more of disappointment than of hope. Early in his career, DuBois was optimistic about overcoming racial divisions. By the end of his life, however, he felt that little had changed. According to Lemert (ibid.), in the end DuBois was no longer an American Negro, any more than he was an African American. He was African and socialist. He called for economic action, for revolution in the colonial system (ibid.). At the age of 93, DuBois left the United States for Ghana, where he died two years later (Macionis 2001).

Critiques

According to Lemert (2002), today DuBois is honoured as much by criticism of his shortcomings as by praise of his genius. Here is a selection of criticisms of his work.

- It could be argued that he was a bit slow in coming to recognize that race was at the basis of the colonial system, and hence at the heart of capitalism and class oppression.
- He has been criticized for never touching upon the psychological effects of the colonial experience that was central to Frantz Fanon's *Black Skin, White Masks* and *The Wretched of the Earth* (see Chapter 5).
- There is also a gendered critique of DuBois. He never even began to see that race and class, and even Africa and the world, present themselves differently to men and women. He did not see gender as one of the differentiating experiences of being black.

Summary

DuBois, then, was an important social theorist. He provided a range of social theories and conducted one of the earliest research projects in urban sociology. He was perhaps also the first theorist to recognize in his social theories the complex interaction of race and social class. Although today his work is central to the study of the sociology of race and ethnicity, at the time of his writings he remained outside the sociological canon.

Anna Julia Cooper (1858–1964)

Anna Julia Cooper was born in 1858, the daughter of a slave. Cooper lived a hard-working and productive life. She was a graduate of Oberlin College, a teacher and the principal of M Street School in Washington, DC. She was also an adoptive mother of five children and a successful doctoral student at the Sorbonne. She was a translator and scholar of medieval French texts and president of an evening college for working-class students (Lemert 1999). Anna Julia Cooper was a feminist and a strong activist in the struggle for the betterment of black people. Her published works, lectures, poems and miscellaneous writings best illustrate her diverse range of ideas. Cooper's thought, in particular her ideas on gender, both contested and reflected the black intelligentsia and black middle-class ideology. She was a much sought-after speaker and was outspoken on subjects such as racism, the status of black women and race- and gender-blind educational systems.

Cooper's achievements were amazing, and she became only the fourth African American woman to gain a PhD. Despite her work on gender, racial inequality and education, until recently Cooper remained outside sociological constructions of the canon. Cooper would possibly not have identified herself as a sociologist. However, this perhaps reflects the barriers to her participation in the sociological community brought about by racism and sexism. She has, however, since been seen as one of the founders of black feminist social thought.

A Voice from the South

In 1892, the year before Durkheim published *The Division of Labour*, Anna Julia Cooper wrote a work that has since become a classic of a different kind. However, during the time of her writing, it was not recognized as a work of classical sociology. Even today not many professional sociologists would recognize her name (Lemert 1995). However, Anna Julia Cooper's *A Voice from the South* (1892) is now considered a classic work in the tradition of black feminist social thought. According to Mary Helen Washington, *A Voice from the South* 'is the most precise, forceful, well-argued statement of black feminist thought to come out of the nineteenth century' (cited in Lemert 2002: 116). In it Anna Julia Cooper, like DuBois, located the conflict of race as being the central American dilemma (Carby 1987).

A Voice from the South, for which Cooper is best known, is structured into two distinct parts. The first provides a solo voice of the black woman, and the second is more broadly expressive of the concerns of the racial and cultural community (Baker-Fletcher 1994). Cooper drew on her experiences as an African American woman to develop her social theory. In this way, her theory foreshadowed the development of a feminist sociological theory based on the interests of women of colour. Cooper's theory differed from that of the white women sociologists of the day. White feminists writing at this time seemed to bathe the issue of domination in themes of evolution and progress. Using race relations as her lens, Cooper explored other social practices of stratification and oppression.

Cooper analysed gender inequality between white women and men and between African American women and men. She also explored the complex relations between race and gender through her own embedded experience in American society. Along with race and gender, her theory also includes social class, exploring relations between capitalists and labour (her terms), class and race in both urban and rural America, class divisions in the African American population, and class, race and gender in educated women's circles and between different societies. In particular, Cooper defended the need for the higher education of women. Here she exposed the ways in which arguments against women's education were tied to ideologies of female sexuality. Academic women were seen as less desirable to men as marriage material. Cooper's analysis showed that the education of women would radically change their social relations with men. However, she replaced the patriarchal emphasis on how men regarded intellectual women with the assertion that higher education made women more demanding of men (Carby 1987).

According to Lemert (2002), when we look back from our positions in contemporary society, Cooper's 1892 book seems to put the words to social worlds that would not exert their influence until the right time. According to him, the book has become a classic today because among the many other works of that era of black feminist writing, none put the basic principle of social theory nearly so memorably as did Cooper (Lemert 1995).

Slavery and the French Revolutionists 1788–1805

At the age of 63, Cooper completed her doctoral degree at the Sorbonne in Paris. Her doctoral thesis, written in 1925 and titled *Slavery and the French Revolutionists (1788–1805)*, focused on the contradiction between black enslavement as an economic resource for eighteenth-century capitalist economies and the democratic revolutionary claims of the French (and supposedly American) revolutions (Ritzer and Goodman 2004a). Here Cooper develops a theory of social organization. She also develops an epistemology for her social critique. Within the dissertation, Cooper identifies society as a system of institutions such as the economy, family, education and religion. She also recognizes that it is made up of stratified groups according to class, race and gender (ibid.). These forms of stratification work in tandem and also interact with one another.

Within this work, Cooper pays significant attention to the cultural themes of masculinity and femininity. She also explores the outcome of these for personality and societal functioning. Within this system, Cooper suggests that order may result from two forms (ibid.). It may result from domination and oppression, which is the case in most of the contemporary world. It may, however, result from a balanced interdependence between all sectors of society. Her criterion for a critical evaluation of society is whether it is characterized by equilibrium or domination, not that it is free of conflict (ibid. 297). Cooper presents an argument here that can be linked again with that of contemporary African American feminism.

Overall, Cooper may not have provided us with a universalistic social theory such as those developed by Durkheim. However, according to Lemert (1995), what Cooper did was to call out of the shadows a historical subject, who (when reflected upon) confounded the very idea of the historical subject. Thus began, or continued, a tradition of sociology that today is not at all restricted to black women. Cooper's position is one that recovers the lost voices of those excluded from long-dominant categories. According to Lemert (ibid.), Cooper, like DuBois, knew that the final measure of the secret of the human subject could not be universal. Just as there is no universal truth to black experience, there is also no single essence to the truth of women's experience (ibid.).

Critiques
The work of Anna Julia Cooper has not, of course, been without criticism. Here is a selection of critiques of her work.

- One of the most frequent critiques of Cooper's work focuses on her acceptance of the white notions of the true womanhood ideal. According to some feminists, she does not seem to imagine black women as the basis of her feminist politics.
- It could be argued that there is a lack of self-criticism in her work regarding the degree to which the black middle class (like her) could actually speak on behalf of the working and poor black people as she did.
- Cooper has also been criticized for failing to fully explore the link between white men's ownership of white women and the political oppression of black men. She recognized the link but failed to explore what was behind it.

Summary
Anna Julia Cooper was a key figure in the attainment of black women's rights in America. She was also a great social theorist. She provides us with an

integrated social theory that takes into account issues of race, class and gender. Her social theories were both political and practical. Historically, however, her work failed to fit into the mould of classical sociology. Although she has become a key figure in the development of black feminism, still only a few sociological theorists to date have tried to write her work back into the history of social theory.

The Hidden Classics and Sociological Theory

The three theorists explored here are but a selection of those writing from behind the veil of exclusion, writing social theories from outside the classical sociological canon. In accounts of the history of sociological theory until very recently, these theorists remained on the outside. However, according to Lemert (1995), despite their sociological exclusion, their insights into the social world were just as valid as those of the founding fathers. The classical theorists wrote sociologies that reflected their times. For example, as argued in the previous chapter, Marx wrote of the alienating effects of industrial capitalism in the 1860s. Weber and Durkheim wrote of the over-rationalizing and anomic effects of bureaucracy and the modern division of labour. This was at a time when Germany and France were struggling to find a new humane solution to their transitions from the traditional social and political cultures while avoiding the terrible costs of world war (ibid. 201–2).

Each of these classical theorists, then, helped develop some key aspect of sociology's classic culture by living in and thinking through the world before them. DuBois, Cooper and Martineau were critical of the powers of modernity, as were Marx, Weber and Durkheim. According to Lemert (1995), they were 'gifted with a second sight', which is not to say that they saw things perfectly, but that they saw the world just as astutely as Marx, Weber and Durkheim. It is just that their vision of the social world was different; their vision, and their social theories, came from behind the veil of racial and gendered exclusion. Why, then, if these theorists wrote such 'profound' social theories, were they excluded from accounts of the classical sociological canon?

Why Were They Outsiders?

The reasons behind the outsider status of the three theorists were diverse. Martineau was excluded by the academy and by the publishing world during the time she was writing. She has remained forgotten in contemporary social theory. According to Hutcheon (1996), the reason for this may have been that the opinion-setters and gatekeepers of her time were all men. She was deemed a masculine woman and ridiculed as a result. Her project on political economy was derided by male intellectuals despite its overwhelmingly enthusiastic acceptance and use by politicians and ordinary citizens. The views on gender spawned by the Enlightenment kept her excluded. As argued in Chapter 2, women were associated with nature and the private realm, whereas men were associated with culture and the public realm. Her work has since failed to be fully uncovered and explored.

DuBois' is a rather different story, though he, too, remained outside the canon at the time of his writing. Many would say this was due to racial politics and the connections he made between eugenics, social theory and Enlightenment thought. He was writing at a time in which social Darwinist approaches prevailed, a time in which western expansion was tied up with racial otherness bathed in exoticism and orientalism. DuBois' social theory questioned this and other social theories of the time; therefore, his work was often excluded. Furthermore, according to Ritzer and Goodman (2004a), the heated political rhetoric of most of DuBois' work is one of the things that would have made it hard in the (modern) past to consider him a sociological theorist. Marx, according to them, had much the same problem, but his work became part of the canon in the United States by about 1970. According to Ritzer and Goodman (ibid.), in part this was because of the recognition that amid all the rhetoric there was a profound theory with a powerful effect on subsequent social thought. DuBois' work, however, remained sequestered within the study of race relations. The profound nature of his work was not acknowledged outside the study of race relations until a decade or two after Marx's work was accorded general recognition as an important theory (ibid.). However, according to Lemert (2002), it was DuBois who had the most staying power out of all the classics. Few of the other social theorists even survived the First World War, which, according to Lemert, in its way killed Durkheim and Weber. Only Freud and DuBois survived to expand their work after the Great War, and, despite his early sociological exclusion, W.E.B. DuBois is now recognized as an important African American theorist.

One could say that the outsider status of Anna Julia Cooper was in part a self-selected one. Her vision and focus remained on her role as a social reformer. However, there are also a number of other reasons why Cooper was kept out. According to Lemert (ibid.), it may be that the importance of her theory is underestimated because her language is so practical, so direct to a reading public, that it was not seen as following established academic conventions (ibid.). She was also doubly excluded from the canon as a result of sexism and racism: Anna Julia Cooper was kept out of the canon because she was both female and black. However, she probably experienced the greatest sense of exclusion from key male race men of the day. In fact, her expulsion from her position at M Street School was brought on by the actions of one of the two race men of the day, Booker T. Washington (ibid.). Much critical attention in African American studies, Carby (1987) argues, has been given to male figures of this period, such as Booker T. Washington and W.E.B. DuBois. Typically, black women have been paid less attention in the academy than black men and are thus doubly excluded. Again, although she remained an outsider to the academy at the time of her writing, she has since come to be seen as an important historical social analyst of black American thought.

From Hidden Classics to Contemporary Insiders

Although these theorists may have been excluded from accounts of classical theory, this is changing. They have in very recent years started (very tentatively) to be rewritten into sociological theory's past (see Lemert 1995, 1999, 2002; Ritzer and Goodman 2004a,c). They have also come to be seen as being of key importance to contemporary sociological theory. This is particularly the case for DuBois and Anna Julia Cooper. Martineau was excluded by the academy and by the publishing world during the time she was writing, but she has since been recognized as an important figure for feminism. However, she has remained largely forgotten within contemporary social theory. The other two, however, have emerged as important figures in contemporary theory.

As is argued in more detail in Part Two, this inclusion of gendered and racial outsiders can be seen as the result of the challenge to social sciences from the women's movement and the impact of the civil rights movement during the 1960s. It also relates, as is argued in Part Three, to the emergence of postmodernism during the 1970s, the deconstruction of the sociological canon and the growth of disciplines such as gender studies, cultural studies and postcolonialism. It is such challenges and changes that have underpinned the inclusion of the work into contemporary theory of those previously classed as gendered or racial outsiders.

The work of DuBois has, for example, been used in many fields in contemporary sociology, African American studies, literary criticism, ethnic and racial studies, and postcolonial theory. According to Ritzer and Goodman (2004a), DuBois' manner of thinking fits in well within contemporary social theory, in particular with those associated with feminist multicultural and postmodern theory. According to them, he is also something of an example of this type of theory. He offered a standpoint theory – a theory that offered a view of society from the standpoint of black Americans and more generally of the world from the perspective of all minority races. Late-twentieth-century thinkers who have adopted the standpoint of black Americans have seen DuBois as a leader in this type of work, and feminists, queer theorists and others also have applauded his efforts (ibid. 305).

Anna Julia Cooper has also proved herself important in contemporary social theory. According to Lemert (2002), Cooper's ideas, though simply put, were an important link in a more than century-long evolution of black feminist social theory from Sojourner Truth's legendary 'Ain't I A Woman?' speech in the mid-nineteenth century to the full expression of black feminist thought in the 1980s. According to him, Cooper anticipated by nearly a century today's debates over the insufficiency of categories such as race and gender, even class, to capture by themselves the complex nature of a woman's social experiences. According to Lemert, from Susan Bordo's gender scepticism to Sandra Harding's idea of the instability of analytic categories, these contemporary theorists are all concerned with the difficult questions Cooper was raising a century earlier (ibid. 115).

Although they were excluded from interpretations of classical theory, then, DuBois and Cooper have been seen as relevant for contemporary theory, especially in the areas of gender studies and race and postcolonial studies. In Chapter 5, however, I explore just how central these theorists and work on gender and race have become within contemporary social theory. I ask whether they are central to the discipline or still sidelined.

Evaluating the Position of the Hidden Classics

Overall, the three theorists explored here were excluded from accounts of classical theory. The failure to engage with these theorists and their work at the time of writing, as argued, undoubtedly relates to the gender- and race-blind nature of the discipline of sociology during the classical era. As we saw in the previous chapter, views of race and gender during this time were often conflicted and deeply engrained in tradition. This can be seen, as I argued in Chapter 2, in the work of the classical theorists who allocated gender and race peripheral positions in their work. We can also see in their work that their views on gender were often caught between notions of female emancipation and a return to nature. In terms of race, their views were often caught between the scientific study of race, the development of social Darwinism, and notions of racial otherness. As a result, race and gender were excluded from the agenda of social theory. It is important to note here that these views were held more widely in society and, thus, also kept women and black academics out of academia more generally during this time. This had implications for the exclusion of authors like DuBois, Martineau and Cooper who were black, female and black female public intellectuals who wrote on issues of gender and race and were subsequently excluded from accounts of classical theory.

However, the failure to include the work of these theorists on these areas within accounts of classical theory has as much to do with the gender- and colour-blind nature of contemporary sociology. Contemporary social theorists writing about classical theory have tended to internalize the views of gender and race held by the classical theorists themselves rather than looking beyond these. They have subsequently failed to explore the deeply gendered and racialized nature of the origins of sociological theory. Furthermore, those writing general accounts of classical social theory are generally white men who view sociology's past as a past largely about European white or Jewish men. Therefore, accounts have come to reflect this. As I have suggested here, and go on to explore in more detail later, on in the book, it is only now, as the sociological canon is being opened up, that these types of writers are being rewritten back into the history of sociological theory.

Within the past two chapters, we have so far focused on classical European sociological theory and the founding fathers. We have looked at those writing sociologically both in Europe and in the United States, such as Martineau, DuBois and Cooper – theorists who have not been explored in the context of the origins of sociology because of their race and gender and work in this area. I want to move on now to explore one of the next key phases in the development of sociological theory, the emergence of the Chicago School.

Changes in Sociology: The Interwar Years

The classical period of sociology started to decline with the First World War. Thereafter came the Russian Revolution and the rise of the Soviet Union. There was a growth of Nazism and fascism in Europe, which led to the Second World War. In between these two wars was the Great Depression, and intellectual life became polarized between socialism and fascism (Sharrock *et al.* 2003b). According to Lemert (1999), during the interwar years 1918–1939 social theory was preoccupied (particularly in Europe) with the turmoil of political instability, depression, fascism and another world war. This period of instability sorely tested the belief of the west in its own abilities to develop successful political and economic systems. Social theories of this time gave voice to the urban poor in newly industrialized cities, to the new marginal working class, to the dislocated in urban areas, to Jewish people suffering under Hitler and to the liberation of what would later be called the third world. The work of the Chicago School reflected this. As the Chicago School focused on urbanization it took race and gender into its remit. Did this mark the end of gendered and racial exclusion?

The Chicago School: A Move to Inclusion?

According to Coser (1979), for roughly 20 years, from the First World War to the mid-1930s, the history of sociology in America can be largely written as the history of the Department of Sociology of the University of Chicago. During this time, the department can be said to have set the tone of sociology. It published the major journal of sociology and assumed presidency of the American Sociological Society. Its members wrote key texts and monographs (ibid.). The Department of Sociology at the University of Chicago was founded in 1892 by Albion Small and was soon a major force in the development of academic sociology, becoming renowned for its empirical studies of urban life (Sharrock *et al.* 2003b). Key interests of the school related to the problems of social change and upheaval, social reform and the establishment of an ordered community. Alongside this there was an interest in the development of sociology as an empirical science. The Chicago School drew on the uniquely American philosophical school of pragmatism, on a sociological interpretation of ecology and on the field methods developed by anthropology, now generally known by sociologists as participant observation (Craib 1992).

Basically, the Chicago School of sociologists was concerned with issues happening in its own city – social change and social order in rapidly industrializing societies – which was what engaged the major European social theorists in the second half of the nineteenth century. However, within the work of the Chicago School there was a much stronger orientation towards empirical research (Sharrock *et al.* 2003b).

In the early work of the Chicago sociologists there was a heavy focus on reformism. The studies that were conducted by the school provided evidence for a critique of racism, industrial exploitation, the depressed wages of immigrants and an educational system that mainly benefited the middle classes. From the beginning, Chicago sociology reflected the idea that the scientific analysis of social problems was a prelude to their solution (ibid.).

Two major figures of the school were W.I. Thomas (1863–1947) and Robert Park (1864–1944). Thomas has been described as the key intellectual force in the early years of Chicago sociology. Robert Park began his career as a journalist, moving into the academic world in 1913 to develop more academically based research. Both theorists felt that Chicago as a city faced numerous problems. In particular, it had problems with social justice, with maintaining social order while enabling individual freedom. Both sociologists felt that social change could not be brought about by legislation alone, that sociological research could make an important contribution to social reform by highlighting social issues as objectively as possible, thus enabling better communication among all social groups (ibid.).

Charles Horton Cooley (1864–1929) was another theorist associated with the Chicago School. His theoretical perspective was related to symbolic interactionism, which was to become Chicago's most important project. Although he held a wide range of views, he is remembered today mainly for his insights into the social-psychological aspects of social life (Ritzer and Goodman 2004c: 196). According to Craib (1992), all discussions of the Chicago School and symbolic interactionism tend to give centre stage to George Herbert Mead (1863–1931). He was not a sociologist but a philosopher. His central work, *Mind, Self and Society from the Standpoint of a Social Behaviorist* (1934), was compiled from his students' lecture notes after his death (Craib 1992). He remains a paradoxical figure in the history of sociological theory, both because he taught philosophy and not sociology and because he published relatively little during his lifetime (Ritzer and Goodman 2004c: 198).

There is not enough scope within this book to discuss the sheer breadth of work from the Chicago School during this period of time. References are provided at the end of the chapter for those who wish to read further on the school. What we are interested in here is the school's focus on race and its relationship to gender. As mentioned in this introductory section, the Chicago School carried out empirical studies that included an analysis of race and racism, thus bringing race to the centre of sociological theory.

Robert Park and the Sociology of Race

The Chicago School carried out a number of studies on urbanization that included an analysis of race, ethnicity and racism. According to Sharrock *et al.* (2003b), one of the first of the Chicago research reports was a policy-oriented study commissioned by the committee of inquiry into the race riots of July and August 1919, first published in 1922 as *The Negro in Chicago: A Study of Race Relations and a Race Riot in 1919* (Chicago Commission on Race Relations 1922). Other studies on city life followed, all focusing on developing an understanding from the actor's perspective (Sharrock *et al.* 2003b).

Another example of an early study undertaken by the Chicago sociologists was one focusing on the sizeable Polish community in the city. The work of W.I. Thomas and F. Znaniecki (1882–1958) on *The Polish Peasant in Europe and America* (1958; first published 1918) aimed to explore the Polish community from the point of view of its members. This was a landmark study in sociology as it was an attempt to integrate social theory and empirical data. As such, it can be viewed as an attempt to move away from abstract theorizing to the empirical study of everyday life. Personal documents were used – in particular letters to and from immigrants in the United States – to explore the Polish community. What the study highlighted was that Polish immigrants brought the traditional values of rural villagers to the United States and felt the contradictions between these and the culture of the American city. There was a lack of correspondence between the two, which led to a sense of social disorganization. Welfare and charity organizations could not recreate the sense of Polish community; hence many Polish immigrants became demoralized (Sharrock *et al.* 2003b).

We can see, then, how the Chicago School was concerned with the city's lack of communication between its diverse groups and how this threatened society. According to Shilling and Mellor (2001: 151), the city constituted 'the natural habitat of civilised man' but contained areas marked by poverty and social problems and populated by immigrant groups. In the absence of the right channels of communication, immigrants could appear alien and threatening to the host community. Communication, then, was viewed as the key medium that could translate cultural differences into accommodation rather than conflict. This assessment was exemplified by Park's landmark study of the immigrant press (ibid.).

According to Park (1972), the immigrant press served two functions. It preserved a language and maintained contact between 'the home countries and their scattered members in every part of the United States', thus providing a firm base for immigrant life. Also, it facilitated assimilation by breeding 'new loyalties' from 'old heritages' (Chicago Commission on Race Relations 1922: 468). Park used the example of foreign newspapers in the First World War to demonstrate his points. He showed how these helped cement relations between immigrant and native populations as they provided information and helped them unite over conflict. Park argued that adequate coverage and accurate reporting of current events were important for assimilation. This notion was based on the assumption that news did not operate on isolated individuals but on the attitudes of people *interacting* in group situations (Park 1972). Such interaction, according to Park (ibid.), enabled people to foster new ties and develop a new collective spirit that maintained social cohesion. These groups were meant to enhance positive relations of interdependence between people in the modern era and provided the impetus behind what Park described as the 'race relations cycle' (Park 1972, cited in Shilling and Mellor 2001: 151). This cycle starts with initial *contact* between people with phenotypical differences viewed in terms of race. The cycle moves through stages of *conflict, accommodation* and *assimilation* (Park 1950: 150). This movement was, for Park, a progressive one.

The key emphasis, then, of Park's analysis of race relations and immigration was on the assimilation of the immigrant population into the host community. As Solomos (1993) notes, assimilationism dominated race research from the late 1940s to the 1960s and consisted of a functionalist view of society and a definition of the race problem as one of integration. As far as this perspective was concerned, 'racial otherness' became relevant to sociology and visible to individuals, groups and politicians only when social actions ascribed an identifiably different immigrant culture 'to the physical traits of a particular social group' (ibid. 16). Those defined as racial others did not, however, have to remain permanent outsiders but could be assimilated into the values of those established within society.

As we can see in our analysis of the Chicago School, race, ethnicity, immigration and racism formed a central focus in its sociology. In contemporary reconstructions of the Chicago School this focus on race has also been widely recognized. Does this mean that there was an opening up of the social theoretical canon to include racial others and to include a focus on racial inequality? Sadly, no: although this school of thought included race in its analysis, we do not see any black sociologists included into the school. Furthermore, although the Chicago School did much to popularize the study of race relations in sociology, it also probably started the growth (which I go on to explore in more detail later) of the study of race relations as a separate field that failed really to penetrate the heart of sociological theory.

Jane Addams and the Chicago Women's School

While men at the University of Chicago were busy building 'the Chicago School', there also appeared a group of women who have become known as 'the Chicago Women's School', who were also creating a sociology and sociological theory. The key founder of the group was Jane Addams (1860–1935). The women worked out of two bases, the University of Chicago and Hull House, the settlement founded by Jane Addams and Ellen Gates in 1889 (Ritzer and Goodman 2004a). Settlement houses were those that white intellectuals from the upper middle classes chose to live in, conducting adult education classes, providing community leadership, establishing Christian role models and advocating celibacy and temperance. They were popular in the nineteenth century in Britain and the United States. Feminists, in particular, were keen on these settlements as they enabled them to move out of the constraints of the repressive Victorian household. Hull House was such a place. In Chicago, Jane Addams championed Hull House for 40 years, and it was America's most successful settlement. It provided a home for many of the female staff at the University of Chicago and for some men (Delamont 2003).

The Chicago women were women connected to the men of the University of Chicago (Deegan 1988) but who formed their real professional and personal networks with each other. This network included women who studied or taught at the University of Chicago and/or lived as residents or conducted research instituted by Hull House. This network included (among others) Edith and Grace Abbott, Jane Addams, Sophonisba Breckinridge, Florence Kelley, Frances Kellor, Julia Lathrop, Annie Marion MacLean, Virginia Robinson, Anna Garlin Spencer, Jessie Taft and Marion Talbot. Jane Addams is the most famous woman associated with the Women's Chicago School. She is, however, much less well known outside the United States. She is remembered in the United States as a pacifist, a settlement worker, a feminist and a social worker, not as a sociologist (Delamont 2003). However, she taught sociology, was a member of the American Sociological Association, published in the *American Journal of Sociology* and identified herself as a sociologist. She edited one of the pioneering studies of urban Chicago, *Hull House Maps and Papers* (1895) (ibid.).

The women of the Chicago School developed a sociology whose purpose was the reform and improvement of society. Despite battling intense sexism in the university and professional life, the women used sociological theory, analysis and research to win numerous victories for the rights of women and for the Progressive Movement (Deegan 1988). The Chicago women helped lead the fight for women's suffrage, factory legislation, child labour laws, protection of working women, aid for dependent mothers and children, better sanitation in the cities, trade unions, arbitration of labour disputes, minimum wages and minimum wage boards. Much of what the women fought for became the stuff of New Deal legislation in the 1930s.

Although these women were connected to the male-dominated Chicago School of sociology, the nature of this link was questionable. It was undoubtedly related to specific theorists and also to particular times, being stronger during the early days of the Chicago School. According to Deegan (ibid.), Charles Zeublin, Charles Henderson, George Herbert Mead and W.I. Thomas all worked with women as colleagues and, to varying degrees, were concerned with women's rights. Mead and Thomas have intrinsically central positions in the study of women as either colleagues or scholars. Deegan argues that in the 1892–1920 era Mead, John Dewey, Thomas and Albion Small shared the social and political goals of the women, especially suffrage, and were happier with a broader, messier sociology that combined university theory with reform campaigns in the city. When these men were gone, their successors were determined to break the link. Deegan claims that these women have in fact been expunged from the history of Chicago sociology, unjustly and because of the active misogyny of Park. She argues that Park was unable to work with women and therefore drove them out of sociology. Subsequently, he wrote up the history of the era, expunging all the women's names and their publications from its history. At the time women thought these were signs of progress, because they gained autonomy and self-determination.

Delamont (2003), however, also points to the split between theory and empirical work that occurred within the Chicago School after 1920. According to her, R.E.L. Faris, Robert Park and Ernest W. Burgess inherited the department, purified it and created a recognizably modern sociology there. In other words, they separated academic sociology as an objective, scientific discipline from social administration, social policy, social work, home economics and political activism of all kinds. This purification of discipline and department involved clearing out all the women lecturers and removing their publications from the canon. In Chicago, there were no women tenured or tenure-tracked in sociology between 1940 and 1960. Delamont (ibid.) argues that this is an ideological division between men in sociology (who wanted their discipline to be university based and detached from political campaigns and social and community action, and theoretical) and women (who wanted to collect data in the city to apply their results to the solutions of pressing social problems). It is in this period that the pioneering women died or retired and were not replaced within sociology departments (ibid. 91).

What we see here is an attempt at the recognition of women and gender by mainstream sociology. However, many members of the male-dominated Chicago School were bound by sexism. As Deegan (1988) points out, sociologists such as Park were keen to keep such women as Addams out by being derogatory about her substantive type of theory and making the division that women do social work and social reform and men do abstract theory. Women's work was therefore relegated to the sidelines and kept out of male-dominated abstract theoretical work.

This attitude is certainly something that developed further in the sociology of the 1970s and 1980s as women sociologists came to be banished to the safe haven of women's studies and later gender studies. However, the work by women of the Chicago School has been erased not only by the Chicago School itself but also by reconstructions of this era. Some of the men of the Chicago School, including Mead, who were sympathetic to the feminist cause have had their views on this erased from constructions of the Chicago School. Furthermore, it is interesting that while race became central to the Chicago School, gender was written off. Abbott (1999: 24) contrasts the 'profound' impact that the literatures on urban issues and on 'race–ethnicity' have had on the history of Chicago Sociology with the lack of impact made by encounters with feminism. It is only in recent years that the work of the Chicago School of women has been reinserted into the canon, and this has been done mainly by feminists such as Deegan (1988) and Delamont (2003).

Conclusion

Within this chapter we have explored the work of a selection of social theorists writing sociologically but writing from outside the canon. As mentioned, these are not the only gendered and racialized outsiders. They are used here as examples, and there are many others just like them. They were theorists who wrote sociologically from the perspective of marginality and exile. They were also social theorists who included gendered and racial analysis into their social theories. They were, however, kept outside the canon both by sociological theorists writing at the time and through contemporary constructions of the classical canon. Despite the wealth of writing focusing on gendered and racial inequalities, the work of these theorists has rarely been touched upon in accounts of sociological theory of this time, although subsequently, and in many cases posthumously, these theorists have been seen as contributing to contemporary social theories.

Within the chapter we moved on to explore one of the next phases in the development of sociological theory, focusing on the Chicago School. The Chicago School, which was the dominant school of American sociology during the interwar years, did encourage new agendas that meant a focus on the marginal and the excluded. There was, then, an inclusion of an empirical focus on race and ethnicity and also the growth of a feminist challenge in the form of the Chicago Women's School. These, however, can be seen as add-ons to the social theoretical canon rather than as providing a major challenge to its key concepts or being integrated into it. This is particularly the case for the Chicago School of women; women were, with time, erased from the canon. Overall, theorists writing from behind the veil of exclusion were still subsidiary with regard to sociological theory and have failed to appear in most central texts on social theory that have been written about this time. It is only with trends in postmodernism and post-structuralism (among others) taking place within sociological theory from the 1970s onwards that some of these theorists and subjects have been reinserted into the canon – but more of that later. For now, we are moving on to explore another important phase in the development of sociological theory, the so-called golden age. In the next chapter we explore the relationship of sociologists writing during the golden age to gender and race. We ask whether race and gender became more central to sociological theory during this time.

Chapter Summary

- Certain theorists who were contemporaries of the classical theorists were excluded from the classical canon because of their race and/or gender.
- These included theorists who offered profound social theories that went beyond the existing social theoretical focus on class to explore the interactions of variables of inequality of race, class and gender.
- They have been kept out of interpretations of the classical canon because of the gender- and race-blind nature of classical and modern sociological theory.
- Their work has since been recognized in a diverse array of fields of study, including contemporary social theory.
- During the interwar years, the Chicago School of sociology emerged, which included empirical work on race. There was also the emergence of a Chicago School of women.
- Race and, in particular, gender, however, still failed to permeate the core of their social theories, and women and black theorists were still marginalized within sociological theory.

Further Reading

G. Ritzer and D. Goodman, *Sociological Theory* (McGraw-Hill, 2004), provides a good broad account of both classical and modern social theory, as does C. Lemert, *Social Theory: The Multicultural and Classical Readings* (Westview Press, 1999). For accounts of race see C. Lemert, *Dark Thoughts: Race and the Eclipse of Society* (Routledge, 2002). For feminist accounts see S. Delamont, *Feminist Sociology* (Sage, 2003). For more general accounts of modern social theory including the Chicago School see W.A. Sharrock, J.A Hughes and P.J. Martin, *Understanding Modern Sociology* (Sage, 2003).

PART TWO

Modern Sociology

4

Theories of the Golden Age

This chapter examines sociological theory in the mid-twentieth century. Accounts of sociological theory during this era present a fragmented picture, identifying a diverse range of sociologists within or on the margins of sociology. Although some theorists were identified as dominant theorists during this era, in accounts of this period there appears to be no clear-cut canon as such. In light of this, the aim of this chapter is not to explore the endurance of a core canon of works as in Chapter 2; rather it explores the diversity of this canon, focusing on a selection of authors who have been presented as sociological during this time. The chapter focuses on the work of some of the dominant and marginal US- and Europe-based sociological theorists of the time. Although some of the theorists discussed here wrote bounded social theories, others were much more politicized. Along with an exploration of the work of a selection of theorists, one of the recurring questions to be explored here is: as sociology engages directly with social and political movements of the mid-twentieth century, does it become more inclusionary of issues of race and gender? Consequently, what does this mean for women and theorists of colour?

The chapter first gives a brief summary of the emergence of modern sociology. This provides a background to the work of theorists writing during this era. The chapter moves on to focus on a selection of theorists writing during this time. It starts with the work of Parsons, exploring the dominance of a grand theory that appeared to be based on very rigid sociological boundaries, social order and a conservative approach to issues of both gender and race. Second, it explores the work of Gouldner and C. Wright Mills, both critics of Parsons' brand of grand theorizing. They themselves were attempting to develop a sociological theory that was more open, politically radical and reflexive. Third, the chapter explores the work of the Frankfurt School. This was a school of theorists who were more critical of the social world and even more attuned to the social and political climate of the time. Overall, as we see, although such theorists as Mills and Gouldner engaged with the social and political movements of the time, their theories still seem to have remained on the whole neglectful of issues of gender and race, in particular gender. Furthermore, although theorists from the Frankfurt School developed pioneering work on fascism, they failed to engage fully with issues of gender. Any improvements, then, in the inclusion of issues of gender and race in sociological theory during this time were at best partial. Sociological theorists' work during this time was still focused mainly on issues of socio-economic forms of inequality.

In the final section of the chapter some conclusions are drawn with regard to Parsons, Mills, Gouldner and the Frankfurt School. The argument is made that although these theorists may have had differential relationships to sociology, and although they may not have been identified as canonical in the same way that classical theorists were, they have nonetheless come to be seen as important figures in the history of sociology's development. They (and others like them) have been written into accounts of the development of sociological theory, whereas others, notably women and black social theorists, are at best sidelined and at worst completely excluded. Thus, the golden age of sociological theory is still presented as one dominated by white men.

The Emergence of Modern Sociology

As argued at the end of Chapter 3, the classical period of sociology started to wane with the First World War. During the period after the First World War came the Russian Revolution and the rise of the Soviet Union and of Nazism and fascism in Europe. This in turn led to the Second World War. In between the First and Second World Wars was the Great Depression, and intellectual life became split between socialism and fascism (Sharrock *et al.* 2003b: 12–13). After the Second World War American sociology became the dominant form of sociology, taking over from European sociology. In terms of the development of sociology this era was characterized by strong attempts to professionalize sociology and further develop sociological theory and methods (ibid. 13).

Sociological theory during this time was marked by diverse trends that reflected the contemporary economic situation. The era after the Second World War was one marked by economic stability. This time has often been referred to as the 'golden age' or 'golden moment' (Lemert 1999: pt 3). This refers to a time when capitalism was booming after the Second World War during the 1950s and 1960s. Sociological theories developing during this time were often called 'theories of the golden age'. An example can be seen in the work of Talcott Parsons, a theorist whose focus on social order fitted in with the economic prosperity of the times.

However, during the 1960s strains in society were also visible. Alongside the growth of capitalism came an increase in migration, transformations in the labour market, movement to cities and so on. The effect of these changes was to put pressure on existing social and political structures, and social and political movements emerged (Callinicos 1999). Questions were raised as to whether economic prosperity was being bought at the cost of political disempowerment or cultural impoverishment (Sharrock *et al.* 2003b).

In the United States, the postwar era brought with it greater acceptance, prosperity and integration of Jewish immigrants. However, this rising postwar prosperity also brought into more central focus the position of black people, who suffered major social, political and economic inequalities. In the 1950s and early 1960s black activist movements began to favour direct action against the sociopolitical arrangements of American society. The women's movement was also bubbling under the surface. Furthermore, the Vietnam War became a focus not merely for opposition to war, especially on the university campuses, but also for much of the discontent about the supposedly benign nature of US society (ibid.).

Several sociological theorists writing at this time wrote theories that engaged with these movements. Two such theorists were C. Wright Mills and Alvin Gouldner, who developed a political sociology. These were theorists who wrote sociologies that spoke to these times, not really to issues of race or gender but rather, as with the classics, to the contemporary socioeconomic situation. During this time there was also a rediscovery of European social thought in the form of Frankfurt School structuralism. The Frankfurt School can be seen as a reaction against the positivism of the then-dominant framework of functionalism (ibid. 13). It offered a damning critique of society, one that spoke to the social movements and engaged with issues of both race and class but not gender.

Sociological theory during this time was beginning to be rocked by the threat of change. As is argued at the end of Chapter 5, sociology was about to be thoroughly challenged by those previously excluded, particularly women and ethnic minorities. However, for now, it was still struggling to maintain itself as a white male domain, a domain which might have reached out to embrace the social and political movements of the time but which nonetheless fell short of full engagement with theorists and theories of race and gender. In this chapter, I explore some of the effects of the politicization of the canon on the relationship between sociological theory and issues of gender and race, with reference to a selection of social theorists writing at this time.

In the next section, however, I begin with a focus on the sociology of the golden age, focusing on the work of Parsons. I explore the key aspects of Parsons' theories that have become best known in books on his work, focusing specifically on his 'grand theory' and some examples of his substantive sociology such as his work on the family. I also explore the issues of race and gender in his work.

Theories of the Golden Age

During the golden age capitalism experienced the longest and most sustained economic boom in its history (Callinicos 1999). According to Callinicos (ibid.), between 1948 and 1973 world gross national product rose by three-and-a-half times. During these years economies enjoyed full employment. There were high growth rates, which made it possible to implement social reforms meeting the basic needs of citizens. According to Callinicos (ibid.), prosperity greatly strengthened the political structures of liberal democracy. Politically and militarily integrated under American leadership through a network of cold war alliances against the Soviet bloc, the western liberal democracies began to emerge as the centre of gravity of world politics (ibid. 227).

Talcott Parsons (1902–1979)

Sociological theories of this time were labelled 'theories of the golden age'. One of the most dominant sociological theories of this time came from an American sociologist, Talcott Parsons. Parsonian sociology enjoyed enormous influence during the 1950s and 1960s. Gouldner at the end of the latter decade wrote: 'More than any other academic sociologist of any nationality, Parsons is a world figure' (1971: 168). According to Callinicos (1999), no doubt his status was to some extent a consequence of the newfound position of the United States as the leading power in the international state system. Parsons' optimistic view of modernity could draw on the real experience of societies that were experiencing prosperity and stability.

Parsons' brand of sociological theory appeared, like Durkheim's, aggressively sociological. The magnitude and detail of his grand theory has led Craib (1992) to call it a filing system of theories. According to Craib (ibid.), Parsons' work dominated social theory for several decades. His theory was a model for the totalizing ambitions of sociological theory as a whole. He produced an immense theoretical framework that claimed to be able to embrace everything in the social world. Parsons' emphasis was on stability and order. He saw social theory as attempting to answer the question of how social order is possible.

Grand Theory

Parsons did not aim to be a functionalist. His main project was an interpretation of classical theory, which appeared in *The Structure of Social Action* (1949). In this work Parsons did not just take a distinctive view of classical European social theory; he also provided a first introduction to it for many Anglo-American sociologists (Sharrock *et al.* 2003b). Parsons starts with the theory of social action. The key feature of this interaction is the relationship between people and features of their environment, both social and natural, to which they apply meaning. The most important features of the environment are people and the interaction between them. In these interactions, norms and values are crucial as they regulate and make predictable the behaviour of others. Socialization ensures that individuals internalize norms and values as they grow up (Abercrombie *et al.* 1988).

The Social System (1951) represents the first full statement of what Parsons calls his 'structural functionalism' (Callinicos 1999: 240). This was widely regarded as his *magnum opus* (Adriaansens 1980: 164). In looking at interaction, Parsons noted that social interaction has a systematic character, hence his use of the term social system. The idea of system gives us the key analogy in Parsons' theory – that of the biological organism or living system. If we take the human body as a system, it can be seen as having certain needs (e.g. food) and a number of interrelated parts (the digestive system, the stomach, the intestines, etc.) that function to meet those needs. Parsons saw a social system of action as having needs that must be met if it is to survive and a number of parts that function to meet those needs. All living systems are seen as tending towards equilibrium, a stable and balanced relationship between the different parts, and maintaining themselves separately from other systems (Craib 1992). The concept that bridges social action and social system is that of *pattern variables*. The pattern variables outlined by Parsons are as follows:

- *Specificity versus diffuseness.* This refers to whether one chooses to engage with others either for general reasons (diffusiveness) or for specific reasons (specificity).
- *Particularism versus universalism.* This refers to the ways in which one may be connected to other people, either by general criteria (universalism) or by criteria specific to that person (particularism).
- *Affective neutrality versus affectivity.* This refers to how one relates to another person, either with neutrality (affective neutrality) or with emotion (affectivity).
- *Performance versus quality.* This relates to the ways in which one decides whether to judge a person by what they do (performance) or by their characteristics (quality).
- *Self-collectivity.* This is a late addition to the set of pattern variables. It relates to whether one puts the interests of oneself before those of the collectivity.

These pattern variables structure any system of interaction. These systems, however, also have certain needs of their own that have to be met.

There are four such functional needs (known as AGIL):

1. adaptation, the need to relate to the environment by taking resources from it
2. goal attainment, the setting of goals for the system
3. integration, the maintenance of internal order
4. latency or pattern maintenance, the generation of motivation to perform tasks.

According to Parsons, in order to meet these functional requirements, groups of actions or subsystems of action develop. For example, the cultural subsystem performs the latency function and the social subsystem performs the function of integration. Each of these subsystems must also face the same four functional needs and subsequently each subsystem can also be divided into four subsystems. In fact, in Parsons' grand theory there appears to be no limit to the subdivisions of systems. Such complexity does make his theory appear, as Craib (1992) argues, like a filing cabinet. In terms of theorizing about social change, Parsons holds that systems of social action tend towards equilibrium, and that social change is the movement from one stage of equilibrium to another (Abercrombie *et al.* 1988). Parsons describes social change as a 'moving equilibrium'. As a result, for Parsons, many of the major changes in western society have involved 'upgrading', building on existing structures rather than overthrowing them, increasing the capacity of the system to manage its functional requirements (Sharrock *et al.* 2003b).

Parsons and Substantive Sociology

Parsons' writings in substantive areas of sociology are much more accessible than his abstract theoretical writings, although his emphasis is the same, the maintenance of social order. Parsons' writings in substantive sociology covered a wide range of subject areas. He wrote on the family, on social status, on the sick role and on education. I give just one brief example here of the family.

The family and its development was one of Parsons' key areas of writing (Parsons and Bales 1956). He argued that the development of the family met (and that only the family could meet) needs for primary socialization and personality stabilization. Primary socialization was the process through which children acquired the basic values of society from their family during early years. Family life also stabilized the adult personality by providing emotional support through marriage and by enabling adults to satisfy their childlike impulses that could not be indulged in the public realm. Parsons' theory of the development of the family was set into a theory of social change. He argued that the extended family found in pre-industrial society was a multifunctional unit that met people's needs. Through modernization the family lost many of its functions to other institutions. Production moved from the home to the workplace. Education and health care were provided by specialist occupations and organizations. The family itself became more specialized around its core functions of socialization and personality stabilization (Fulcher and Scott 2003).

For Parsons, the nuclear family suited the needs of industrial society. Roles within the family were specialized. There was one adult member who would be the breadwinner; the other would rear children. The family would be geographically mobile. Status within the nuclear family, according to Parsons, was ascribed and depended on who you were, whether you were a wife, husband or child. If family units and work units crossed over, as they did in earlier societies, this would lead to tension and conflict between the value systems of work and the family. With the nuclear family, these two worlds are kept separate and linked only by the male breadwinner, who is both family member and the income-generator. This balance between the two realms, according to Parsons and Bales (1956), maintains equilibrium.

Gender, Race and Parsons

Parsons' work has been heavily criticized for being gender blind. According to Johnson (1989), in the 1960s and 1970s feminists joined others in various progressive movements in criticizing Parsons for his 'ahistorical' and 'functionalist' approach. Parsons' association with functionalism and especially his statements concerning the positive functions of a gender-based instrumental/expressive division of labour within the family seemed to do nothing but justify the status quo. In 1953 Mirra Komarovsky published *Women in the Modern World: Their Education and Their Dilemmas*. This book challenges Parsons' belief in the naturalness of conventional gender roles. In *The Feminine Mystique* Betty Friedan (1963) also offered a direct critique of Parsons' work. She documented the emotional and intellectual oppression that middle-class women were experiencing during that time because of limited life options.

Parsons did also write on issues of race, although, again, as with the classical theorists, this was not a central issue in his work and he was conservative in his approach. In particular, Parsons wrote on fascism. In his essay 'Democracy and social structure in pre-Nazi Germany' (1942), he saw fascism as derived from the right as a result of its connections with existing conservative and elite political groups. Drawing on Weber, he thought that the masses were susceptible to fascism through the process of rationalization brought on by modern capitalism. The strains of a modernizing society affect social groups differently. Certain groups (e.g. youth in pre-Nazi Germany) are put under pressure and are therefore easily drawn into fascism and other radical ideologies. Anomie and a lack of identification with stable institutions such as 'the family' lead people to be susceptible to radical ideologies such as fascism. Parsons' wartime work also included a study of racial patterns in Cambridge housing, as he collaborated with a liberal organization combating racial antagonism and violence (Brick 2000). He also edited the book *The Negro American* with Kenneth Clarke (1966), an early leader in the civil rights movement.

Parsons does, then, appear to have recognized that there were possibilities for strains (relating to ethnicity and gender) to develop within the social structure, creating dissatisfaction among some (Sharrock *et al.* 2003b). However, according to Parsons, such strains would engender changes in society as 'corrective responses', which would eventually dissolve the strains themselves. These changes, however, would fall well short of a revolutionary transformation of the whole of society. Therefore, while Parsons recognized issues relating to gender and race, his position on these issues was ultimately one that fostered a conservative approach to social change rather than a revolutionary one.

Critiques

Along with the critiques of Parsons already mentioned, there are a number of other, more general criticisms levelled at Parsons. Here is a selection.

- His theory places its emphasis on equilibrium, balanced exchange and functional relationships. This does not take into account social conflict.
- He fails to explore the differences between biological, living systems and social systems. This results precisely in a generalization of a theory of persons to a theory of society. People are, among other things, biological organisms, but it does not automatically follow that the same is true of societies (Craib 1992).
- His is a grand theory of little empirical use.
- He gives too much emphasis to norms and values around which the action system and social system are organized. According to Lockwood (1964a,b), there is another factor at work in social life, what he calls the 'material substratum'; for example, people do not just go to work because they adhere to a system of norms and values but because they have a material interest (Craib 1992: 53).
- He is unable to reconcile action theory and system theory and in effect sees individual action as structurally determined.

Summary

Parsons was the dominant figure in sociology during the 1950s and 1960s. He focused on providing a totalizing theory of society as a whole, a theory that was undoubtedly economic in focus. Although we can see that Parsons did write on the issues of gender and race, these were not central to his work. Like the classical theorists before him, his views on gender in particular are somewhat traditional, and although he did recognize the strains in society he did not want to see any particular revolutionary change either for women or for ethnic minorities. I want to move on now to look at two theorists who were more political in their social theories and possibly more marginal in relation to the sociological canon.

Crisis and Hope in the Sociological Canon

As argued in the introduction to this chapter, by the 1960s black activist movements and protests against the war in Vietnam were challenging the stable picture of modern society, and there emerged a number of critical sociological theories that opposed the conservatism of structural functionalist theories including those of Parsons. Sociology was repoliticized (Sharrock *et al.* 2003b). In his attempts at grand theory, Parsons paid little attention to the broader political context during his time of writing. Other theorists writing at the time felt that in order for sociology to sustain itself as a discipline, it must engage in more concrete terms with the political and social contexts in which it existed. As is shown in this section, this can be seen early on in the work of C. Wright Mills and latterly in the work of Alvin Gouldner. These were theorists who drew on the classical tradition; their aim was to bring politics to the centre of social theory. Both critiqued Parsons and grand theory, and both sought a more reflexive sociological project. Within this section again I focus on the ways in which these authors are presented in contemporary constructions of their work, as fiery political characters who offered a direct challenge to Parsons. In doing so, I also ask whether, in their engagement with the social and political movements of the time, they were more inclusionary of issues of gender and race.

C. Wright Mills (1916–1962)

According to Crow (2004), Mills stands out as an important figure in sociology both because of what he said and because of the way in which he said it. Mills was often referred to as 'the sociologist in anger' (Cuzzort and King 1989). Becker (n.d.) calls Mills 'an intensely American sociologist, steeped in the perspective of philosophical pragmatism'. Mills was critical of the existing sociology of the time. He engaged in an ongoing battle with sociologists at one end of the continuum who were 'all theory' and those at the other end who were 'all statistical fact'. He calls the first 'grand theory', by which he meant theories that are couched in an abstract level conceptually. The latter he called 'abstracted empiricism' – the practice of accumulating quantitative data for its own sake. Mills instead developed a politically based sociology. There were elements of Marx in his theory of social change, but Mills saw student protest not proletarian revolution as leading the way to a more equal society. He is best known for his book *The Sociological Imagination* (1959), in which he developed a reflexive approach to sociology that contains both structure and agency. The aim of the sociological imagination, according to Mills, was to look beyond the world as it is taken for granted.

Taking It Big

Mills, following on from his heroes, who were pre-eminently Marx and Weber, wanted to ask the big questions about society. In fact, he frequently talked about 'taking it big' (Mills, cited in Wakefield 2000: 8). Like his heroes he wanted to look at the big issues of the time, such as the direction of history and the deep fractures of class and ideology, issues that gave an age its distinctive character. According to Becker (n.d.), this tendency in Mills' thought went off at the deep end in the final years of his life, when he planned gigantic, undoable comparative sociologies of the entire world.

In his theories Mills hit hard on the injustices of the social order. He argued that existing conventional social science actually perpetuates inequality rather than challenging it. According to Mills, being a sociologist gave one the tools to challenge and change such inequality. According to Gitlin (n.d.), for the political generation trying to find bearings in the early Sixties, Mills offered a light of radicalism. Mills was also paradoxical, but this, according to Gitlin, was part of his appeal. He was a radical disabused of radical traditions, a sociologist fed up with the way sociology was going, an intellectual who was often critical of intellectuals, a defender of popular action as well as a craftsman, a despairing optimist and a vigorous pessimist.

During his career as a sociologist Mills wanted to reach wider audiences than the classroom. He wanted to do so by engaging with readers more actively. As a result of the goal of creating a 'public sociology', Mills spoke broadly to a wide educated public not only through his books and journal articles but also by writing for national and left-wing newspapers and magazines. Mills' project of public sociology meant that ideas were presented in a common everyday language because their audience was not a narrow, educated elite but ordinary people. According to Mills, if intellectuals were to gain more power, then they needed to develop the capability of speaking to a wider audience, addressing popular awareness (Crow 2004).

The Sociological Imagination

According to Lemert (1995), *The Sociological Imagination* was the clearest, most enduring statement of Mills' many recommendations to the new left. Within the book Mills defined the sociological imagination in terms that appealed to young men and women already familiar with an increasing number of social criticisms of American life in the years following the Second World War. According to Lemert (ibid.), the sociological imagination that Mills envisioned was not so much an academic attitude as a practical moral vision.

In *The Sociological Imagination*, Mills advocated sociology as the study of the relationship of individuals' experience of society and history. According to Mills, the sociological imagination is simply a 'quality of mind' that allows one to grasp 'history and biography and the relations between the two within society' (Mills 1959: 3, 6). *The Sociological Imagination* provided a historical interpretation of the evolution of the social sciences in America. It was a vigorous polemic against the dominance of functionalism (grand theory) and empiricism in sociology. In the introduction to *The Sociological Imagination*, Mills wrote:

> We have come to know that every individual lives from one generation to the next, in some society. That he lives out a biography, and that he lives it out with some sequence. By the fact of his living he contributes

however minutely to the shaping of this society and to the courses of its history, even if he is made by society and its historical push. (ibid. 12)

Mills shows that by unifying biography and history we are forced to place our own individual experiences and attitudes in the context of social structure and that societies themselves are not unique but have to be placed within historical context (Marsh 2000). This reflexive approach to sociology that Mills introduced in *The Sociological Imagination* has come to have an enduring effect on the sociological canon.

The Stratification Trilogy

During the late 1940s and 1950s, Mills wrote what has become known as his 'great stratification trilogy' (Horowitz 1983: 282). This trilogy consisted of *The New Men of Power* (1948), *White Collar* (1951) and *The Power Elite* (1956). In *White Collar* he looked at the social characteristics of the American middle class. Within *The Power Elite* he focused on the power structure of the United States as an integrated array of elites in different areas. C. Wright Mills took a critical approach to the organization of power in the United States. In particular, he addressed three interlocked aspects of power: the military, corporate and political elites. In the book Mills argued that America had moved somewhat towards a mass society. At the end of the road was totalitarianism as in Nazi Germany or communist Russia. Although he recognized that America had not got there yet, he thought it was well on its way (Crow 2004).

The Power Elite built on the two other works, *The New Men of Power* and *White Collar*, in which Mills presented the working and middle classes as misperceiving their positions. Unlike Marx, Mills appeared not to believe in the expectation of growing class consciousness and mutual support. Rather, according to Crow (ibid.), Mills felt that workers had been depoliticized by the pursuit of status and by consumerism, to which they turned in what Mills felt was a futile search for individual fulfilment (ibid.). Mills did not seem to think that workers and their organizations were the route by which Americans would sort out their problems, at least not while there was an acceptance of subordination when they dealt with the power elite.

Despite this, Mills was always hopeful that things would be different. Sociology, according to him, has a key role to play in imagining alternatives. This applied at both a personal and a social level as for Mills the personal was caught up with the public issues of the time. The examples that he cited of unemployment, war, divorce and urban sprawl were things that he felt people did not need to feel were beyond their control. The sociological imagination had the capacity to bring hope to individuals. It could encourage them to think in ways they had not thought before. It could challenge the brainwashing to which Mills argued people had become exposed.

Listen, Yankee!

Having completed the great stratification trilogy, Mills in the years between 1957 and 1960 sought a wider turf upon which to exercise his political imagination (Horowitz 1983). In 1958 he wrote *The Causes of World War Three.* This was a negative book with what Horowitz calls 'a holocaust message' (ibid. 292). The main message was that there was another war on the horizon, one which must be prevented. What eluded Mills at this time were the positive forces of change. He located his positive vision with a vengeance in the Cuban Revolution (ibid.). In August 1960, he went to Cuba to find out for himself what Cubans were thinking, what their revolution meant. *Listen, Yankee!* is his report, written in the language of the Cuban revolutionary. According to Horowitz (ibid.), the key to *Listen, Yankee!*, which was published in 1960, is Mills' internalizing of the experience of others. He writes as a partisan. This literary device was part of an ongoing effort by Mills to reach a wide mass of people through the medium of the paperback. In his two final years, Mills became more of a public figure; his tracts against the cold war and US Latin American policy were more widely read than any others.

Critiques

There are a number of critiques levelled at Mills. Here is a selection.

- Mills attempted to strike a balance between being a professional sociologist and a public speaker. He sometimes got this wrong and was criticized as a result. His public voice often excluded him from academic debate and the academic jargon in which he often spoke sometimes alienated him from the public.
- He was criticized for his political views. For example, he was often criticized (even by fans) for his argument for the need for America's unilateral disarmament. It was said that such disarmament would leave a power vacuum that the Soviets would step into.
- Mills was accused of having too much faith in government and politicians.
- Mills can also be seen to attribute too much power to certain countries (e.g. Russia, the United States and countries of Europe), ignoring other countries.
- He was criticized for his emphasis on the importance of intellectuals as agents of change (Gouldner was also criticized for this).

Alvin Gouldner (1920–1980)

According to Piccone (1986), the contributions of Gouldner are exceptional. His first two books on labour relations and bureaucracies became sociological classics. His later contributions on Marxism and the role of intellectuals, according to Piccone (1986), provided the main parameters for the crucial issues facing sociology and public discourse during the twentieth century. According to Giddens (1987), Gouldner had an extraordinarily productive and intriguingly heterodox career. Like Mills he was interested in the work of Weber. He criticized sociologists' attempts at value-freedom. Like Mills, he attacked functionalist theories, highlighting the ways in which they under-estimated tension and conflict in society. Nonetheless, he oriented his work clearly towards the main body of professional sociologists especially in the United States (ibid.).

Early Works

In his early works such as *Patterns of Industrial Bureaucracy* (1954) and *Wildcat Strike* (1955), Gouldner explored parts of Weber's theory of bureaucracy in relation to labour relations, management and control. He highlighted the possibility for working-class action and industrial disruption. He also ex-plored aspects of Weber's sociology of religion in *Notes on Technology and the Moral Order* (1962). Here he argued that certain moral orders, for example the Apollonian, were causally important in the development of technology. This, according to Gouldner, was because the attributes of Apollonianism such as moderation, reason and activism enabled men to control impulses that otherwise might threaten instrumentality. Gouldner, who studied under Merton, stood out in the field of industrial sociology through the 1950s into the early 1960s (Chriss 2002).

Within his career, he underwent an important change of direction during the 1960s, when he turned to theoretical debates with Marxism and scientific sociology. Like Mills, he turned towards a critical and reflexive sociology. During his earlier career, Gouldner had embraced positivism. Although he was critical of Parsons' functionalism and like-minded social theories, from at least the mid-1950s these criticisms were nevertheless written in a tolerant tone that reflected Gouldner's continuing immersion in what he later came to deride as 'establishment' sociology (ibid.).

In 1965 he published *Enter Plato*, where he broke with the usual run of top-ics with which his sociology colleagues were concerned. This book focused on tracing the origins of European social theory in the classical age. Here he ap-plied sociological understanding to a key phase in the emergence of western culture. The book was, according to Giddens (1987), directed towards high-lighting the roots of Enlightenment reason, which were seen as involving an ap-propriation of classical thought and, at the same time, a rejection of it. Modern social science as an inheritor of the Enlightenment had lost a reflexive sense of the conditions of its own production. According to Gouldner, in Plato we still find an account of the relation between the knower and the known, whereas in later developments of European social thought, the position of knower disap-peared from view (ibid.).

Reflexive Sociology

Gouldner's most famous work is undoubtedly *The Coming Crisis in Western Sociology* (1971). It is a major study of functionalism and Marxism. Here he was concerned with progressive social change and specifically with the role of intellectuals in directing and contributing to change (similar to Mills). He called upon sociologists to be more reflexive about their theories and roles in society. At the time Gouldner wrote the book, the United States was still at war with communism. There was the war in Vietnam and resulting student protest. According to Lemert (1995), today many might be shocked by the audacity of the book's assumptions. Lemert (ibid.) argues that the assumptions made by Gouldner in the book were that sociology was a subject of general human interest, that a crisis in sociology would be central to the cultural and political crises then already defining social life. Gouldner also argued in the book that resolution of such crisis would require a renewal of sociology in which critical reflection on one's personal life would join and inspire rigorous analysis of the big historical structures of society. During the early 1970s thousands of young women and men read the book as part of a struggle to figure out what had become of the hopes that had moved them through much of the previous decade (ibid.).

In his book, Gouldner concluded, similarly to Mills, by recommending a reflexive sociology. He argued that such a reflexive orientation to life would transform the sociologist. It would penetrate deeply into the sociologist's daily life and work. It would make the sociologist more sensitive, raising self-awareness to a new historical level. Although the idea of a reflexive sociology was aimed at professional sociologists, it was rooted (as was Mills' imagination) in practice. According to Mills, individuals are most free when they reflect on themselves with a critical eye. According to Giddens (1987), reflexive sociology was for Gouldner very much bound up with a focus on the role of intellectuals in the shaping of modern culture and in the production of ideologies. His programme of reflexive sociology can be seen as an attempt to alert theorists to the hidden or tacit dimensions of their theories (Chriss 2002). This theory of reflexivity was a continuing theme in Gouldner's work. In 1973 he wrote the book *For Sociology*. In it he treats the discipline as supplying a reflexive perspective of social life that will lead political action towards Enlightenment ideals (Hammersley 1999).

Marxism and the New Intellectuals
In his later works in the late 1970s and early 1980s, Gouldner wrote more on Marxism. Like many others theorists, Gouldner saw Marxism as contradictory as a body of thought. In *The Two Marxisms* (1980), he discussed what he referred to as two types of Marxism. The first was a scientific Marxism. According to Gouldner, scientific Marxists see the development of capitalism and its transcendence by socialism as dependent upon a series of objectively founded changes. For them, the transcendence of capitalism and emergence of a socialist society are determined by laws of development. The second body of Marxists, the critical Marxists, on the other hand see Marxism overall as a

means of understanding history in order to change history (Giddens 1987). Gouldner also wrote on the role of intellectuals in the twentieth century. According to Giddens (ibid.), Gouldner attributes a pervasive importance to intellectuals. In Gouldner's work they form the core of a new class that is ever more likely to replace the old propertied classes.

Critiques

As with Mills and Parsons, a number of critiques can be levelled at Gouldner. Here is a selection.

- Gouldner's work on Marxism is often seen as unoriginal and as not dissimilar to that of many theorists before him.
- His notion of ideology is ambiguous and baffling (Giddens 1987). He sometimes calls it 'stunted reflexivity', but Giddens asks, 'what makes it stunted?'; he sometimes calls it 'limited rationality', but Giddens asks, what is 'full rationality'? (ibid. 270).
- The term 'intellectual' is a vague category. Very often it seems to mean all those who have been through some process of higher education. Sometimes Gouldner distinguishes intellectuals from the intelligentsia, with the former being a much narrower concept than the latter. But this distinction is by no means always observed in what he has to say (ibid.).
- What does he mean by class when he talks about the 'new class'?
- According to Hammersley (1999), Gouldner is inconsistently reflexive, preserving his own position from the corrosive effects of the kind of sociological analysis he applies when criticizing others.

Mills and Gouldner: Sociological Outlaws?

Mills and Gouldner have been presented here as controversial figures. They developed a radical critic of existing sociological conservatism such as that found in the functionalist theories of Parsons. Their social theories were much more radical than those of Parsons. As a result, they occupy a much less central position within sociology than Parsons (although they have both had a lasting effect in sociology). For example, Mills occupied a peripheral position within American sociology. According to Becker, this was due to Mills not really deciding whether he wanted to be a political speaker or a professional sociologist;

> Mills wanted to be a respected professional, in a field in which professionalism was coming to be defined in a narrowly disciplinary way, and a speaker on the big contemporary issues at a time when success with those narrow disciplinary concerns disqualified you as a speaker, almost by definition. (Becker n.d.)

Mills therefore failed ultimately to bridge the two fields wholeheartedly, never fully addressing the social and political issues of the day nor ultimately being

taken seriously as a professional sociologist. However, as Becker argues, perhaps because of Mills' ambivalence about whether to be an engaged political
thinker or a professional sociologist, he never did what he would have had to
do to make the world accept him as a top-notch professional sociologist.

According to Giddens (1987), Gouldner was, by all accounts, one of the
major figures in sociology in the period after the Second World War. He
never ceased to regard himself as first and foremost a sociologist and to the
end of his life defended the centrality of sociology to the understanding of
modern culture. However, others have questioned this supposed centrality.
Piccone (1986), for example, saw Gouldner as the brilliant and troublesome
outsider. He argues that although increasingly cited by intellectuals in general, his sociology has not received the attention that it deserves from other
sociologists. According to Piccone (ibid.), this had nothing to do with the
books themselves or with changes in the intellectual climate. Rather, it must
be explained primarily in terms of an ongoing resentment within the profession towards an innovative sociologist who never missed the chance to step
on the toes of whoever happened to be in the way. As a result, Gouldner was
for the most part during the last decade of his life isolated by the profession.
His own self-description as a 'ridge-rider', an 'outlaw' or an 'artist' meant that
he felt at odds with the profession of sociology which consisted of many
people imprisoned by their own careers (ibid.).

Thus, as mentioned initially, during this era theorists such as Mills and
Gouldner, who were attempting to develop a more reflexive and radical
canon, were marginalized from the canon as a result. However, these theorists still classed themselves as professional sociologists, and in accounts of
modern sociology they are still identified as key authors in the history and
development of the discipline. Their theories also reflected other sociological
theories written at the time in that they still, despite their focus on social and
political movements, managed to bypass issues of race and gender, as is
explored in the next section.

Race, Gender and the Work of Mills and Gouldner

Although Mills' and Gouldner's theories were socially and politically motivated, there were limits to the extent of this. For example, neither wrote
specifically on the racial politics involved in the civil rights movements or on
feminism associated with the women's movement. In unpublished letters,
Mills wrote of his disdain for racial inequality. He wrote ardently about the
need to see all people as equal regardless of colour. In his own words, however,
he took no interest in this issue in his published works:

> The point is I have never been interested in what is called 'the Negro
> problem'. Perhaps I should have been and should be now. The truth is,
> I've never looked into it as a researcher. I have a feeling that it would be

'a white problem' and I've got enough of those on my hands just now. (Mills, cited in Mills and Mills 2000: 314)

Both theorists produced theories that spoke to the liberation movements of the time. The sociological imagination, for example, with its emphasis on the relationship between personal and public issues, enabled the possibility of exploring the position of men and women and people of different ethnic and racial backgrounds. Within sociology at this time, however, it was still a male white vision. Sociology did not relate specifically to black people or women's experiences. Similarly, the reflexivity in Mills' and Gouldner's work failed to be linked with the reflexivity found in the work of second-wave feminists.

According to Delamont (2003), the existence of feminism went quite unsuspected by such theorists as Gouldner (1971), who did not see the absence of women or the existence of sexist stereotypes as a problem endemic in western sociology. According to Delamont, Gouldner neither recognized the deeply engrained sexism of sociology in the 1960s nor queried the lack of women in the discipline, especially the lack of women in tenured posts in elite universities, and the management of the learned societies. Mills was just as sexist as Gouldner. This sexism is apparent in a rather damning review Mills wrote of Simone de Beauvoir's book *The Second Sex*, published in 1949. His review is a critical one, which is interesting as she is much more positive about his work (Mills and Mills 2000) (a point explored in further detail later). The central question of de Beauvoir's book, according to Mills, is: 'How can a human being in a woman's situation attain fulfilment?' (Mills 1963: 339). According to Mills, what de Beauvoir is after is what the Soviet revolution promised, that is, women raised and trained like men, working under the same conditions and overall sexual liberty recognized by custom. According to him, it is not just women's situation that she should be lamenting but also the human condition. He argues that in writing about the second sex de Beauvoir should have paid more attention to the first sex (men) and to human beings in general. He argues that she generalizes too much about women's condition and does not classify women based on their experienced situation. He concludes by saying that the book is 'verbose, even padded' (ibid. 346).

In conclusion, although Mills and Gouldner developed a more political and radical canon, they did not really address key issues of race and gender. They held similar views to Parsons on gender, but their work on race was certainly less developed than his. This is interesting as they both offered theories that were more radical than Parsons' and seemed so much more engaged with social and political movements of the time. However, rather like the classics (and Parsons), their focus was still specifically on socioeconomic issues and inequalities. In the next section I want to move further from the dominant American sociologists of the time to look at those who stood at the intersections of sociology and other disciplines. Did those on the disciplinary borders produce sociological theories that engaged more thoroughly with issues of gender and race?

Gloom and Despair: The Frankfurt School

Although American sociology seemed to dominate the sociology scene during this time, there was also in the 1960s a resurgence of interest in the European tradition of social theory. In particular, there was a rediscovery of European social thought in Frankfurt School structuralism. This provided a more politicized and gloomy version of sociological theory than Mills or Gouldner. Although American sociologists such as Mills and Gouldner made clear critiques of American society, it has been argued by many that the Frankfurt School provided the most systematic critique of western society during this era (Callinicos 1999).

The Frankfurt School is the collective name given to a group of German intellectuals who wanted to re-evaluate Marxist theory. They became known as the Frankfurt School because many of them were associated with the Institute of Social Research at the University of Frankfurt. The institute was founded in 1923 and consisted mostly of Jewish scholars, the majority of whom went into exile in 1933 to escape the Nazi regime. They spent the following years in the United States and returned to Frankfurt in 1949 (Sharrock *et al.* 2003b). Thinkers included in the school were Theodor W. Adorno (philosopher, sociologist, musicologist), Walter Benjamin (essayist and literary critic), Herbert Marcuse (philosopher), Max Horkheimer (philosopher, sociologist) and later Jürgen Habermas.

The main interests of the Frankfurt School were in developing a critique of economism in Marxist theory. They emphasized the importance of culture rather than economics and produced influential studies of music, literature and aesthetics. They wanted to develop an appropriate epistemology and critique of capitalist society. They attempted to incorporate psychoanalysis into Marxist theory, filling the gaps left by orthodox Marxism. They attacked instrumental rationality as the basis of capitalist society. Unlike many Marxists before them, they were pessimistic overall about revolutionary change. In this section it is possible only to scratch the surface of their work, extensive as it was. Readings for those who wish to explore their work more thoroughly are provided at the end of the chapter. In particular, the question to be addressed within this section is: did their position of exile make the Frankfurt School more attuned to issues of gender and race than the other theorists explored so far?

Relationship to Sociology
There has been much controversy over the disciplinary basis for the work of the Frankfurt School. After all, these were theorists who were not located just

in sociology. According to Sharrock *et al.* (2003b), these were not much concerned with the development of academic sociology like Mills and Gouldner. Their aspirations were far wider than sociology, and they made influential contributions to the areas of economics, politics, history, psychiatry, literature, music and other fields. Like Simmel before them, they identified the importance of culture as well as of economics. According to Morrow and Brown (1994), it is possible to identify variants of critical theory in all of the social science disciplines.

Nevertheless, according to Morrow and Brown (ibid.), sociology does have a strong case for centrality. Sociology is concerned ultimately with the theory of society and the problems of society as a whole, including crisis. This is what concerns the critical theorists of the Frankfurt School. The ideas of the Frankfurt School have had an enduring impact on the development of sociology, and many of these ideas themselves emerged in response to the major works of the 'classic' sociological theorists, notably Marx and Weber. Thus we can see that these theorists were located even further away from dominant sociology at this time than Mills and Gouldner, yet they still maintained links with the discipline and have come to be key figures in the development of sociology.

The Early Years

The first director of the institute was the Austrian economist and historian Carl Grünberg. Under Grünberg's directorship, the institute pursued research of a broadly orthodox Marxist character. He was replaced as director by Max Horkheimer in 1930. Horkheimer, as a philosopher, intellectually reoriented the institute. In his inaugural lecture of 1931 he proposed a programme of collective research directed at specific social groups, particularly the working class, that could elucidate the problem of the relationship between reason and history (Callinicos 1999). According to Callinicos (ibid.), the theoretical starting point for the institute under Horkheimer's leadership was provided by Lukacs' *History and Class Consciousness* (1971). The central essay, 'Reification and the consciousness of the proletariat', demonstrated that it was possible for Marxist philosophy to be carried out at as great a level of sophistication as philosophy. It also offered a strategy in which bourgeois society was conceived as a totality that was united by the structure of reification. Every aspect of social life 'reflected the commodity fetishism arising from, at the core of the capitalist mode of production, the transformation of the worker into a marketable object' (Callinicos 1999: 249).

During the late 1930s with the regression of the Soviet revolution to Stalinism, the Frankfurt School abandoned a specifically Marxist political position. They still strongly opposed the negative effects of capitalism. However, they turned in their analysis to an exploration of the newfound stability of capitalism, which they attributed partly to the rise of the welfare state and the ability of the new mass media (culture industries) to distract working-class audiences from what were held to be their real interests. During this time they also turned their interests to issues of race. In particular, in their work they engaged with debates on the role of fascism. In 1947 Adorno and Horkheimer wrote *The Dialectic of Enlightenment*, which provided a valuable early account of the role that anti-Semitism played in the politics of fascism (Solomos and Back 1996).

Furthermore, this was a time during which they conducted such studies as *The Authoritarian Personality* (1950), an empirical study that concerned itself with the question of what had led to the acceptance by the masses of authoritarian politics. What made people obedient and what, in particular, made some of them into the kinds of people who would persecute Jews and staff the concentration camps? (Sharrock *et al.* 2003b: 88). The study found that the authoritarian personality was a mix of servility and resentment including traits of conventionalism, submissiveness, aggression, intolerance, anti-Semitism, ethnocentrism, intolerance of ambiguity and conceptions of social relations as power relations, regarding the world as a dangerous and violent place (ibid.). This type of personality was seen as arising from an upbringing within a family structure where relationships between parents and children were structured in a very hierarchical way. Overall, the study paid little attention to the structure of wider society within which such personalities were formed (ibid.).

Later Years

According to Craib (1992), the fortunes of critical theory have fluctuated since the end of the Second World War. After being a marginal and largely philosophical interest for many years, it became surprisingly popular during the 1960s and 1970s. It provided not just a way of thinking for political activists in the student movement but also a means by which radical academics could find a basis for their work (ibid.). The Frankfurt School provided an alternative vision.

During this time, work coming out of the Frankfurt School included Marcuse's famous book *One Dimensional Man*, published in 1964. According to Sharrock *et al.* (2003b), Marcuse influenced some of the key radicals in the protest movements for racial equality and opposition to the Vietnam War. His ideas gained prominence as these two movements fused into general hostility towards the political and economic system of the United States and Europe.

Marcuse took on board these changes and updated the school's position. Marcuse felt that the aim of theory was not to assist the existing society to administer itself better within its limitations but actually to change society and get rid of inhibitions on freedom (ibid. 98). According to him, totalitarianism was creeping up on the advanced societies. These societies were becoming totalitarian themselves in much more subtle and covert ways. According to him, society is one-dimensional because it allows thought and imagination only within one dimension. This is a dimension that is needed by, and compatible with, the existing system, a dimension that reabsorbs any potential critical thought into its own terms. The contentment of postwar capitalism was, therefore, mere conformism and complacency that was actively reinforced by repressive tolerance (ibid. 99).

Gender, Race and the Frankfurt School

As argued initially, the members of the Frankfurt School can hardly be seen as professional sociologists although they have been taken up in contemporary debates in sociology. They were self-confessed outsiders who sat on the margins of a multiplicity of disciplines. Their position as Jewish exiles gave them the ability to look in from the perspective of the outsider. This perhaps is what enabled them to deal more wholeheartedly with the racially motivated movements during the 1960s. They managed to address issues of race found in the civil rights movements in their mainstream theories much more than Mills and Gouldner, who, although they spoke of the movements and incited passion among radical protesters, did not really engage with the specific issues of racial inequality in their work. The Frankfurt School did this; for example, in *The Authoritarian Personality*, Adorno *et al.* provided an analysis of the type of person who is involved in ethnic and racial persecution. This was an analysis, moreover, that was based on empirical explorations.

However, while their position as exiles gave them a greater insight into issues of race, Frankfurt School members were quite conservative when it came to gender. As Craib (1992) argues, the question that half of its readership might ask the Frankfurt School is 'what about women?' According to Craib, the answer in the work of the Frankfurt School is 'not a lot' (ibid. 222). Within *The Authoritarian Personality* we get a glimpse of their ideas of gender relations within the family. Implicit in their arguments is the idea that we need to return to proper patriarchal family relations. We see nothing in their work that addresses specifically the issues raised by the women's movement. As a result, while they, more than the other theorists, discussed and engaged with the racial politics of the day, their theory on gender was as rigid as Parsons' work on the family. Their supradisciplinary position, then, gave them a greater insight into the position of some sociological outsiders, but in many ways they remained as exclusionary as the others.

Critiques

According to Craib (1992), the Frankfurt School's work came under attack from two main directions: from those they labelled as positivist social scientists and from Marxists. According to Craib, the basic criticism from both sides is the same (although expressed differently) – that is, critical theory is empty speculation.

- From the point of view of conventional social scientists, critical theory has no foundation in the real world. It cannot be tested and confirmed or refuted against any external measurement. It is obscure, over-complex and self-indulgent. From this perspective much of it can be seen as logically meaningless, even when translated into intelligible terms.
- The Marxist critique argues that critical theory represents a return to classical idealist German philosophy. Because of this, it cannot provide us with knowledge about the world or an analysis of real social structures. It is abstract and connected to high culture with no basis in practical politics (ibid. 223).

Summary
The Frankfurt School, then, stood on the fringes of sociology and provided some of the most profound and critical social theories of the time. Its members spoke candidly to the political situation of the time and wrote their social theories from their position as exiles. As such their theories very astutely address issues of racial otherness. They did, however, remain as gender blind as the other theorists discussed.

Evaluating Modern Theorists

The aim of this chapter has been to look at sociological theory in the mid-twentieth century. Although, as argued in Chapter 2, the classical canon must be seen as fluid and subject to reinterpretation, there is still a canon of work identified as classical. However, when it comes to accounts of sociological theory during the 1950s and 1960s there is no attempt at identifying a core canon. Rather, in accounts of social theory during this time a diverse range of sociologists within or on the margins of sociology are presented. Although some theorists, such as Parsons, were identified as dominant theorists during this era, others, including Mills and Gouldner, are identified as working on the fringes of sociology. Furthermore, some theorists, for example the Frankfurt School, worked in a number of disciplines, with sociology being only one. However, all the theorists discussed here are written into the history of modern sociology as important figures. For example, no one would think of teaching the sociology of the 1950s without looking at Parsons' grand theory. Sociology textbooks without Mills' 'sociological imagination' would seem empty. How could one explore the crisis faced by sociology in the 1960s without Gouldner, and how could any analysis of modern culture without the Frankfurt School appear anything but incomplete? These theorists have had a lasting impact on sociology and although they are possibly not viewed as canonical in the same way that the holy trinity are, they are nonetheless crucial to the telling of the discipline's history.

During the time that these theorists were developing their social theories, there were, of course, a number of other sociological theorists writing. As mentioned in the introduction to this chapter, space constraints mean that we could explore the work of only a selection of theorists in the chapter. There are, however, a number of other theorists who are included in accounts of the history of sociology's modern past. For example, symbolic interactionists including Howard Becker or structuralists such as Levi Strauss all form an important part of the history of sociological theory in the mid-twentieth century. These, along with various other structuralists, ethnomethodologists and symbolic interactionists, are all important figures written into the history of modern sociological theory. Like the theorists discussed in this chapter, race and gender are also excluded or sidelined within these theorists' work. Nonetheless, in accounts of modern social theory, a diversity and broad range of theorists are acknowledged and their works explored.

However, although the diversity of the canon is recognized in the telling of sociology's history, there remain curious omissions, most notably of theorists of gender and race. There were a number of theorists writing at the same time as those discussed above. These were women, or theorists of colour, writing on issues of race and gender, such as Hannah Arendt, Franz Fanon and Simone de Beauvoir. These authors were writing thought-provoking and challenging sociological theories that are just as worthy of our attention as those of the theorists discussed in this chapter so far. These theorists, however, have been excluded from accounts of the history of sociological theory's modern past.

Such exclusion, as argued in previous chapters, can be related to the status of issues of race and gender during the time these theorists were writing. It also relates to the subsequent gender- and race-blind nature of contemporary interpretations of modern sociology. As argued throughout this chapter, although some sociological theorists writing in the mid-twentieth century included an analysis of race into their social theory, gender was still excluded from sociological theory. The main focus of sociological theory was social class. Both gender and race as issues of study and theorists of gender and race have, then, been excluded from sociological theory at this time. Furthermore, this lack of interest in issues of gender and race by theorists of the golden age is something that has been internalized by contemporary theorists writing past histories of the discipline. Consequently, contemporary authors have failed to include theorists of gender and race and issues of gender and race within their own reconstructions of modern sociological theory.

Although some feminist theorists, such as Simone de Beauvoir, have very recently started to be incorporated into accounts of modern sociological theory, such incorporation is still in its infancy, and most authors like her remain excluded. It is to an exploration of the work of those authors excluded from the golden age of sociological theory and the reasons behind their exclusion that we turn in the following chapter.

Conclusion

This chapter has focused on mid-twentieth century sociological theory and on theorists such as Parsons, Mills, Gouldner and the Frankfurt School. Despite their varying relationships to sociology during this era, the theorists discussed in this chapter have been seen as key figures in the development of sociology. They have been accepted as such because of the nature of the topics they were writing on and the fact that they were male and white. In short, they have been accepted as key because of the sexism and racism of the sociological canon.

The work of the sociological theorists explored here (and others like them who were writing at the same time) focused centrally on issues of economic stability (Parsons) and inequality and social unrest (Mills, Gouldner and the Frankfurt School). However, dimensions of power and inequality in texts on modern theory are most associated still with class analysis. The sociological theorists discussed above have written to varying degrees on other issues such as gender and race. However, as argued, their focus on these issues was often peripheral compared with their interests in other areas. Furthermore, gendered others were often banished from the public realm in accounts of the works of these modern theorists. Thus, although there is a slight improvement in the incorporation of issues of race and gender into sociological theory during this time, it is still limited.

In the next chapter we focus on an exploration of the theories of those who provided a voice beyond the boundaries of sociological theory, that is, who spoke from completely outside the canon. They were women and people of colour who were kept out of sociological theory because they were women, because they were black, and because their work explored these issues. These were the theorists who spoke truly from a position of exile, who had much to tell us about the social world at that time but whose stories were seen as invalid by established sociology.

Chapter Summary

- During the mid-twentieth century a fragmented picture of sociological theory appears:
  - Parsons focused his social theories on social order and stability.
  - Mills and Gouldner focused on a repoliticization of sociological theory.
  - The Frankfurt School focused its social theories on a society characterized by gloom and despair.
- During this time some theorists, such as those in the Frankfurt School, provided explorations of race in their work on fascism.

- However, during this time, all the theorists included in this chapter wrote in ways that reinforced gender inequality.
- Furthermore, in the work of most of the sociological theorists discussed here, economic forms of inequality were still dominant.
- Women and theorists of colour were still excluded from sociological theory at this time.

Further Reading

For a good account of Parsons' theories see D. Layder, *Understanding Social Theory* (Sage, 1994). For good accounts of a range of theorists including Mills and Parsons see G. Crow, *The Art of Sociological Argument* (Palgrave Macmillan, 2004). See also A. Callinicos, *Social Theory: A Historical Introduction* (Polity Press, 1999). For accounts of the Frankfurt School see D. Held, *Introduction to Critical Theory* (Polity Press, 1980). For general accounts of modern social theory see W.A. Sharrock, J.A. Hughes and P.J. Martin, *Understanding Modern Sociology* (Sage, 2003).

5

Race, Gender and
Sociological Outsiders

The previous chapter argued that although some sociologists working during the 1950s and 1960s began to turn towards the social and political situation of the time, most focused on the socioeconomic situation. Despite the civil rights and women's movements, sociological theorists did not really engage wholeheartedly with issues of racial and gendered inequalities or with authors who put these issues at the centre of their social theories. Any attempts at the inclusion into the canon of authors writing about these issues were at best partial. To play on the title of Mills' (1959) book, there were limits to how far the 'sociological imagination' would stretch. As argued previously, this was a result not just of the sexism and racism of the sociologists discussed, such as Parsons, Gouldner and Mills, but also of the gender- and race-blind nature of contemporary constructions of sociology's past. In accounts of the history of sociological theory, social class has been the central focus of interest, and issues of gender and race have been marginalized or excluded.

During the mid-twentieth century, while authors such as Mills and Gouldner were writing about the economic issues of the time, there were authors writing their social theories from the perspective of gendered and racial inequality. The aim of this chapter is to explore the work of some of these social and political writers who were black or women (or both) and whose general social theories included an analysis of gender and racial inequality. It focuses on the work of Hannah Arendt, Frantz Fanon and Simone de Beauvoir. All were developing sociological theories and unearthing social inequalities of sociological interest, yet all remained outside the boundaries of sociological theory. They were theorists who have been kept out of sociology, as argued in the previous chapter, partially by sociologists writing at the time whose views were often gender and race blind. Leading on from this, theorists such as Arendt, Fanon and de Beauvoir have also been kept out of the canon by those writing contemporary accounts of sociological theory's modern past. As is argued in Chapter 6, this has changed somewhat within contemporary social theory as some past and present outsiders are now inserted into reconstructions of social theory. However, until very recently, most accounts written on modern sociological theory have provided a very white male portrayal of sociological theory, one that fails to include these theorists in accounts of the

1960s sociological canon. These theorists have, however, since become key figures in social and political thought.

This chapter focuses on several issues. First, it outlines the theories of a selection of modern sociological outsiders: Hannah Arendt, Frantz Fanon and Simone de Beauvoir. It explores their relationship to sociological theory and their outsider status. The chapter asks why, despite the profound nature of these theorists' work, they were kept outside sociological theory and subsequent interpretations of sociological theory of the mid-twentieth century. It also explores the changing nature of their relationship to social theory through a focus on their relationship to contemporary social theory, gender and ethnic and racial studies. In the later part of the chapter, the crisis faced by sociology during the late 1960s and early 1970s is explored, along with the subsequent feminist challenges to sociology and the growth of ethnic and racial studies. Within the chapter we explore the effects of these challenges on sociological theory. We ask whether, with these challenges, gender and race are now centralized within sociological theory. Consequently, what are the implications for women and theorists of colour?

Race, Gender and Sociological Exclusion

Hannah Arendt, Frantz Fanon and Simone de Beauvoir have all become central figures in the history of social thought. They were all writing around the same time as Parsons, Mills, Gouldner and the members of the Frankfurt School. They wrote sociologically about issues of inequality and they all wanted to work towards a fairer world, just like Mills and Gouldner. However, they all remained outside sociological theory during the time they were writing and were also excluded from subsequent accounts of the sociological theory of the mid-twentieth century. It could be argued that these were theorists who were telling the stories of the world through the experience of exile and exclusion. In this way, although their stories were different from those of people working within the paradigm of sociology, they were just as valid. As with the case of the outsiders discussed in Chapter 3, including DuBois and Martineau, some contemporary theorists have started to recognize this fact. For example, Lemert (1999: 19) suggests that some of the best social theorizing comes from people at the margins because their need to make sense of the world may be more pressing than is that of more privileged groups. Within this section of the chapter I explore the work of some theorists who remained outside sociological theory during the mid-twentieth century, starting with the work of Hannah Arendt.

Hannah Arendt (1906–1975)

According to Whitfield (2002), Arendt was a political theorist with a flair for grand historical generalization; she was a cultivated intellectual and a

German-trained scholar whose exile gave her insights into the experience of
the excluded. Hannah Arendt was born in Hanover, in Wilhelmine Germany.
She was raised in Koenigsberg, by parents with Russian-Jewish backgrounds.
After graduating from high school in Koenigsberg in 1924, she began to
study theology at the University of Marburg. In 1929, Arendt completed her
dissertation on the idea of love in the thought of St Augustine and earned her
doctorate. Arendt became a political activist when the National Socialists
took power and helped the German Zionist Organization to publicize the
plight of the victims of Nazism. She researched anti-Semitic propaganda, for
which the Gestapo arrested her. However, she won the sympathy of a Berlin
jailer, was released and escaped to Paris, where she remained for the
remainder of the decade (ibid.).

Eventually Arendt managed to flee to America. While living in New York
during the rest of the Second World War, Arendt worked on the book that
became *The Origins of Totalitarianism*. It was published in 1951, 10 years after
she arrived in the United States. Arendt also secured US citizenship during
this time and went on to become one of the most prominent intellectuals within
the United States. Arendt was the first woman to become a full professor (of
politics) at Princeton University. She then went on to teach at the University
of Chicago, Wesleyan University and finally the New School for Social
Research.

Without doubt, Arendt was a formidable social and political theorist, one
who has had a profound influence on contemporary social and political
theories, feminist social theories, and ethnic and racial studies. She has, however,
remained outside accounts of sociological theory during the mid-twentieth
century, when she wrote extensively. This is interesting as, out of all three
theorists explored here, Arendt was the most conservative and the most in
keeping with the grand theoretical agenda of the time. Within this section I
explore some key aspects of her work and look at the contributions she has
made to social theory.

Totalitarianism

The Origins of Totalitarianism traces the steps towards the distinctive twentieth-
century tyrannies of Hitler and Stalin. It looks at how wounded western civilization and human status itself had become. Within the book Arendt
demonstrated how embedded racism was in central and western European
societies and how imperialism experimented with the possibilities of un-
speakable cruelty and mass murder (Whitfield 2002). Within the text, what
appears to Arendt to be totally without precedent is not so much the shock-
ing numbers of people massacred under the conditions of the death camps
as the fact that this took place as a systematic attempt to destroy them as
juridical, moral and human beings (Wilkinson 2004: 119). The terrible

specificity of the evil of totalitarianism is based in its ambition to render all people equally *superfluous*, 'such that the very category of "being human" is violated and destroyed to the point of utter meaningless' (ibid. 120). It is in this quite particular sense that she understands the Nazi crimes as crimes against humanity (Bernstein 1996). According to Wilkinson (2004), Arendt's efforts to disclose the radical novelty of the evil of totalitarianism were recognized broadly as a great advancement in the struggle to understand the nature of the violation that took place at camps such as Auschwitz.

There are a number of themes that appear in her early work that seem to influence Arendt's political writings in general, for example, the quest for a humane and democratic public life, the factors that came to threaten it, the conflicts between private interests and the public good and the intensity of patterns of production and consumption that destabilized the world.

The Rise of the Social

What has become particularly interesting sociologically is Arendt's work on the rise of the social. In the book *The Human Condition* (published in 1958), Arendt was concerned primarily with the problem of reasserting politics as a valuable realm of human action, praxis and the world of appearances. She wrote about the loss of public space under the conditions of modernity. The book is an anti-modernist treatise that focuses on the rise of the social realm to the detriment of public space.

What is crucial to this work is what Arendt calls the 'rise of the social'. By this she means the institutional differentiation of modern societies into the narrow political realm on the one hand and the economic market and the family on the other (Benhabib 1992: 90). As a result of the rise of the social, economic processes, which had previously been confined to the realm of the household, emancipate themselves and become public matters. The same historical process that brought forth the modern constitutional state also brings forth society. This is the realm of social interaction, which interposes itself between 'households' on the one hand and the political state on the other (ibid. 90). Arendt is highly critical of this development. According to her, the rise of the social realm is the result of the tendency for life-sustaining labour increasingly to define human purpose. This is at the expense of human involvement in broader political action. As a result, a labouring society becomes one that resembles a large machine with humans as replicable parts that are expected to behave by conforming to certain rules (Hansen 2003: 28). As I go on to explore in the next section, Arendt's conceptualization of the rise of the social is something that has been both contested and admired by contemporary feminist social theorists.

In *The Human Condition*, Arendt also discusses the rise of the social sciences in conjunction with the rise of society. In particular, she sees economics as the representative of the social sciences *par excellence*. She is critical of the use of statistics that is found in the social sciences:

> The laws of statistics are valid only where large numbers or long periods are involved, and acts or events can statistically appear only as deviations or fluctuations. The justification of statistics is that deeds and events are rare occurrences in everyday life and in history. Yet the meaningfulness of everyday relationships is disclosed not in everyday life but in rare deeds, just as the significance of a historical period shows itself only in the few events that illuminate it. The application of the law of large numbers and long periods to politics or history signifies nothing less than the wilful obliteration of their very subject matter, and it is a hopeless enterprise to search for the meaning in politics or significance in history when everything that is not everyday behaviour or automatic trends has been ruled out as immaterial. (Arendt 1958: 42–3)

This critique of the social sciences could be one reason why Arendt is left out of accounts of social theory. However, such a critique is not dissimilar to Mills' critique of abstracted empiricism. Unlike Mills, though, Arendt was never included in the sociological canon. The critique Arendt develops of such empiricism provides a valid critique of statistics that could have been used in sociological debates on methodology. Her work in this area has, however, failed to be explored within debates on sociological method.

Race, Gender and Conservatism

Arendt has often been criticized for a certain conservative element in her work. For example, in charting the rise of the social at one level, according to Benhabib (1992), Arendt seems to praise the antagonistic political space of the Greek *polis*. According to Benhabib (ibid.), the political space of the *polis* was only possible because large groups of human beings, such as women, slaves, labourers, non-citizen residents and all non-Greeks, were excluded from it. However, their 'labour' for the daily necessities of life made possible the 'leisure for politics' that the few enjoyed. In contrast, the rise of the social was accompanied by the emancipation of these groups from inside the household and by their entry into public life. This can at times make Arendt seem undemocratic. Furthermore, some theorists writing about Arendt's theory identify a certain conservatism and alignment with imperialism in her work. Singh (2002), for example, argues that Arendt strongly attacked the discourse of violence (more of which in the next section) embraced by the new left and anti-colonial and black activists during the 1960s, while 'largely acceding to the euphemistic account of French and US warfare in Vietnam as "intervention in the Vietnamese civil war" rather than as perpetration of a still-repugnant and exceedingly violent, imperialist project' (ibid. 175).

In light of this, Arendt's work seems somewhat dismissive of what we are concerned with here in this book (e.g. the emancipation of marginal groups). In her views on the rise of the social she seems perhaps to take on the view of the more conservative sociologists whom we critiqued in the last section, such as Parsons. There are criticisms against her reliance on the rigid distinction between private and public particularly from feminists who argue that the confinement of the political to the realm outside the household has been part and parcel of the domination of politics by men and the corresponding exclusion of women's experiences of subjection from legitimate politics (Hansen 2003).

However, this is perhaps an over-simplification of Arendt's theories. As Benhabib (1992) points out, it is misleading to read Arendt as a nostalgic thinker. Arendt's views on the loss of public space and the rise of the social are not nostalgic but rather should be viewed as an attempt to think through changes in history. According to Benhabib (ibid. 92), we must learn to identify those moments of rupture, displacement and dislocation in history. This is about remembering creatively, putting together the members of a whole, a rethinking that sets free the lost potentials of the past.

As Hansen (2003) points out, plurality is also a key theme in Arendt's work. She suggests that we are 'strangers for ever'. The reality is that everyone is alike but no one is exactly identical to anyone else. Individual human beings, not an abstract, generic humanity live on earth and inhabit the world (ibid. 27). This emphasizes the acceptance of plurality in Arendt's work. Respecting plurality means that we accept others and their differing atrributes. We are connected through our differences and not despite them. According to Hansen (ibid.), for Arendt plurality makes solidarity possible. All in all her politics is about a certain kind of solidarity, a solidarity of strangers who are neither for nor against but, rather, with one another as sharers in freedom of a common world (ibid. 29). In these themes of worldliness and plurality Arendt dealt uniquely with the issues of similarity and difference, of how to work together while recognizing and appreciating difference. These are issues that have become central to contemporary debates in social theory on identity and to postmodern debates on race, ethnicity and gender more generally.

Critiques

Although Arendt's political and social theories have been applauded, she has also been subject to numerous critiques. Here are just some of the criticisms that have been levelled at her work.

- Some people argue that as a defender of the *polis* as a political standard, Arendt holds an elitist and even anti-democratic and hierarchical view of politics (Hansen 2003).
- Some argue that she defends a potentially immoral conception of political action. According to Hansen, the target here is the antagonistic element in Arendt's understanding of action. This supposedly exempts it from everyday moral and legal restraints that ensure that we respect the dignity of others, while in pursuit of our own goals (ibid. 29).

- It could be argued that Arendt is insufficiently attuned to the realities of social and political power, and consequently indifferent to the complex array of political identities in modern societies (ibid. 30).
- As argued earlier, there are criticisms against her reliance on the rigid distinction between private and public, particularly from feminists who argue that the confinement of the political to the realm outside the household has contributed to the exclusion of women from politics.
- She was critiqued for venturing that the evil of Nazism was 'banal'. According to Wilkinson (2004), this was seen as an act of bad faith and by some as a lack of sympathy for the victims.

Summary

Overall, Arendt has come to be seen as one of the most significant intellectuals of modern times. She was a female theorist whose social theories were broad and all encompassing. However, despite her 'grand theoretical' approach (not dissimilar in scale to Parsons'), which made her popular within the political realm, her accounts of racism and her social theories more generally never quite entered the boundaries of sociology during the time she was writing or in reconstructions of social theory during that age.

Frantz Fanon (1925–1961)

Frantz Fanon was a psychiatrist, a revolutionary and a writer. He wrote two key texts on anti-colonialism that have made a significant contribution to postcolonial studies. Fanon was from the French colony of Martinique. He left Martinique in 1943, when he volunteered to fight with the Free French in the Second World War, and he remained in France afterwards to study medicine and psychiatry in Lyon. He began to write political essays. He has been influential in both leftist and anti-racist political movements. His work stands as an important influence on contemporary postcolonial theorists (e.g. Homi Bhabha and Edward Said).

Fanon was a member of the National Liberation Front and participated in the violent struggle that led to the liberation of Algeria from French colonial rule in the 1950s. As a practising psychiatrist he also studied the effects of racism on the minds and personalities of its victims in Northern Africa. In the last years of his life Fanon devoted most of his time and energies to the liberation of Africa as a whole and its eventual unification. This gave Fanon a vantage point from which to undertake an analysis of both colonialism and racism. His work has been controversial. According to Alessandrini (1999), particularly controversial were his opinions on violence, the need to rethink class struggles in the colonial context and the relative revolutionary potential of colonized agricultural workers and the proletariat. His theories have had a long-lasting influence in cultural and postcolonial studies and have spawned their own academic subject area, 'Fanon Studies'. Within this section I explore some key aspects of his work.

Black Skin, White Masks

In 1952 Fanon published *Black Skin, White Masks*. According to Macey (2000), this book is really without precedent. It reflected Fanon's own frustrations with racism. The text was part manifesto, part analysis. It presents Fanon's personal experience as a black intellectual in a white world. It also elaborates the ways in which the colonizer–colonized relationship is normalized in psychology. As a young man, Fanon thought of himself as French because of his education and background. Therefore it was a shock to Fanon to encounter French racism. However, it is this encounter that shaped his theories about culture. Fanon endowed his medical and psychological practice with the understanding that racism generates harmful psychological effects that blind the black man to his subjection to universalized white norms. It also alienates his consciousness. According to Fanon, a racist culture inhibits psychological health in black men.

In the introduction to the book, Fanon asks, 'What does the black man want?' His question is not posed within a unified notion of history or a unified concept of man. According to Bhabha (1987), who has written extensively on Fanon, it is one of the original and disturbing qualities of the book that it rarely historicizes the colonial experience. According to Bhabha (ibid.), there is no grand narrative or realist perspective that acts as a background to social and historical facts against which the problems of the psyche emerge. The alignment between self and society or history and the psyche is questioned through Fanon's identification of the colonial subject. This colonial subject is historicized as it becomes diversely inscribed in the texts of history, literature and science; the colonial condition is invoked through image and fantasy (ibid.).

Colonization and Decolonization

In 1961, Frantz Fanon wrote *The Wretched of the Earth*, one of a growing number of social theories of the black decolonizing revolution that were increasingly read in Europe and the United States (Lemert 1995). According to Lemert (ibid.), although he was culturally light years away from the world of C. Wright Mills, Fanon wrote with sociological imagination of the issues that explain the troubles of colonial subjects in rebellion. In the book, Fanon urged colonized peoples to rid themselves of their degradation through enacting collective violence against their European oppressors. Using the United States as an example, Fanon warned of the dangers of a nation achieving national liberation before achieving maturation in the development of its own culture. Fanon's writings in themselves served as a source of intellectual inspiration for the US civil rights movement and subsequently the women's liberation movement (Poulos 1996).

According to Lemert (1995: 6–7), there could hardly be a more perfect application of Mills' ideal of joining reflexive biography to the critical history of social structures, although reconstructions of social theory during this era failed to see this. Ideas like Fanon's soon came back to the Euro-American world. By 1965–70, the non-violent civil rights movements had collapsed, giving way to a new, more aggressive social theory of the world (ibid.). As Fanon used the sociological imagination to define the hope of the colonized, so black revolutionaries applied Fanon, and theorists of the colonial situation, to the European and American situations (ibid.). For a period in the late 1960s his name and ideas were invoked by a bewildering variety of causes and groups. He was both a thinker and an activist and wrote about the social situation of the time.

Expanding Marxism

Fanon in his work drew heavily on Marxism and adapted Marx's theory to take on a more global and racial dynamic. According to Wyrick (1998), Fanon believed that colonialism is the bedrock of capitalism, which is the engine of western democracy. He also believed that colonialism is global robbery. Thus any political systems built on it are always corrupt and serve to maintain and exploit an underclass (ibid. 122). As a result Fanon saw socialism, a system whereby the state maintains the control of the production of goods and also redistributes wealth among the people equally, as a good alternative to capitalism (ibid. 123). Socialism was both a practical and an ethical solution for developing countries. However, for Fanon socialism for developing countries must be different from that in developed countries because of differences in economic and social organization. As a result, he advocates stretching Marx's original theory.

Fanon agreed with Marx that history developed dialectically, through factional struggle. But whereas Marx was concerned here with the warring factions in terms of economic class, Fanon claimed that race was the key categorical term in colonial situations. And, unlike European class structure, which branches from a single geographical area, colonial 'race structure' depend on geographical difference (ibid. 124). There is also a difference in approach to historical materialism. For Marx, at the centre of history was the material relationship between people and the means of production. As argued in Chapter 2, for Marx, the model for these relationships was nineteenth-century European industrial capitalism. Within the context of nineteenth-century capitalism, mechanization already mediated between the worker and his labour. Fanon believed underdeveloped countries were in a much less developed stage of production (ibid. 127). Rather than taking over the channels of production in the same ways as Marx suggested in nineteenth-century Europe, developing countries needed to change everything. They needed to re-examine their country's soil and mineral resources along with re-evaluating the nature of the export process itself (Fanon [1961] 1963). (Furthermore, Fanon did not trust a European historical narrative, even the revolutionary one as outlined by Marx (Wyrick 1998). This was because, as discussed in Chapter 2, for Marx all history is the history of class struggle; for Fanon, however, the history of colonialized peoples would be the 'history of resistance' to colonial invasion and domination (Fanon 1961: 69). Fanon also felt that Marx's base–superstructure model did not really apply to the masses in colonized countries. He felt that in capitalist societies, the superstructure fosters respect for the established order. This in turn creates an atmosphere of submission and inhibition around the people being exploited that lightens the task of policing them. However, the difference for Fanon between this and the colonial context is that, in a colonial context, colonial rule operates not through managing 'consent' but through inflicting terror and despair (Wyrick 1998: 131).)

His theory thus offers an alternative vision to Marx's focus on class revolution, just as Mills and Gouldner offered a fresh reading of Marx. However, whereas Mills' and Gouldner's adaptations can be seen in accounts of sociological theory of the 1960s, Fanon's racialized interpretation remains outside interpretations of the canon at the time.

Third Worldism

According to Wyrick (1998), Fanon saw the anti-colonial struggle as being at a crossroads: decolonization can lead either to new and different forms of cultural, political and economic oppression or it can lead to positive personal, national and global changes. He suggested that hope lay in bringing together the common interests of nations comprising the 'third world'. According to Fanon, it was from the third world that a new idea of human being would arise (ibid. 143).

Fanon found the concept of a 'third world' useful because for him it went beyond restrictive forms of nationalism and essentialized pan-Africanism or pan-Arabism (ibid.). Third world countries, according to him, were united by a common relationship to their colonial past and in their neocolonial present and future. More importantly, however, Fanon saw the third world as an oppositional space. He saw it as a place of resistance against threats from more powerful countries. According to Fanon, through growing rich and powerful the first world deliberately underdeveloped its colonies, leaving them no money or infrastructure and no coherent middle class (ibid.). As a result, in Fanon's eyes Europe owed the third world.

Fanon believed that the third world held a strategic position of non-alignment with either the first capitalist world or second socialist world. This enabled underdeveloped nations to get assistance from both. He sees this also as a political position that would ensure independence and that would lead to global justice and historical change (ibid.). This is an innovative position that, again, is not referred to in the rewriting of the 1960s sociological canon.

Critiques

Fanon Studies has become a huge and contested area as Fanon has been read, reread and critiqued from a number of angles. Here are some of the key critiques.

- For Bhabha (1987), among others, the relationship between colonizer and colonized is more complex, nuanced and politically ambiguous than Fanon recognizes in *The Wretched of the Earth.*
- Marxists often criticize Fanon for simply replacing the analysis of class with that of race, thus ignoring his own class position.
- There appears at times a contradiction between his radical criticism of colonialism and the holistic nature of his cultural criticism.
- Fanon's vision for social change has been critiqued as somewhat utopian. Social change in the third world as he predicted has not happened, and these countries still remain in poverty in comparison with the west.
- Fanon's work has often been critiqued for being gender blind as it focuses only on black men. However, many have argued that this fails really to appreciate Fanon's contradictory and troubled views on women.

Summary

Fanon produced interesting and innovative sociological theories during the 1960s. Psychology and his medical background influenced his approach. Furthermore, he produced important developments in Marxist theory. However, although Fanon has become a prominent contributor to contemporary postcolonial studies, his work on race, similar to that of DuBois before him, never reached the boundaries of social theory during his lifetime.

Simone de Beauvoir (1908–1986)

According to Evans (1996), when Simone de Beauvoir died in 1986 she was hailed as the greatest feminist of the twentieth century, if not ever. She was born in Paris to a bourgeois family. Much of her early life was spent in rebellion against the constraints of bourgeois manners. From her youth onwards, de Beauvoir focused her energy on the problem of defining, and living, the authentic human life (Lemert 1999). She attended the Sorbonne in Paris, where she met Sartre, gaining her aggregation in philosophy in 1929. Following this, she taught in schools and lectured on a part-time basis before launching a monthly literary review along with Sartre in 1945. De Beauvoir began her publishing career with a work of fiction, *L'Invitée* (She Came to Stay) in 1943, then turned to writing philosophy with *Pour une morale de l'ambiguité* (The Ethics of Ambiguity) in 1948, following this with *The Second Sex.* This latter book, published in 1949, was her most famous work, in which she stated that 'one is not born a woman; one becomes one'. Women are the 'other', the sex defined by men and patriarchy as not male, and consequently they are viewed as subordinate. De Beauvoir became involved in the women's movement in the late 1960s and began to be a campaigner for women's rights, particularly on issues such as abortion and sexual violence.

De Beauvoir's other works include a four-part autobiography, a novel called *The Mandarin* and *The Coming of Age*, a novel about ageing and society. She also wrote *A Very Easy Death*, a book about the death of her mother. One of her final novels was a diary recording the death of her friend and lover Sartre, called *Adieux: A Farewell to Sartre.* De Beauvoir moved continually between fiction and non-fiction, philosophy and essays, but throughout all ran an existentialist thread and recognition of 'the other'. In sum, de Beauvoir was a French philosopher, novelist and essayist.

The works of de Beauvoir are hugely important for contemporary feminism. De Beauvoir has consistently challenged the taken-for-granted attitudes of western bourgeois society; she remained an active critic of the society she inhabited (Evans 1996). Some feminists also promote her as a 'founding mother' (Moi 1994). During the feminist critique of malestream sociological theory in the 1970s and 1980s, de Beauvoir's work became central. However, at the time of the writing of *The Second Sex*, apart from occasional reviews of her books by sociologists such as Mills, her work on women's position in society remained outside the sociological canon. She has, however, more recently been inserted into some accounts of the development of social theory (e.g. Lemert 1999; Evans, in Stones 1998).

The Second Sex

The Second Sex (1949) is the book that de Beauvoir will be remembered for most. She herself, however, felt that too much attention had often been paid to her writings on women and too little to other aspects of her work. According to de Beauvoir, the book was not written as part of a subconsciously feminist stance. Simone de Beauvoir's conscious engagements with feminism came after the book's publication. It was not until the early 1970s that de Beauvoir became involved with active feminist politics. One could say that she was in a way co-opted into a movement that she had inspired and helped to establish.

In *The Second Sex* de Beauvoir argued that man has appropriated the status of the active, observing *self* and designated woman as the passive, observed other (Shilling and Mellor 2001: 129–30). Although becoming a woman involves 'apprenticeship' (learning passive roles, etc.), de Beauvoir insisted that this socialization is based on the bodily differences between girls and boys (ibid.). For de Beauvoir, biological difference is of key importance in explaining women's position. However, according to her, biology is not enough of an answer. De Beauvoir argued that women are created as 'other', a process that begins with constraints on girls during socialization. Sacred authority figures surround and reveal the future for girls, whereas boys are encouraged to 'break away' to discover and project themselves on the world. Whereas boys are introduced to violent sports, girls are directed towards passive activities (ibid. 130). De Beauvoir argued that women in society are kept as 'other'. She argued that within the social world, there are those who occupy the position of the 'essential', the universal and the human and there are those who are defined, reduced and marked by their (sexual, racial, religious) difference from what is the 'norm', the universal. Although the achievements of 'others' may not always be dismissed, they are always seen as different, specialist and peripheral.

De Beauvoir's answer to the 'woman question' was with the adoption by women of male habits and values. She encouraged women against womanhood, instead advocating economic independence and emotional autonomy. She argued for a rejection of traditional femininity. Basing her analysis on existentialist principles and values, de Beauvoir argued that women should reject their subordinate position and take their place in the public world of men as independent individuals. According to C. Wright Mills (1963), as argued in Chapter 4, what de Beauvoir was after was what the Soviet revolution promised – that women be raised and trained like men, that they have the same working conditions, rights and sexual liberty as men (ibid.).

As argued, *The Second Sex* has become de Beauvoir's most famous piece of work and has been of central importance to the development of feminist theory. Her personal life, however, has sometimes led feminist theorists to question her feminist credentials.

A Reluctant Feminist

De Beauvoir was 'discovered' by feminism in the late 1960s and annexed for feminism. However, her view of the world gave rise to numerous problems about how she could be described as a feminist and how her work could be used to demonstrate a theoretical tradition in feminism. She appeared to have worshipped intellectual men. In particular, she saw Sartre's work as most important and put him on a pedestal. Like many women, she underestimated her own achievements and had negative views about women's bodies, a view later overturned by the French feminists (among others). These views led some to wonder whether she was really a feminist.

According to Lemert (1999), some are inclined to fault de Beauvoir's feminist credentials because of her relationship to Sartre. She seemed, at times, to have ceded too much to him. According to Lemert (ibid.), the relationship was, however, complex, and hurt ran in both directions. Evans (1996) also points out that we can defend de Beauvoir's admiration for the outstanding figures of the western academy by pointing out that when she was writing, at least in the period up to the mid-1960s, there was no visible feminist tradition for her to refer to (as demonstrated in Chapter 4). Her education was by men and about men. Women simply did not appear in her world except as her friends or lovers. De Beauvoir, like everyone else in the west, had to live in the moral climate of the 1950s, which was deeply conservative and in many ways socially reactionary.

According to Evans (ibid.), in making de Beauvoir, or any woman, a feminist icon, there are always dangers of refusing the problems that her life raises. We nonetheless need to appreciate the radical nature of her theories at that time, which have been of crucial importance to the development of feminist theory and feminist sociological theory.

Autobiography

As mentioned in the introduction to this section, another key area of de Beauvoir's writings was biography. She wrote four biographical pieces about herself: *Memoirs of a Dutiful Daughter* (1959), *The Prime of Life* (1962), *Force of Circumstance* (1965) and *All Said and Done* (1974). According to Evans (1996), as de Beauvoir entered the public world through the publication of *The Second Sex* and her political involvements, so the accounts of her life that she provided changed. *Memoirs of a Dutiful Daughter* and *The Prime of Life* are essentially about a girl and a woman living a 'private life' but determinedly making statements about the public world and attempting to theorize human relations within it. According to Lemert (1999), *The Prime of Life* is one of the best narrative descriptions both of her relationship with Sartre and of her life in Paris before during and after the Second World War. *Force of Circumstance* and *All Said and Done* are very much about a publicly known woman whose life is recorded in the international media and is increasingly the subject of comment and evaluation.

According to Evans (1996), both *Memoirs of a Dutiful Daughter* and *The Prime of Life* end on a note of liberation. In the first volume de Beauvoir is 'freed' from her family by success in higher education and through meeting Sartre. In the second, de Beauvoir as a French woman is literally freed by the end of the Second World War and the liberation of Paris in 1944. The later two books end on a more ambiguous note. The conclusion to *Force of Circumstance* suggests reservations about the experiences of her life, while *All Said and Done* is about the death of God. Overall, de Beauvoir presents her life as an exercise in personal emancipation. However, this is an exercise left unresolved (ibid.). De Beauvoir also wrote an account of her mother's death into a separate volume of autobiography, *A Very Easy Death*. This suggests to the reader an organizing worldview that placed the death of a mother in a distinct category (ibid.). This particular text has been cited in contemporary research on the sociology of death. Her biographies overall have come to be explored by contemporary feminist sociologists working in the area of biography and narrative.

Critiques

De Beauvoir has been critiqued from a number of directions. In particular she has been critiqued for a lack of context in her work. Here are some critiques of her work.

- First, de Beauvoir takes for granted a great deal about western bourgeois culture that feminists, from a range of viewpoints, might now question.
- Second, her statements about women's positions and politics are frequently made without reference to the context in which these issues arise.
- She argues for women to reject femininity, to control nature by culture, but can it be controlled? And how? More important, do we want to control it?
- Jean Bethke Elshtain (1981, cited in Tong 1992: 211–12) made three major points in her critiques of de Beauvoir's *The Second Sex*.

  - The first is that the book is not accessible to the majority of women. Her ideas are often abstractions that arise not from women's experience but from philosophers' armchair speculations.
  - The second major point in Elshtain's critique concerned her objections to the ways in which de Beauvoir treated the body. In *The Second Sex* women's bodies appear negative, dirty, insignificant, burdensome and alienating. De Beauvoir distrusted the body. Women's individuality, or personhood as she saw it, were won at the cost of rejecting their reproductive capacities.
  - Finally, Elshtain criticizes de Beauvoir for valorizing male norms and characteristics. According to de Beauvoir, women achieve success through being like men, not through celebrating their difference. This is something critiqued by psychoanalytic feminism.

Summary

As mentioned, then, de Beauvoir wrote groundbreaking social theories, in particular focusing on women's positions in society. Male social theorists writing during the 1950s and 1960s were reticent in engaging with her work. Also, it is only recently that we have seen her being inserted into accounts of modern sociological theory. She has nonetheless been recognized as an important figure in contemporary sociological theory, in particular for feminist social theorists.

Outsider Visions and Sociological Theory

According to Lemert (1995: 5), if Mills taught sociology as an act of the sociological imagination in which individuals reflect critically on the relations between their 'personal troubles' and 'the public issues of social structure', then sociology occurs wherever such imagination takes place. In this sense, sociology in those days can be found in the work of Arendt, Fanon and de Beauvoir. However, despite the fact that the work of these theorists can be seen as a practical application of the sociological imagination, they were not recognized as sociological theorists. Those sociological theorists writing at the time, such as Parsons, Mills and Gouldner, failed to fully engage with the work of authors like these. Furthermore, these outsiders (and theorists like them) have also until very recently, as mentioned, remained outside most contemporary reconstructions of sociological theory of that time. Within the next section I want to ask why this was the case.

Why Were They Outsiders?

The outsider status of the theorists discussed in this chapter can be related in part to a self-identified outsiderness. For example, none of these theorists discussed here identified as a sociologist. Simone de Beauvoir identified herself as a philosopher, essayist and novelist, not a sociologist. Frantz Fanon was a psychiatrist, political activist and theorist, and Hannah Arendt was a political theorist. However, as discussed back in Chapter 2, practically none of the classical sociologists identified themselves as sociologists – certainly not Marx or Weber – yet their sociological theories have been seen as canonical. The non-identification of theorists as sociologists has never stopped some theorists being viewed as central to sociological theory. The theories of Arendt, Fanon and de Beauvoir were sociological in nature. Why, then, were they left out of sociological theory during the time they were writing and why have they been left out of accounts of sociological theory's modern past?

The failure to engage with de Beauvoir undoubtedly relates to the sexist nature of the discipline during this time. Such sexism could also be seen to be one of the reasons for the failure of the discipline to engage with Arendt's more general sociological theories, as was the case with Martineau's theories on political economy a century before. When it comes to Arendt, we must also acknowledge that she was in part probably cast out of the canon because of her critical views towards the dominant trend of empiricism within the social sciences at the time. However, this was not the only reason; sexism would also have played a role in her exclusion. Male sociological theorists did not acknowledge women theorists during the mid-twentieth century. As argued in the previous chapter, male sociologists writing during this time failed to pay any attention to issues of gender more generally, and when they did, as with Mills, this was in a sexist manner. Although male theorists were writing during times of upheaval, during the women's movement and civil rights movement, they preferred instead to model their notions of gender on 1950s ideologies. Such ideologies supported a natural division of labour between the sexes, a division that kept women in the private realm and men in the public realm. Thus, malestream social theorists writing at this time failed to engage with feminism. Women theorists and their work were excluded as a result. For Fanon particularly (but also for Arendt), there was also the issue of race. As explored within this chapter, both these theorists included an analysis of race in their social theories. However, as argued in the previous chapter, race was not seen as a key fundamental variable of social theoretical analysis during the mid-twentieth century. With the exception of the Frankfurt School, this is reflected in sociological theory during the 1950s and 1960s, despite the fact that the civil rights movements at this time placed the issue of race in a central position.

Again, as argued previously, the lack of interest in issues of gender and race by theorists of the golden age is something that has been replicated in contemporary accounts of modern sociological theory. Rather than questioning the treatment and place of women and theorists of colour and issues of gender and race, in social theory during the mid-twentieth century contemporary theorists simply accepted it. Consequently, contemporary authors have neglected to include theorists of gender and race and issues of gender and race within their own reconstructions of sociological theory during the mid-twentieth century. Their accounts of sociological theory's modern past have tended to reflect the position and interests of white men. As a result, race and gender were excluded from the agenda.

As we have seen in previous chapters there has for a long time been a reluctance to rethink the origins and implications of sociology's way of thinking, and thus the field has been defiantly resistant to sociology that is being done outside the organized profession of sociologists (Lemert 1995). As argued throughout this book, we can see that sociology has for a long time resisted taking feminism into account. According to Lemert (ibid.), if anything, sociology has been even more unwilling to read with definitive seriousness the writings of social theorists working on race or sexuality. This can be seen in the failure to engage at this time with the most prominent practical sociologists working outside the discipline, theorists such as Arendt, Fanon and de Beauvoir who were writing their social theories beyond the boundaries of sociological theory. However, although these theorists have been ignored in relation to sociological theory during the mid-twentieth century, they have since been recognized as important to aspects of contemporary social theory, particularly in relation to gender studies, ethnic and racial studies, and postcolonial studies.

From Modern Outsiders to Contemporary Insiders

Although these theorists may have been excluded from accounts of modern sociological theory, their theories have come to inform the work of contemporary sociological theorists. For example, de Beauvoir's work went on to become central to the second-wave feminist critique of malestream sociology. De Beauvoir has also more recently been included in texts about key thinkers in sociological theory (e.g. Evans, in Stones 1998).

Hannah Arendt never seemed to elicit the engagement of sociologists writing during the golden age. She has since, however, become a more central figure in contemporary sociological theory. Social theorists working in the area of race have taken up her historical accounts of race and racism. Her work on the rise of the social realm has also been taken up by contemporary feminists, such as Benhabib (1992), who focus on the issue of gender and public space. Arendt's theories on social and public space offer contemporary feminist social theorists new ways of conceptualizing the public and private realms. Other, male social theorists have recognized the influence of Arendt upon their own work. For example, Habermas has recognized Arendt's influence on his own theory of communicative reason and discourse ethics. Other social theorists, both critical social theorists and postmodernist thinkers, have also drawn on her theory of judgement in their own work. She has also been taken up in a number of other areas of sociology, for example in recent work on the sociology of suffering (e.g. Wilkinson 2004).

Frantz Fanon, again, was not included in accounts of sociological theories of the 1960s. However, he has become a central figure in contemporary black social thought. We often find him now in profiles in social theory (e.g. Lemert 1999). Fanon's work has been widely drawn on, both politically and academically. After his death it held particular value for leaders of the Black Panther Party in the United States and other revolutionaries. It was influential on political theory, cultural studies and postcolonial studies. He has influenced the work of some key theorists in postcolonial studies (e.g. Homi Bhabha and Gayatri Chakravorty Spivak to name but two) and the black British left (e.g. Stuart Hall, Paul Gilroy and Hazel Carby) (Alessandrini 1999). He can also be found in the contemporary social theories of Lemert (1995), who takes a multiculturalist approach to social theory. Given the breadth and complexity of Fanon's work, he will surely continue to be relevant in a wide range of disciplinary fields.

Evaluating Modern Outsiders

Overall, the three theorists explored here were excluded from accounts of modern sociological theory. The failure to engage with these theorists and their work at the time of writing, as argued, undoubtedly relates in part to the gender- and race-blind nature of the discipline of sociology during the mid-twentieth century. Although it is important to recognize that other factors played a role in the exclusion of these theorists from sociological theory (e.g. self-perpetuated outsider status), gender – and race – did play an important role. As we saw in the previous chapter, views of race and gender during this time were often conservative. This can be seen, as I argued in Chapter 4, in the work of theorists including Parsons, Mills, Gouldner and the Frankfurt School, who allocated gender no role in their work and race only a peripheral role. We can see that the work of sociological theorists during this time was still focused on socioeconomic issues of inequality. Furthermore, this lack of interest in issues of gender and race by theorists of the golden age is something that has been internalized by contemporary theorists writing past histories of the discipline. Consequently, although contemporary authors may see these authors as relevant to the development of contemporary social theory, they have not included theorists of gender and race and issues of gender and race within their own interpretations of sociological theory's past. Their accounts of sociological theory's recent history have tended to reflect the position of white men. As a result, race and gender have been erased from the agenda of modern sociological theory.

It is important to note here that these views on race and gender were held more widely in society during the early part of the mid-twentieth century. At least in the period up to the mid-1960s, gender ideologies were based on a rigid division of labour whereby the woman's place was in the home. Furthermore, views on race before the civil rights movements served only to situate people of colour in positions of subservience. Thus, there were not many women or people of colour who were able to gain academic posts, certainly not tenured positions, in universities during the 1950s and 1960s. However, during the late 1960s and 1970s the women's movement and the civil rights movements started to have effects on the position of women and black people within academia and within sociology specifically. These movements fostered a vehement challenge to sociological exclusion, one that would challenge the race- and gender-blind nature of the discipline. In the next section I explore this challenge to sociological theory and ask whether it was about to end the exclusion of gender and race and black and female sociological theorists.

The Challenge to Western Sociology

Despite, as argued over the past two chapters, the somewhat varied engagements of theory in the 1950s and 1960s with the social movements of the time, these movements ultimately did have a long-term significant effect on sociology. The most obvious one, according to Callinicos (1999), was a stimulated renaissance of Marxist theory as it sought to liberate itself from the confining association with the official communist parties aligned to Moscow. After the upheavals of the 1960s, structural functionalism was seen as no longer plausible (ibid.). The turmoil and social and political movements of the 1960s led to further change, spawning a war on social science disciplines such as sociology. It is this war on social sciences and the subsequent effects on sociology that we are interested in here.

The attack on disciplines such as sociology came from a variety of angles. In particular, women attacked sociology for what was seen as its refusal of women both institutionally and theoretically (Evans 2003). This attack was furthered by challenges from gay people and people of colour, who also voiced their dissatisfaction. Sociology was accused of having refused to acknowledge or study the worlds of those people who were not heterosexual, white or male. It was accepted that sociology had always included the working class in its vision, but that vision had been one that had defined social exclusion or social disadvantage largely in terms of discrimination in the labour market. A new agenda began to challenge existing sociology (ibid.). There was a growth in gender studies and the study of race and ethnicity within sociology, which enabled those writing from behind the veil of exclusion to speak. Did this challenge finally put an end to sociological exclusion based on gender and race? This question is explored in the following two sections.

The Feminist Challenge to Social Theory

According to Jessie Bernard (1989), the 1970s and 1980s marked a series of eye-opening experiences for a generation of women activists. These were women who had been trained in the civil rights and anti-war movements who, despite their contributions, were nonetheless finding themselves victims of male sexism. These women found themselves excluded from leadership positions within such movements. Their eyes were opened to the 'taken for granted sexism' and to the real nature of their relationships to men (ibid.). The 1970s thus proved to be an amazing decade for women. During this period, an expansion in higher education meant that more women were included in academia. Furthermore, a number of feminist journals were launched between 1968 and the 1980s (e.g. *Feminist Studies, Women's Studies* and *Signs*). These were places where women could unearth inequalities and express their plight.

During this time there emerged a proliferation of feminist perspectives, including those that sought to adapt existing malestream theories. For example, Marxist sociologies were based on assumptions about the primacy of the mode of production; however, they emphasized class rather than gender relations in the productive process. Feminists challenged this during the 1970s through developing forms of Marxist feminism focused on gender, while sharing Marxism's emphasis on the mode of production (Shilling and Mellor 2001). Other perspectives, including radical feminism, also emerged in the 1960s and became influential in the 1970s (ibid.). Radical feminism examines the sexed nature of social action. In doing so, it prioritizes patriarchy over capitalism and sexual over economic relations. It emphasizes the control men have over women's bodies through the institutions of marriage, motherhood and heterosexuality (ibid.).

Psychoanalytical feminism also rose in the 1970s and became popular in the 1980s. Psychoanalytical feminism looks at gender identity through the complex cultural, interpersonal and symbolic mediation of biology. In particular, psychoanalytic feminists focus on how psychic processes are mediated through traditional male–female sex roles or through linguistic symbolization of culture. These symbolic media both direct and repress childhood experience and provide a libidinal and psychic basis for the sexual division of labour (ibid.).

Along with the growth of a diversity of feminist theories there was also a proliferation of feminists who specifically challenged malestream sociology from the late 1960s onwards in both Europe and the United States. As mentioned in the previous chapter, this started in 1963, when Friedan published *The Feminine Mystique*. In this text, Friedan provided a feminist critique of theorists such as Parsons. She argued that Parsonian structural functionalism was a pseudo-science, describing 1950s America as if it were an example of human achievement. Those not conforming to this vision were labelled 'deviant' (Delamont 2003: 16). Friedan argued that Parsons' sociology was taught in an oversimplified way to thousands of young women in courses on the family and marriage. Friedan's critique was particularly good in exposing how easily functionalist ideas about gender slid from description to prescription (ibid.).

There was a proliferation of critiques on malestream theory after this, in the United States in the work of Jessie Bernard and in Canada in the work of Dorothy Smith. In the United Kingdom Ann Oakley provided a stunning critique in *The Sociology of Housework* (1974) of existing malestream sociology. In the introduction to this book, Oakley wrote a critique of existing sociological theory from classical theory onwards. In conventional sociology Oakley saw women as taking the position of 'ghosts, shadows or stereotyped characters' (ibid. 1). The gender-blind nature of conventional sociology she attributed to three aspects: 'the nature of its origins, the sex of its practitioners, and the ideology of gender roles, borrowed from the wider society, which is reproduced uncritically within it' (ibid. 21). She also looked at the gender-blind nature of a variety of substantive areas in sociology, including work and the family. Her strategy for confronting this sexism during this time involved looking through women's eyes at the occupation of housewife (ibid.). According to Crow (2004), Oakley's work presents a direct challenge to existing understandings, and as part of this process she aims to rescue the discipline of sociology from the hands of those sociologists who suffer from what she calls the 'sociological unimagination'.

In light of these critiques, little by little sociological theory came to recognize feminism as intrinsically worthy of incorporation into the discipline. However, feminist theorists such as those named above were mostly banished to the safe haven of women's studies and later gender studies. While men carried on with the business of doing highly abstract social theories, and women became linked yet again with substantive issues, gender and women's studies became a comfortable add-on to malestream sociology but did not challenge or threaten it. Women sociologists, according to histories of sociology, remained focused on gendered inequalities. Gender inequalities failed to be centralized within sociological theories and remained on the sidelines of the discipline. Such a relegation of female theorists and issues of gender can be seen from this time onwards on many core courses on social theory. Gender and women sociologists were haplessly tacked on to the end of a long and distinguished history of male social theorists. Thus, although feminist social theorists might have induced a major overhaul of mainstream sociology, they were still put in their place, and their views were still secondary to male abstract theories.

The Growth of the Sociology of Race

There was also during this time a critique of existing sociology as race blind and a resulting growth in the sociological study of race and ethnicity. According to Stone (1977: xiii), the Second World War marked a major turning point for race relations. Several fundamental forces influenced both the popular conception and the academic study of race and ethnicity, for example the revelation of the Nazi genocide in Europe, the leap of Afro-Asian societies out of colonial racial domination into national integration and the continuing flow of migrants across national and regional frontiers in all parts of the world. These all highlighted a sense of racial and ethnic awareness and raised it to an issue of national and international concern. According to Stone (ibid. xiii), alongside these changes, sociologists (writing at this time) became increasingly aware of the possible contribution of the study of race and ethnic relations to the core field of sociology. Sociologists, as a result, according to Stone (ibid. xiii), were forced to re-examine their basic tools and concepts when applying them to cultures and situations significantly different from their own. What came out of this process was the emphasis on alternative strands of thought within the mainstream of contemporary sociology (ibid. xiii). Thus, during this time there was a growing recognition of race as a theoretical concept and, more generally, an increasing interest in the sociological study of race and ethnicity.

According to Solomos and Back (1996), a number of early studies of what came in Britain to be called 'race relations' were carried out in the 1950s and 1960s by scholars such as Michael Banton, Ruth Glass, John Rex and Sheila Patterson. The majority of these studies during this time focused on the interaction between minority and majority communities in employment, housing and other social contexts. Furthermore, in the United States from this time onwards, there were a number of studies that looked at the role and impact of the civil rights movement and anti-discrimination legislation on the position of African Americans (ibid.). During the 1970s and 1980s, the sociology of race relations turned to structural explanations, linking itself more clearly with the concerns of sociological theory. According to Solomos and Back (ibid.), John Rex made the most sustained effort to bring a class perspective to the study of race relations. Rex's text on *Race Relations in*

Sociological Theory (1970) has been very influential in this area and it remains one of the most ambitious attempts to provide a theoretical grounding for research in ethnic and racial studies (ibid.). Studies focusing on structural explanations were of key importance during this time and helped to merge the concerns of sociological theory and the sociology of race.

Overall, from the 1960s onwards one could witness the growth of interest in the theorization of the study of both the new forms of migration and settlement as they were being experienced in Britain and elsewhere and other types of race relations. From this period onwards, race and ethnicity became a thriving subfield of sociology. It connected itself to structural explanations of sociological theory and had a diversification of interests. But this is exactly what it was still at this time: a *sub*field. Despite the recognition of race as a key theoretical concept, it was still sidestepped by those writing mainstream social theory. While white men carried on with the business of doing highly abstract social theories, the field of race and ethnicity, like gender and women's studies, became a comfortable add-on to mainstream sociology. The concepts of race and ethnicity failed to be centralized within sociological theory. Ethnic and racial studies was seen to focus on its specialized critique of 'racial inequalities' not on groundbreaking generalist social theories.

Conclusion

Within this chapter I have explored the work of a selection of sociological theorists writing sociologically but writing from outside the canon. As argued, these are not the only gendered and racialized theorists who were writing from outside the boundaries of sociological theory. There are many others just like them. However, as argued previously, space constraints within the book mean that it can explore the work of only a few. The theorists discussed here wrote sociologically from the perspective of marginality and exile. They were also social theorists who included gendered and racial analysis into their social theories. They were, however, kept outside the canon both by sociological theorists writing at the time and through contemporary constructions of the golden age canon. Despite the wealth of writing focusing on gendered and racial inequalities, the work of these theorists has rarely been touched upon in accounts of sociological theory of this time, although subsequently and posthumously these theorists have been seen as contributing to contemporary social theories.

As discussed, the social movements of the 1960s did encourage new agendas and challenges to social theory from the marginal and the excluded. There was then during the 1970s a growth in the critique of mainstream theory from women and people of colour. There also emerged a growth of gender and the sociology of race and ethnicity in both the United Kingdom and the United States. These, however, remained during this time add-ons to the social theoretical canon rather than being integrated into it. Theorists writing from behind the veil of exclusion were still subsidiary with regards to sociological theory and failed to appear in most central texts on social theory at this time. However, as a result of trends in postmodernism and post-structuralism (among other approaches) taking place within sociological theory from the 1970s onwards, this was about to change. The next chapter explores these changes, focusing in particular on their effects on race and gender and women and black theorists.

Chapter Summary

- During the mid-twentieth century, there were a number of sociological theorists writing from beyond the boundaries of sociological theory.
- The examples of such theorists given here are Hannah Arendt, Frantz Fanon and Simone de Beauvoir.
- All three theorists were writing profound social theories just as worthy of our attention as those explored in Chapter 4.
- They were kept outside because they were either black or female.
- Sociological theory at this time was gender and race blind. Accounts of this modern era of social theory have tended to reflect this in their interpretations.
- During the late 1960s and early 1970s a challenge to sociological theory arose. There was a growth of feminist sociology and the sociology of race and ethnicity.
- However, the concepts of race and gender still failed to be centralized within sociological theory, and black and female theorists still remained excluded from sociological theory.

Further Reading

For accounts of Arendt see L. May and J. Kohn (eds.), *Hannah Arendt: Twenty Years Later* (MIT Press, 1996). For good accounts of Fanon see A. Alessandrini, (ed.), *Frantz Fanon: Critical Perspectives* (Routledge, 1999). For a good account of de Beauvoir see M. Evans, *Simone de Beauvoir* (Sage, 1996). For an account of the feminist challenge to social theory see S. Delamont, *Feminist Sociology* (Sage, 2003). For a history of ethnic and racial studies see J. Solomos and L. Back, *Racism and Society* (Macmillan, 1996). For a general account of these issues see C. Shilling and P. Mellor, *The Sociological Ambition: The Elementary Forms of Social Life* (Sage, 2001).

PART THREE

Contemporary Sociology

6

Postmodernism and Social Theory

In the preceding chapters, I focused on sociological theory in the mid-twentieth century. I also explored the subsequent crises within sociology that led to significant changes in sociological theory, looking again at sociological insiders and gendered and racial outsiders. In this chapter, I want to move on to look at contemporary social theory. Many argue that trends towards postmodernism from the 1970s onwards have led to a deconstruction of the sociological canon. The deconstruction of the discipline has meant an emphasis on interdisciplinarity and a shift in focus for sociology from traditional forms of inequality to an emphasis on *difference* and diversity. According to Mouzelis (1991), such a shift can be seen in the movement away from sociological theory to social theory. This, according to him, indicates a move from substantively linked theory to speculative philosophizing, and from a disciplinary emphasis on economics to a focus on culture. This in turn for Mouzelis leads to an excessive focus in sociological theory on epistemological or ontological questions. However, such a shift has also led to the opening up of sociological theory to further include issues of gender and race and those theorists previously classed as outsiders.

The aim of this chapter is to explore the status of contemporary social theory, paying particular attention to the repercussions of postmodernism for those theorists previously excluded, that is, women and theorists of colour. The chapter also explores the effects of postmodernism on the areas of gender and race. These are areas that have, as shown throughout the book, previously been sidelined within sociological theory. The key question to be asked within this chapter is: now that sociological theory has been deconstructed and opened up, does this mean an end to sociological outsiders? Is it an end to the exclusion of theorists because of their race and gender? Also, does it mean that the areas of race and gender have become more central within social theory?

The chapter is split into several sections; first, it looks at changes that have taken place within sociological theory over the past 20 years. It also focuses on the deconstruction of sociological theory, exploring the impact of postmodernism on the discipline and on gender and race. Second, it explores the ways in which this opening up of sociological theory has meant that disciplinary insiders, marginal figures and outsiders are now found alongside one another in accounts of social theory. This is explored through a focus on the work of a sample of theorists now found side by side in texts on social theory. I explore the work of three contemporary social theorists: Anthony Giddens, Donna Haraway and Stuart Hall. The aim here is not to explore the work of postmodern theorists per se, but rather to look at the work of a range of social theorists (some may class themselves as postmodern) who can be found in contemporary social theory as a result of shifts occurring because of postmodernism. The theorists chosen are but a selection of theorists writing contemporary social theory. As shown, they are all very different theorists writing from different perspectives and backgrounds, but they nonetheless can all be found in accounts of contemporary theory. The chapter moves on to look at the position occupied by women and theorists of colour within social theory. Are they now centralized within the discipline? Or is there a hierarchy between those considered mainstream white male sociologists and those previously situated as racial and gendered outsiders? The chapter begins with an exploration of changes in sociological theory over the past few decades in order to give a background to the arguments

Changes in Sociological Theory

According to Elliott and Ray (2003), over the past 20 years social theory has undergone dramatic changes. There has been a widespread sense of disillusionment with classical forms of social thought (Marxist, Durkheimian, Weberian) and a significant proliferation in new conceptual approaches. This diversification has ranged from the re-examination and revitalization of older traditions of thought to the elaboration of new standpoints, including cultural studies, postfeminism and queer theory (ibid. xi). There has been a shift in emphasis from the economic to the cultural, provoking authors to write about the 'cultural turn' within the social sciences. Alongside this, theorists and theoretical schools of thought previously ignored or marginalized have been rediscovered and reinterpreted, creating new approaches in the process. As I go on to explore in this chapter, the rise in postmodernism has also had a profound effect on the social theoretical canon. With its emphasis on decentred subjectivity, difference, otherness, ambiguity and ambivalence, in accounts of contemporary social theory the coherent and cohesive canon of a century before has been blown apart.

As argued in Chapters 2 and 4, changes in social theory reflect changes in society itself. According to Elliott and Ray (2003), the rapid expansion in competing versions of social theory results from broad-ranging changes in social relations in modern institutions. For example, they argue that the analysis of postmodernism as a core concern of social theory developed because of the impact of globalization, transnational finance and capital movements, as well as global civil society. Indeed, according to them, an array of social developments and political transformations – including new information technologies, the hyper-technologization of war and the proliferation of globalized risk – have been critical to both disciplinary specialization and interdisciplinary studies within the academic humanities and social sciences (ibid. xi–xii). They argue that social theory, despite being thrown into disarray in terms of the established canon, has consequently been equally reinvigorated or reinvented. Indeed, contemporary social theory has underpinned academic output in fields as diverse as gender studies, cultural studies, film studies, psychoanalytic studies, communications and media studies, postcolonialism and queer theory (ibid. xii).

This chapter is largely concerned with the impact of postmodernism on social theory. It focuses on the way in which the social theoretical canon has been opened up to include those previously excluded, focusing in particular (as throughout the book) on issues of gender and race. I start by looking at the effects of postmodernism on sociological theory.

Postmodernism and Sociological Theory

What is postmodernism? According to Delamont (2003), at its simplest, postmodernism is a challenge to the consensus among the educated classes in the western capitalist nations, since the Enlightenment at the end of the eighteenth century, that universal, objective scientific truths can be reached by scientific methods. Doubts about the modernist project have encouraged many authors to challenge the triumph of progress and the validity of scientific knowledge. Postmodern theorists argue instead that we have entered a new age, the postmodern condition, which has generated a much more relativistic view of the world (Marsh 2000). The rational and the rigid guidelines of the grand theories and meta-narratives of modernism have been swept away and replaced by the irrational and flexible elements of a far more relativist position in which 'anything goes'.

Those social theorists working within a postmodern framework have opposed traditional sociological theory as it existed in the past. According to Mouzelis (1994), postmodernism and post-structuralism oppose conventional social theory on three fronts: they are against foundationalism and universalism; they are against the notion of the centred subject, favouring social practices instead; they are also against the notion of representation and empirical reference, in particular questioning the very existence of a social reality out there for sociologists to study. According to Mouzelis (ibid.), the three theoretical orientations of postmodernism examined above lead to a view of the social as a set of discourses that cannot be conceptualized in either hierarchical terms or in terms of such conventional distinctions as micro–macro and agency–structure or, finally, in terms of the institutional differentiation in modern societies between the economic, political and cultural

spheres. Consequently, postmodern and post-structuralist thinkers completely
ignore the boundaries between social science disciplines. Postmodernists
view with disdain the artificial classification of knowledge into separate
disciplines. Instead, they emphasize the pluralistic character of knowledge.
As a result, postmodernism entails a deconstruction of the boundaries between disciplines such as sociology, philosophy and linguistics. This enables
a more eclectic approach to social theory, one where we are able to pick and
mix from a range of theories. It has also enabled previous theoretical outsiders to become part of the discipline.

This rise in theories of postmodernism, deconstruction of the canon and
collapse of disciplinary boundaries has been accompanied by what has
become known as the 'cultural turn', a movement from the economic and
social to the cultural. According to Barrett (1998), this turn has both theoretical and empirical aspects. It reflects awareness that culture was marginalized in the work of the classics, Marx, Weber and Durkheim. Furthermore, it
recognizes that in the late twentieth century, technological and social
changes have made the media and culture in general more important and
thus highlights the need for sociologists to recognize this (ibid.). Overall, the
cultural turn and a more general postmodernist critique of knowledge have
contributed to the weakening of paradigms for social scientific research. This
has led in turn to the growth of cultural studies – a term that covers a range
of analytic approaches including feminist, postcolonial, gay and lesbian, multicultural and even revived versions of materialist enquiry inspired by British
Marxism.

However, according to Elliott and Ray (2003), although some theorists
wish to celebrate postmodernity or modernity becoming conscious of its own
limits, others see various dangers in these developments, notably relativism.
In particular, some theorists are critical of the effects of postmodernism on
sociological theory. For example, in *Back to Sociological Theory* (1991)
Mouzelis argues that the development of sociological theory has been ham-
pered. This, according to him, is because it has been absorbed into social theory more generally conceived (see McLennan 1995). This is a change brought
about by postmodernism and the deconstruction of boundaries, and it presents a problem for the professional identity of the discipline since it is no
longer clear how sociology as a specific intellectual pursuit is to be distinguished from any other. More important, the slide into social theory removes
what is specific to substantively oriented discourses, since these are in effect
all brought under the dominance of philosophy. Mouzelis suggests that the
discipline draw in its boundaries and halt the trend towards speculative
philosophizing.

There is not space within this chapter to explore fully all the implications
of postmodernism for social theory or necessarily to explore the work of postmodern theorists themselves. Readings are provided at the end of this chapter
for that purpose. Rather, the aim is to look at the impacts of postmodernism

for those previously classed as outsiders because of gender and race and the subjects of gender and race. Because of the emphasis on the deconstruction of sociological theory brought about by postmodernism, it is no longer tenable for social theory to exclude in the ways it has previously. This is what we are concerned with here. Sociology, it would seem, has at last been opened up to theorists of gender and race. According to Game (1991), the social world is one comprised of a multiplicity of orders, different ways of meaning, that inscribe and are inscribed in different structures of desire. Through the process of deconstruction, such a multiplicity of voices, including those from a gendered and racial point of view, become able to speak within sociology. Before I go on to look at these voices within social theory, I look more specifically at the impact of postmodernism on race, gender and class.

Postmodernism, Class, Race and Gender

Changes in sociological theory and postmodernism have heralded a number of changes in the positions of the areas of class, gender and race. As argued throughout this book, for a long time class has been seen as a central element in the development of the discipline. Class and socioeconomic patterns of inequality are central themes in sociological theory from the founding fathers onwards. This is particularly the case in British sociology. There has, however, over more recent years been a retreat from class analysis in the discipline. According to Skeggs (1997), the retreat from class has occurred across a range of academic sites. This retreat from class can be linked to the crisis within Marxism itself during the 1990s, in which it was said to be unable to cope with the complexities of modern life (Solomos and Back 1996). As argued in Chapter 1, those retreating from class either ignore it or argue that class is becoming increasingly irrelevant. The retreat, Crompton (1993) suggests, is the sociological equivalent of the 'new individualism', a movement strongly evident in many postmodern theories (cited in Skeggs 1997: 7). Thus, while some theorists have called for a radical revision of class analysis (Castells 1983), a great deal of postmodernist theorizing just dismisses class as irrelevant. The concept of difference has come to stand in, in many cases, for inequality (Skeggs 1997).

Under the effects of postmodernism, there has been a move towards cultural analysis whereby class analysis has lost favour and race and gender have become popular theoretical and substantive areas, along with queer theory and similar disciplines. Many have seen postmodernism as having a positive effect on gender and race. With regard to gender, Evans (2003) argues that the work of postmodern theorists has been theoretically crucial to feminism in that 'through "powerlessness" (or theories of discursive practices) feminists have been able to identify the resistance to patriarchy which feminism always provided and to enhance and express those ideas which allow women, and the interests of women, a space in the social world' (ibid. 93). Postmodernism has, therefore, been invaluable to feminist academics because it provides feminism with theoretical legitimacy. 'If others (that is, male others) are 'using' the theoretical space of postmodernism then there is no reason why feminists should not have access to those unpoliced vistas' (ibid.).

However, not all feminist theorists take up this positive view of the effects of postmodernism on gender. Many feminist theorists highlight a number of negative issues associated with it. For example, Fox-Genovese questions the timing of postmodern theory: 'Surely it is no coincidence that the Western white male elite proclaimed the death of the subject at precisely the moment at which it might have had to share that status with the women and peoples of other races and classes who are beginning to challenge its supremacy' (1986: 134). More important, there are intellectual doubts and the feeling that postmodernism undermines the potential for radical social change. Feminist sociologist Dorothy Smith (1999: 97–8) has two main objections to postmodernism. She argues, first, that postmodernism has imported the 'universalized subject of knowledge' although it opposes it. Second, by prioritizing language/discourse, postmodernism inserts a gap between the practices of people's everyday lives and the language that postmodernism studies (cited in Delamont 2003: 146). For Smith, this imprisons the sociologist in an abstract world and prevents the sociologist from focusing on the real world in which people actively practice their lives. However, overall, whether the impact of postmodernism on feminism is seen as good or bad, one thing it has done, as argued by Evans (2003), is to open up a space for women. In particular it provides space for women social theorists to speak.

Postmodernism has also had an impact on the study of race and ethnicity within sociology. Most notably, in the study of race there was a movement towards a focus on postmodern difference (Alexander and Alleyne 2002). Again, thoughts on the impact of postmodernism on race and ethnicity are mixed. hooks (1990) identifies some positive aspects. She argues that radical postmodernism calls attention to those sensibilities that are shared across the boundaries of class, gender and race and that could be fertile ground for the development of solidarity and coalition. For example, she argues that postmodernism, with its emphasis as outlined above, may offer us insights that open up our understanding of African American experience. According to her, postmodern critiques of essentialism that challenge notions of universality and static, over-determined identity within mass culture and mass consciousness can open up new possibilities for the construction of the self and the assertion of agency. However, again, as with gender, there are also critiques of the effects of postmodernism on race. Stone (1998) argues that postmodernism emerged and raised high hopes of providing a new intellectual framework, a paradigm for a non-ideological age. However, according to him, it has often turned out to be intellectually vacuous and morally corrupt. Furthermore, concerns have been expressed that euphemisms of diversity, emphasized in postmodern studies on race, can actually act as a smokescreen for the entrenchment of inequality (S. Smith 1993).

Views on whether postmodernism has been a positive force for gender and race remain mixed. However, as argued, one of the outcomes of the changes to social theory is that the canon has been opened to include those previously seen as outsiders. Postmodernism has given women and theorists from ethnic minorities a space from which to speak. Furthermore, with the shift in focus from forms of inequality focused mostly on social class to an analysis of *difference* and diversity that takes multiple forms, the axes of gender and race have come to the fore.

As argued above, there may be problems with this emphasis on diversity, and the position of gender and racial outsiders may also still be one based on the sidelines (as explored later). However, postmodernism has nonetheless shifted the emphasis of study from social class to race and gender, and from a focus only on white male theorists to one including women and black social theorists. As a result, we can now open a textbook on contemporary social theory and see female social theorists alongside key male theorists, writing their social theories from the position of racial and gendered *difference*. Open any reader on contemporary social theory and you will find Donna Haraway nestling next to Anthony Giddens, whom you will also find next to Stuart Hall. Similarly, women and black theorists from the past are now being rewritten into sociology's history. This is mostly done by American theorists such as Ritzer and Goodman (2004c) and Lemert (1995, 1999). Such a deconstruction of the canon brings untold dangers as far as such theorists as Mouzelis (1991, 1994) are concerned because it threatens the very cohesiveness of the sociological canon. However, sociological theory has now been opened up and we see theories and theorists included in the canon who would previously have been seen as outsiders. It is to an exploration of the work of contemporary theorists that we now turn.

Contemporary Social Theorists

As the sociological canon has been opened up, textbooks on sociological theory are now filled with people who are not sociologists. Sociologists' accounts now sit next to those by anthropologists, literary theorists, cultural critics and the like. Furthermore, those theorists who are black or women, who write from behind the veil of exclusion, can now be found inside accounts of sociological theory. Those who would previously have been seen as sociological 'outsiders' now form part of the discipline. Furthermore, the white male social theorists who would previously have ignored issues of gender and race in their theories have now, in some cases, started to write on these issues. These changes in social theorizing do not involve what concerns Mouzelis (1994), that is a move from substantive theory to speculative philosophizing, but rather in many cases they involve an increase in the links made between social theory and the substantive world.

Within this section I explore the work of three theorists: Anthony Giddens, Donna Haraway and Stuart Hall. They can be viewed as a mainstream British white male theorist, an American feminist theorist and an Afro-Caribbean cultural theorist. As mentioned previously, the aim here is not necessarily to explore the work of postmodern theorists per se but rather to look at the work of a range of social theorists (some may class themselves as postmodern) who can be found in the contemporary canon as a result of shifts occurring because of postmodernism. The theorists chosen are but a selection of theorists writing contemporary social theory; I could have included dozens more, for example, from Pierre Bourdieu to Judith Butler, from Michel Foucault to Trinh T. Min Ha. However, as argued throughout the book, I have myself to take part in a process of selection. These theorists all occupy key positions within contemporary constructions of social theory. This is despite the fact that they are clearly not all sociologists.

The question one might ask is: how does this inclusion differ from the inclusion of Marx and Simmel in the founding paradigm a century before? Just as Hall and Haraway do not see themselves as sociologists, neither did Marx or Simmel, as shown earlier. Contemporary inclusions of outsiders are different: first, because these 'outsiders' are not white (or Jewish) men but are theorists who are women or who are black and so on; second, because writers such as Hall and Haraway (and many others like them) also include race and gender in their social theoretical analysis. As argued throughout the book, theorists were often excluded and cast outside the sociological canon because they wrote on such issues. This clearly marks a major transition in the discipline, which places those previously seen as outsiders on the inside.

Anthony Giddens (1938–)

According to Craib (1992: 111), 'Giddens's work is remarkable – not only for its quantity, but also for the range of ideas it brings together; not just as theory, but as studies of world history; it is remarkable, too, in that Giddens has become the first British social theorist in recent times to have an international reputation.'

According to Elliott (2001), Giddens' writings on the classics and his contemporary social theory have had a profound impact on conceptual debates in the social sciences over recent decades. He is above all a grand theorist who engages with a wide range of theoretical frameworks from interpretive sociology, critical theory, ethnomethodology and systems theory to psychoanalysis, structuralism and post-structuralism. He has an impressive academic profile. He taught for many years at King's College, Cambridge, where he was professor of sociology in the Faculty of Economics and Politics. He then went on to become the director of the London School of Economics. He is also founder, publisher and editor of Polity Press, one of the most 'ambitious and interesting publishers of books in social theory' (Lemert 1999: 487).

Giddens' first widely read book was *The New Rules of Sociological Method* (1976). The book is an attempt to reformulate sociological reasoning, in this instance by re-examining the idea of interpretive or hermeneutic sociology. According to Lemert (1999), this was Giddens' first statement of structuration theory, which is systematically worked out in *The Constitution of Society* (1984). It is his theory of structuration, wherein he tackles the perennial sociological problem of action and structure, for which he is perhaps most famous in sociology. Reflexivity came to be a central issue in his work. In the 1990s he focused on reflexivity, modernity and modernization. He has also moved on more recently to provide critiques of radical politics. He is both a social and political theorist and has come to be viewed as a central figure within British sociology. In this section on Giddens I focus the discussion on the analysis of his theoretical contributions to sociology and modern social thought, paying attention to both the strengths and limitations of his social theory. In doing so, I give a brief overview of key aspects of his work.

Theory of Structuration

In reference to Giddens' structuration theory, Craib states, 'although his style – and to a lesser extent his way of thinking – is different to Parsons, structuration theory should be considered on a par with structural-functionalism' (1992: 111). It is an attempt to maintain a conception of society as a whole, while holding on to the insights of the 'linguistic turn' in philosophy, and particularly ethnomethodology in sociology. The problem of the relationship between action and structure is one that has long been central to debates on sociological theory. Many theorists have asked whether structures dominate and exist outside individuals. Are individual agents set apart from, or are they part of, the reproduction of those structures? Social theorists have often tended to focus on the importance or dominance of one over another; Giddens, however, wants to deal with both. He argues that we must go beyond dualist approaches to structure and agency and look instead at the ways in which these are constitutive of one another.

According to Giddens, people are knowledgeable about the social structures they produce and reproduce in their conduct. In light of this, the central task for the social theorist is to understand how action is structured in everyday contexts of social practices, while, at the same time, recognizing that the structural elements of action are reproduced by the performance of action. In the theory of structuration, Giddens puts forward the argument that the dualism of agency and structure should be understood as complementary terms of a duality because social structures are both constituted by human agency and at the same time the medium of this constitution. This theory of structuration is something that has been explored by many sociologists and is often applied in empirical settings.

Modernity

In Giddens' later work he focuses on the issues of modernity, reflexivity and the self. He does this in such books as *The Consequences of Modernity* (1990) and *Modernity and Self-Identity* (1991). What Giddens does in these texts is develop an analysis of the complex relation between self and society in the later modern age. According to Elliott (2001), Giddens is wary of Weber's portrait of the iron cage of bureaucracy. He also rejects Marx's equation of modernity with capitalism.

The key to Giddens' theory of modernity is reflexivity. Giddens argues that social practices are constantly examined and reformed in the light of continuous information about those very practices. In the process, the character of such practices is changed. Giddens sees modern society as being like a juggernaut: 'it is not just that more or less continuous or profound processes of change occur; rather, change does not consistently conform either to human expectation or to human control' (Giddens 1991: 28). In *The Consequences of Modernity*, we also see Giddens' defence of what he calls radicalized modernity (Lemert 1999: 487). In effect, Giddens argues that modernity opens new and different opportunities for human fulfilment. In modern society people may be displaced from local communities, but they are remembered in world culture in ways that can be liberating. This is an example of a reflexive social theory recursively producing a theory in the world of the reflexive (ibid.).

In *The Transformation of Intimacy* (1992), Giddens connects the notion of reflexivity to sexuality, gender and intimate relationships (Elliott 2001). In light of modernization and the decline of tradition, argues Giddens, the sexual life of the human subject becomes a 'project' that has to be managed and defined against the background of new opportunities and risks, including, for example, artificial insemination, AIDS, sexual harassment and the like (ibid.). Giddens argues that we live in an era of 'plastic sexuality', an era when sexuality is open and freed from the constraints of reproduction. According to Giddens, 'The emergence of what I term plastic sexuality is crucial to the emancipation implicit in the pure relationship, as well as to women's claim to sexual pleasure. Plastic sexuality is decentred sexuality, freed from the needs of reproduction' (1992: 2). Overall, Giddens argues that the transformation of intimacy, in which women have played a key role, holds out the possibility of a radical democratization of the personal sphere.

Radical Politics

In his more recent works Giddens has turned to a focus on radical politics. In *Beyond Left and Right: The Future of Radical Politics* (1994), Giddens argues that we live in a radically damaged world for which radical political remedies are required that go beyond the neoliberalism offered by the right or reformist socialism offered by the left (Elliott 2001: 298). In light of this, Giddens provides a detailed framework for the rethinking of radical politics. At issue, in Giddens' eyes, are both risk and reflexivity. According to Elliott (ibid.), it is against a backdrop of risk, reflexivity and globalization that Giddens develops a new framework for radical politics. The core dimensions of Giddens' blueprint for the restructuring of radical political thought include the following claims, usefully outlined by Elliott (ibid. 298–9) and summarized here:

- We live today in a society that is post-traditional. This does not mean a society in which there is no tradition but rather one in which tradition is forced into the open for public discussion. Reasons or explanations are increasingly required for the preservation of tradition, and this should be understood as one of the key elements in the reinvention of social solidarity. Tradition is refashioned to build new types of solidarities, for example in new social movements (peace, ecology, human rights, etc.). The opposite of this can be seen, according to Giddens, in the rise of fundamentalism, which forecloses questions of public debate and is nothing other than tradition defended in the traditional way.
- Radical forms of democratization fuelled by reflexivity are at work in both personal and political life. There is, according to Giddens, a democratizing of democracy, by which he means that all areas of personal and political life are increasingly ordered through dialogue rather than pre-established power relations. According to Giddens, the mechanisms of this have already been set in process, from the transformation of gender and parent–child relations to the development of social movements and self-help groups.
- The welfare state requires further radical forms of restructuring, and this needs to be carried out in relation to wider issues of global poverty. Here he urges a move away from a top-down approach to the dispensation of benefits to a more 'positive approach' – welfare that is concerned with promoting autonomy in relation to personal and collective responsibilities and that focuses centrally on gender imbalances as much as class deprivations.
- The prospects for global justice begin to emerge in relation to a 'post-scarcity order'. Here Giddens is not suggesting the end of scarcity but rather that scarcity is coming under more reflexive scrutiny itself. Several key transformations are central here. The entry of women into the labour force, the restructuring of gender and intimacy, the rise of individualization as opposed to egoism and the ecological crisis have all contributed to a shift away from secularized Puritanism towards social solidarity and obligation.

Critiques

As Giddens has been so prolific and such a high-profile social theorist, he has also been subject to a vast amount of wide-ranging criticism. Here I explore just some of the critiques made of his theories.

- Many sociologists do not feel that Giddens really transcends the problem of agency and structure in his theory of structuration. Authors such as Archer (1990) have criticized Giddens' structuration theory. She feels that we must not merge agency and structure, as does Giddens. Rather, she argues they must be kept analytically distinct in order to analyse core methodological and substantive problems effectively.
- The extent to which Giddens' largely generalized social theories, such as structuration theory, can be empirically operable is questionable.
- Giddens has also been critiqued for his theory of the self. Critics have seen the reflexive project of self-making and self-actualization as individualist. As a result, Giddens' theory of the reflexive self is seen as fitting too neatly with the liberal ideology of individualism.
- Critics have also focused on the notion of subjectivity in his work. Craib (1992) argues that Giddens' failure to appreciate the unconscious dynamics of subjectivity and intersubjectivity limits the strengths of his social theory.
- Leading on from this, some theorists have been more critical of his use of theoretical fields of thought such as psychoanalysis. Critics are concerned that Giddens' appropriation of psychoanalysis is too narrowly focused on the functioning of the unconscious within social processes (see Elliott 1994, 1996).

Summary

Within this section, I have focused on a key contemporary British social theorist who appears frequently in readers on contemporary social theory. Giddens offers grand theories in the manner of the classics before him. He does, however, unlike many earlier social theorists discussed throughout this book, include an analysis of gender and sexuality in his social theories. These theories form a part of his social theories on modernity and his more recent work on politics. I now want to move on to consider another figure who we see frequently in accounts of contemporary social theory but who until recently would have been excluded from sociological theory.

Donna Haraway (1944–)

Unlike Giddens, Donna Haraway would not be regarded traditionally as a sociologist. Like Arendt or de Beauvoir before her, she could be seen as a sociological outsider. The difference is that now – unlike Arendt and de Beauvoir, who remained outside the discipline of sociology – Haraway is included in accounts of contemporary social theory. Haraway was trained in the history and philosophy of science. She holds a PhD in biology from Yale. She teaches in the History of Consciousness Program at the University of California – Santa Cruz (Lemert 1999). Her background in biology influences many of her social theories and is what marks her social theories out as so original.

Her influence is felt widely in cultural studies, women's studies, philosophy, political theory, primatology and literature. In *Primate Visions: Gender, Race and Nature in the World of Modern Science* (1989), she combines literary theory, political philosophy, and American history to explore the world of primatology. Among her often cited and highly influential articles is 'Manifesto for cyborgs' (1985), initially published in *Socialist Review*. This tract offers a highly original approach to social theorizing, one that includes an analysis of a number of different forms of social interaction, including human and machine. Another key work is 'Situated knowledges', first published in *Feminist Studies* in 1988, within which we can see her development of the idea of the partial perspective. This had a profound impact on feminist theory and the sociology of science. Within this section on Haraway, as with Giddens, I explore some key aspects of her work.

Nature, Culture and Technology

As an American biologist and cultural critic, Haraway has produced a widely read body of work. She has aimed at reconfiguring the relationship among nature, culture and technology. In *Primate Visions* (1989), she deconstructs the opposition of nature and culture, human and animal. Within the book, she maps primate studies over the course of history and across disciplinary boundaries. She starts in the early twentieth century with European male researchers studying within a naturalist framework. She goes on to explore cultural research among non-Euro-Americans and women. Finally, she focuses on feminist science fiction and the fictional narratives that appear there. Within the book Haraway denies any attempt to outline an objective study of the history of primate studies. Haraway includes anti-racist, anti-colonial, pro-feminist and pro-animal rights issues in her list of influential bodies of knowledge. According to Claudia Springer (1996), this book is among the most carefully researched analyses of how scientific knowledge has complemented both patriarchal and racist ideologies.

In her later work such as *Simians, Cyborgs, and Women* (1991), she deconstructs the opposition of nature and technology, human and machine (Clough and Schneider 2001). Haraway uses the metaphor of the cyborg to discuss the relationships among science, technology and 'socialist-feminism'. She takes the view that hi-tech culture challenges and breaks down the old dualisms of western thinking such as the mind–body split, Self–Other, male–female, reality–appearance and truth–illusion. According to Haraway, we are no longer able to think of ourselves in these terms or even, strictly speaking, as biological entities. Instead, she argues that we have become cyborgs, mixtures of human and machine, where the biological side and the mechanical/electrical side have become so inextricably entwined that they cannot be split.

According to Kirby (1997: 146), the cyborg is a creature that appears to offer a good representation of contamination. In its bizarre unity, animal melds with human; silicon and metal meld with bone and muscle. Haraway (1991) celebrates this cyborg as a creature that is sheer excessiveness; its combination of the monstrous and illegitimate offers new political horizons (Kirby 1997: 146).

Situated Knowledges

Another area in which Haraway has been influential is the debate on standpoint epistemologies. According to Clough and Schneider (2001), it was Sandra Harding who brought together the works of a number of feminist theorists who were engaged in criticisms of the positivistic, empiricist practices of science. She also firmly set in place a desire and a hope for a feminist 'successor science', an empirical science that, according to her, would be characterized by a 'strong objectivity' only when the standpoint of the scientist or research is made evident. Standpoint epistemologies, as they became known, were thus elaborated (ibid.).

Haraway's contribution to debates over standpoint epistemology comes from what she has called the 'partial perspectives of the situated knowledges'. This is laid out in her essay 'Situated knowledges' (1988), where Haraway puts over the perspective that feminists should not give up on science altogether. She insists that as well as exposing the historical and ideological specificity of scientific practices and deconstructing their absolute authority, feminists should also aim to give a better account of the world (Clough and Schneider 2001: 342). Such an account, however, comes with the recognition of the irreducible difference and radical multiplicity of local knowledges. Haraway thus accepts a version of scientific realism; however, it is one that is expressed in partial visions or partial perspectives. This takes us away from relativist approaches and what Haraway calls the 'god trick', that is, seeing everything, everywhere from nowhere. Hence she stresses partial views not the view from above. Under situated knowledges and the partial perspective, according to Clough and Schneider (ibid.), the familiar scientific term 'objectivity' is rescued but with a profoundly and consequentially altered meaning.

Although many researchers have taken up the partial perspective in sociology and other disciplines (my own work included; Reed 2003), partial perspectives are nonetheless problematic and epistemologically demanding (Clough and Schneider 2001). The partial perspective framework could also be critiqued for its evasion of research responsibility. On the one hand academics and researchers can emphasize commonality when it suits, and on the other hand they can highlight diversity if issues of responsibility come to light. This is something to be aware of when adopting such an approach.

A Sociologist?

Although not working within a strictly sociological paradigm, Haraway has much to offer sociology and sociological theory because of the unique ways in which she combines nature, technology and culture in her social theories. According to Clough and Schneider (2001), Haraway's work reminds social theorists that there are 'actants' and 'agencies' other than human. In Haraway's work, human and non-human agencies are mixed in 'material-semiotic entities'; these are techno-scientific knowledge objects such as the gene, the database, the chip, the fetus, the immune system, the neural net and the ecosystem. 'Given their dynamism, material-semiotic entities are social processes, embedded in or productive of, social contexts that have traditionally not been the subject of social theorising' (ibid. 340).

As a result of this we can see that Donna Haraway's social theories urge sociologists to rethink social theory in terms of a more complex sociality than that currently explored (ibid.). She also encourages us to think about the ways to jump from one scale of sociality to another. According to Clough and Schneider (ibid. 340), she thus promotes a 'risky' interdisciplinarity in order to engage critically the dynamism of various contexts at various scales of sociality and also to strive in every context for a critique of domination in categories of sex, gender, race, class, ethnicity and nation. In her reconfigured relationship of nature, culture and technology, Haraway challenges familiar epistemologies and ontologies on which the majority of social theory is based (ibid.).

The influence of Haraway's sociology does not end here. More broadly, Haraway can be seen to have a significant impact on the sociology of science. Few have been more influential than Donna Haraway in developing a cultural criticism of science and scientific knowledge that examines dominations of class, race, gender, sexuality, age and nation. In doing so, Haraway has raised difficult questions that point to ways that scientific knowledge and work are interwoven with a broad range of local and global practices of exploitation and domination.

Critiques

When looking at reviews of the work of Donna Haraway, it is rare to find criticism of it. However, below are listed some of the key critiques that have been levelled at her work.

- Many of her critics take aim at the complexity of her social theories. Haraway's essays are challenging for the average reader. Haraway does not seem interested in simplifying her arguments for the sake of broadening the appeal of her work.

- Haraway's work has been critiqued for leaning too heavily on the ideal of political correctness.
- Haraway fails to explore the relationship between the cyborg and the 'other'. The focus is on the hybridity of the cyborg itself and on its lack of origin.
- Haraway in her work on the cyborg attempts to dispense with history and origin. This, according to Kirby (1997), is unsuccessful because the nature of origin cannot be separated from the question of identity itself.

Summary

Haraway, then, provides a social theory that takes us beyond the traditional relationships of humans and society to incorporate much more complex notions of sociality. Along with this social theory she also offers a gendered critique in her theories on the partial perspective. Although Haraway may not have been included in previous accounts of sociological theory, we can now find her work in many key texts on contemporary sociological theory. She has become a very respected intellectual who contributes to a wide variety of fields.

Stuart Hall (1932–)

Stuart Hall was born in Jamaica; he came to England in 1951, studying at Oxford University. He has worked at the Centre for Contemporary Cultural Studies (CCCS) at Birmingham University and at the Open University, from which he retired in 1997. He has also sat on the Runnymede Trust's commission on the future of multiethnic Britain. Like Haraway, Stuart Hall would previously have been classified as a sociological outsider. According to Rojek (2001), Hall's work can be understood as an exercise in revisionist Marxism. His theories, as Lemert (1995) would argue, are written from behind the veil of his own exclusion; according to Rojek (2001), his interest in social exclusion and the character of class rule are the tangible result of his expatriate experience. Indeed to go back to the earlier work of DuBois, Hall could be seen to be gifted with 'a second sight'. His work includes a focus on diaspora culture, hybrid formations and a general interest in the politics of difference. He is also concerned with the shifting balance of power between the established and outsiders.

Hall's influence is extremely wide and can be seen to span a number of areas such as social theory, cultural studies, ethnic and racial studies, postcolonial studies, media studies, crime and deviance, and youth studies. According to Barrett (1998), Hall is certainly a key figure in contemporary sociology; however, he is not trained in the discipline and his agendas are very different from those of mainstream sociology. His work has been largely directed towards the development of cultural studies, now recognized as an independent discipline. According to Barrett (ibid.), however, it is a sign (as argued here) of the current pluralism and interdisplinarity within contemporary sociology that Hall is such an influential figure.

The Public Intellectual

According to Kenny (2003), Hall has been one of Britain's most prominent and charismatic 'public intellectuals' since the 1950s. Hall has contributed much to the reformulation of the moral and political thinking of the political left in Britain, and elsewhere, over the past 20 years. He is widely regarded as one of the founding fathers of cultural studies, and his writings have also exerted enormous influence within the fields of sociology and social theory. He has achieved a readership beyond the academy as well as within the political realm.

According to Kenny (ibid.), Hall's political and intellectual thinking developed in discrete phases of his intellectual career: in a series of collective projects at the CCCS in the 1970s; in the 1980s in a number of widely read essays in *Marxism Today*; more recently, during the 1990s onwards, in a number of contributions to emergent intellectual debates about cultural analysis, social change and ethnic identity. However, as Kenny (ibid.) points out, these phases of his writing career were prefigured by some of Hall's lesser-known essays from the late 1950s and early 1960s, specifically those written for the journals of the New Left movement. In the 1950s Hall joined forces with E.P. Thompson, Raphael Samuel, Ralph Miliband, Raymond Williams and John Saville to launch two radical journals, *The New Reasoner* and *New Left Review*. His work during this time combines reflections on the limitations of the base–superstructure model of Marxist thought with sociological essays on the cultural changes sweeping across Britain in the 1950s (ibid.).

According to Kenny (ibid.), it was his analysis of Thatcherism that brought Hall's thinking to a wide and public audience and that established him as a controversial and important presence on Britain's intellectual scene. In January of 1979, before the election of the Conservative government in Britain, Hall published an analysis of 'The great moving right show' in the magazine *Marxism Today*. The article outlined his position on Thatcherism and its wider political implications, particularly for the left (Barrett 1998). Hall regarded the politics of the revamped Conservative Party as an attempt to construct a new 'hegemony' within British political life, to legitimate new kinds of solutions to the problems of relative economic decline and social fragmentation (Kenny 2003: 157). Hall viewed Thatcher's interventions on race, national identity and crime as attempts to connect deeply rooted prejudice and sentiment to a Thatcherite perspective. Hall's aim during these years was to foster a deeper understanding in the communities of the left of the politics of Thatcherism. He also wanted to reconfigure the political imagination of the Labour Party, encouraging it to engage with the realities of conservative hegemony (ibid.).

Contemporary Cultural Studies

In 1964 Hall co-wrote *The Popular Arts*, which resulted in him being asked to join the CCCS. In 1968 Hall became director of the Contemporary Cultural Studies Unit. During his time at the CCCS, Hall engaged with the writings of a number of Marxist theorists in the west European tradition, such as Louis Althusser and Antonio Gramsci (Kenny 2003). According to Kenny (ibid. 156), within the centre Hall and other colleagues began to suggest that the political instability of the late 1960s and early 1970s amounted to a crisis of 'hegemony' (a Gramscian term). This meant that the balance of the relations of class forces had been upset, and consequently the state was drawn more and more towards the coercive rather than the consensual (ibid.). What was to become a key text in the sociology of crime and deviance, race and ethnicity, media and youth studies arose from this, entitled *Policing the Crisis* (Hall *et al.* 1978). This was a political and theoretically diverse exploration of the interrelated discourses about crime, youth delinquency, and race within Britain during this period (Kenny 2003).

During his time at the CCCS, Hall took a leading role in the founding of cultural studies (Lemert 1999). According to Barrett (1998), Hall is so important to the founding of the discipline that he virtually *is* cultural studies. In his writings here he drew on Marxism and on the work of Foucault. Cultural practices, according to him, should be understood as signifying practices not as objects whose meaning and identity can be guaranteed by their origin or their intrinsic essences (Hall 1997). According to Hall, the analysis of culture should involve the interpretation of the cultural ideological field within which the struggle over meanings occurs. These struggles take place in a field of relations that are established through prior struggles for domination and that always show evidence of resistance (Kenny 2003: 158). Ideology is central to understanding why cultural practices come to possess certain meanings and not others. The task of the cultural analyst is to illuminate the discursive operations whereby ideological values are produced in texts and also to look at the multiple ways in which human agents receive these (ibid.).

New Ethnicities and New Times

In particular, from the 1970s onwards Hall began to write prolifically on race, ethnicity and identity. According to Rojek (2001), during this time race and ethnicity were supplanting class at the forefront of his intellectual interests. The civil rights movements of the 1950s and 1960s, as argued in Chapter 5, and the emergence of postcolonial studies meant a destabilization of white power. During the 1980s and 1990s people began to write about diaspora and issues of hybridity. It was during this era that Hall began to write about 'new ethnicities'. According to Hall, new ethnicities were based, first, on a recognition of difference and, second, on an acceptance of the signifying system as arbitrary (Rojek 2001). Here Hall denies the essentialist nature of race, arguing that race should instead be seen as a matter of cultural construction. According to Rojek (ibid.), he is also concerned to demonstrate that racial identity is an unstable category and that questions of race always intersect with issues of gender, class and sexuality. Within the framework of 'new ethnicities', there is no essential racial or ethnic identity outside social, historical and political processes (Solomos and Back 1996).

In 1989, Hall co-edited another key text with Martin Jaques, called *New Times*. Here Hall seeks to emphasize continuity with Gramscian analysis (Rojek 2001). He suggests that the twin characteristics of new times are, first, the recognition that subjects of power must be conceptualized in pluralist forms and, second, the pronounced cultural layering of social, political and economic struggles (ibid. 367). In Hall's mind the 'new times' thesis reinforces the duty of the organic intellectual to be at the vanguard of knowledge and generate debate with regard to shifts in the social, cultural and economic formation of power. However, according to Rojek (ibid.), in its denial of the struggle between capital and labour as the engine of social change, and in its espousal of 'the politics of difference', Hall's thesis abandons the central tenets of classical Marxism. Rather, in *New Times*, transformative action should be studied on a variety of fronts – for example, the struggles of new ethnicities, feminisms, the gay and lesbian movement, ecological protest groups, animal rights groups and so on (ibid.).

Critiques

As with Giddens, appraisal and critique of Hall come from a wide variety of areas. According to Kenny (2003), the most controversial of Hall's ideas are those that have the most direct political bearing. Not surprisingly, then, Hall has come in for a number of criticisms.

- Some critics have argued that, in his development of 'hegemony', Hall was guilty of overlooking Gramsci's commitment to the decisive nucleus of economic relations. This made his analyses not sensitive enough to the role of social and economic determinants in contemporary politics (ibid. 159).
- According to Wood (1998), Hall's approach to hegemony slides ambiguously between reading hegemony as either concentrated state domination or freewheeling discourse. Consequently, Hall in some ways reinforces the discursive turn in contemporary cultural studies, despite his own explicit criticisms of this development (ibid.).
- Hall is often criticized for his overemphasis on the coherence of Thatcherism. Some authors have argued that Thatcherism was always far more diverse than he suggested.
- Hall and some of his collaborators were never really clear on whether the 'new times' were independent from, or the consequence of, Thatcherism (Kenny 2003: 159).

Summary
Whatever the critiques of Hall, Haraway and Giddens mentioned above, they
are all important theorists and all three can be seen within constructions of
the contemporary social theoretical canon. The incorporation of black and
female theorists such as Hall and Haraway into contemporary social theory
alongside existing white male theorists such as Giddens would, then, seem to
mark a transition in sociological theory. This transition reflects a movement
away from from gendered and racial exclusion towards a more inclusive discipline. What I want to move to ask now though is whether this means an end
to gendered and racial outsiders. Do the voices of the excluded now speak
from the same vantage point as those previously classed as insiders? Furthermore, are the areas of gender and race now centralized areas of analysis
within social theory?

Is This the End of Sociological Outsiders?

The deconstruction of the contemporary canon has had three main consequences. First, there has been a shift from sociological theory to social
theory. Second, there has been a movement away from a dominant focus on
economics to one on culture. Third, and most important for the argument
developed here, this has meant a shift away from a bounded sense of sociological theory that kept certain people in and others out to a social theory
that celebrates difference and incorporates theorists of race and gender and
topics of race and gender. It is the aim of this section to ask whether this
means an end to sociological outsiders.

When we look at accounts of contemporary social theory we can see that
those figures who once would have been excluded because of their gender or
race have now become insiders. Some social theorists are seen as more sociological then others. Giddens, for example, would be considered as the most
sociological mainstream sociological theorist of the examples above. However, the other two are highly respected figures in their fields with significant
status, and the label 'sociologist' in this sense seems arbitrary. However, the
question I want to ask here is whether they all have the same status within
contemporary social theory.

It is clear that the position of those previously cast outside sociological
theory has improved with the deconstruction of sociological theory. We cannot dispute that postmodernism has opened up the canon to include outsiders. It has also created a space for the analysis of gender and race within
social theory, as argued previously. There are, however, limits to this inclusion. It would seem, for example, that although those writing social theory
from the position of gendered or racial exclusion are included in accounts of
contemporary social theory, they are still somehow sidelined within it.
Although feminist sociological theory has expanded into the mainstream

(women do now appear in mainstream texts), the expansion is limited. According to Bordo, the fathers of postmodernism are, after all, also the sons of the Enlightenment man, the inheritors of both his privileges and blind spots (1997: 210). Women theorists, even if they are placed in contemporary books on social theory, are still seen primarily as just 'doing gender' and nothing else. Male social theorists are apparently without gender and thus write much broader-ranging social theories. As a result, according to Bordo (1997), feminists are often shown as engaging in a specialized critique, the specialized critique of gender. Through the effects of postmodernism, as argued previously, this is a critique that can no longer be ignored within mainstream social theory. However, it is one whose implications are contained, self-limiting and of insufficient general consequence to amount to a new knowledge of the way culture operates (ibid. 193).

Similar points can be made with regard to black social theorists. According to Bordo, every time black authors are quoted it is only for their views on race. As with gender, black social theorists are shown as engaging in a specialized critique, the specialized critique of race and ethnicity. Through postmodernism, as argued previously, the shift towards an emphasis on *difference* and diversity may have bought race and ethnicity further into the realms of social theorizing; thus race and ethnicity can no longer be ignored within mainstream social theory. However, they are still sidelined and still the domain of authors of colour, who apparently, like women, have little to say about broader theoretical issues. Thus, the otherness of black is perpetuated (ibid. 194).

Furthermore, when we look at the rewriting of social theory's past, women and authors of colour appear to fare no better. Although those rewriting sociological theory's past may have added accounts of women and other minorities, this is only as an appendage not, as Parker (2001) argues, integrated into accounts of the classics.

Women and black social theorists are sidelined on the fringes of social theory, as are the areas of gender and race more generally. Race and gender as fields of study have grown and have been recognized by social theory as important. Over the past few decades, for example, interest in the areas of both race and gender has increased. These areas have expanded academically as vibrant areas of study. According to Banton (2001), ethnic and racial studies have flourished recently because students have wished to attend courses, and publishers to market books, discussing what are represented in ordinary language as important problems. The demand for information and analysis has been more political than a search for knowledge for its own sake. Similar points can be made about gender studies. Both of these are multidisciplinary subjects that can be likened to areas, such as criminology, in which scholars trained in different disciplines meet (ibid.). However, they have often been sidelined within social theory and are added on to various disciplines.

The growth of these fields is certainly impressive; however, the way they are offered as specialist critiques merely reinforces their marginality. These two areas have never seemed to hold the transformative capacities or grasp the centrality of social theory in the way that social class did. Although this may be a sign of our postmodern times, which emphasize difference, it nonetheless reinforces their marginality.

So it would seem, as argued by Parker (1997), that contrary to popular belief sociological theory has not been transformed by feminism, cultural studies or ethnic and racial studies. Instead, these strands of thought have remained outside the discipline's mainstream, as it refuses to weave them into the pattern of its work (ibid.). As argued earlier in the chapter, Mouzelis (1991, 1994) was clearly worried that the deconstruction of the canon would mean that sociological theory would lose its specificity. As can be seen here, however, little seems to have changed. In terms of the make-up of the social theoretical canon, those occupying dominant positions are still largely white men who mainly address issues of gender and race in only a cursory fashion. From this analysis, then, it would seem that despite the opening up of the canon, and despite the fact that authors writing from the position of the excluded may now be allocated a place in social theory, their positions are still marginal, as are the areas of gender and race.

Conclusion

This chapter has focused on the deconstruction of sociological theory. It has explored the impact of postmodernism on sociological theory and the ensuing focus on diversity and interdisciplinarity. As we can see, in these terms it is no longer feasible for sociological theory to exclude, and this can be seen in the proliferation of the many texts on social theory, each filled with a broad and diverse selection of writers from a variety of different disciplines. As shown, contemporary texts on social theory now include women theorists and black theorists alongside those who have traditionally dominated social theory – white male theorists. It includes those writing from the position of gendered and racial exclusions.

Furthermore, as we have seen in this chapter, postmodernism has enabled the incorporation of key conceptual areas such as race and gender within social theory. This has enabled the areas of gender and race to become part of social theory. However, as discussed, there is still the question of how integrated the accounts from those previously seen as outsiders are, and it still seems that the areas of race and gender are sidelined. I concluded that within sociological theory there is still a hierarchy of theorists. Women or those writing from ethnic minority groups are still marginalized and still allocated the role of offering a specialized gendered or racial critique rather than being seen as offering more generalist social theories. In the following, and final, chapter we ask the questions: How can we bring women, black theorists and other outsiders into a more integrated canon, one not based on hierarchy? In doing so, can we also make gender and the study of race more central to social theory? If so, how will this affect the practice of social theory in the future?

Chapter Summary

- Shifts towards postmodernism from the 1970s onwards have had a profound effect on social theory and on gender and race.
- With its emphasis on deconstruction, postmodernism has enabled the opening up of sociological theory to include those previously viewed as outsiders.
- Furthermore, postmodernism has created a space for the analysis of gender and race within sociological theory.
- This has meant that those gendered and racial outsiders whose position and focus on gender and race kept them out of sociological theory in the past have now been incorporated into social theory.
- A range of theorists are now incorporated into social theory. These include white men, women, theorists of colour and so on.
- However, both women and theorists of colour are still sidelined within social theory, as are the areas of gender and race.

Further Reading

See E. Elliott and L. Ray, *Key Contemporary Social Theorists* (Blackwell, 2003), and A. Elliott and B.S. Turner, *Profiles in Contemporary Social Theory* (Sage, 2002), for good accounts of contemporary social theory. See also C. Lemert (ed), *Social Theory: The Multicultural and Classic Readings* (Westview Press, 1999), for contemporary and classical theorists. See G. Ritzer and D. Goodman, *Modern Sociological Theory*, 6th edition (McGraw-Hill, 2004), for basic accounts of postmodernism. See N. Mouzelis, *Back to Sociological Theory: The Construction of Social Orders* (Macmillan, 1991), and N. Mouzelis, *Sociological Theory: What Went Wrong? Diagnosis and Remedies* (Routledge, 1994), for a critique of the effects of postmodernism on social theory. See S. Delamont, *Feminist Sociology* (Sage, 2003) for a feminist account. See J. Solomos and L. Back, *Racism and Society* (Macmillan, 1996) for an account of race.

7

Beyond Sociological Exclusion

The previous chapter argued that contemporary social theory has been opened up as a result of the deconstructive process inherent in post-modernism. This has meant that those authors working from behind the veil of exclusion have now been included into accounts of sociological theory. This relates not only to contemporary social theory. Some sociologists are now reinterpreting and broadening out their accounts of sociological theory's past. However, many theorists who write accounts of the discipline's past history still seem to focus predominantly on those authors who are presumed to be canonical. Furthermore, as argued in the previous chapter, when we look at contemporary social theory, although outsiders are now included within it, they are still marginalized. Despite the deconstruction of the canon, there is still a hierarchy of theorists. Women and those writing from ethnic minority groups are still marginalized and still allocated the role of offering a specialized critique, rather than being seen as offering more generalist social theories.

As argued in Chapter 6, the advent of postmodernism has meant that the focus on gender and race has increased in sociology. However, these areas are still seen also as offering specialist critiques and are viewed as subsections of sociology rather than as being central to social theory. The aim of this chapter, then, is to explore the following questions: How are we to proceed with both past rewrites of sociological theory's origins and the future of social theory? How can we make the contemporary constructions of social theory more inclusionary and the rewrites of the past more diverse? If we open up the canon of the past to include a wide range of authors, what are the implications for those existing theorists identified as classics or canonical figures? What about the contemporary canon? How do we move beyond an exclusionary social theory to one that not only includes theorists of gender and race but also incorporates these topics fully into its analysis?

This concluding chapter aims to develop ways forward. The chapter begins with a focus on the canon of the past and outlines the ways in which social theory must be opened up to explore the multiplicity of possible sociological histories. Within this section, I also look at what this means for those existing constructions of sociological theory's past. The second, and longest, section of the chapter focuses on the future of contemporary social theory. In this section I explore several means by which social theory could develop in ways that are non-exclusionary. First, within social theory, racial and gendered outsiders must be centralized and viewed as equal to other theorists within existing mainstream social theory. In this sense, existing mainstream social theorists need to do two things. They need to recognize that gender and race are important areas that need to be just as central to their social theories as any other topic (white men, after all, are not devoid of race and gender). Following on from this, although it must be recognized that white men do not write their social theories outside gender or race, it must also be recognized that female and black authors do not write social theories that are just about race or gender. Both of these issues taken together, I hope, will go some way towards preventing issues of gender and race and women and black theorists being sidelined and placed in unequal positions in comparison with white male theorists.

The chapter moves on to put forward a further suggestion for a more inclusive social theory. It promotes the role of the public social theorist in rendering issues of gender and race more visible both academically and publicly. Here I encourage a more publicly focused social theory, one that engages with, and speaks publicly to, issues of race and gendered exclusion. As I argue, many contemporary social theorists writing from the position of exile and exclusion (e.g. Stuart Hall) address a variety of academic and public audiences about issues of race. This, as I argue, can only be a good thing in challenging the existing unequal position of women and people from ethnic minorities within society in general, and in academia specifically, and thus should be further promoted. Third, in dealing with the gender- and race-blind nature of social theory within this section, the chapter also suggests the adoption of a more empirically focused social theory, one that relates theory more broadly to substantive concerns.

In making these recommendations, the chapter also recognizes the limitations to the extent of change in social theory based on the continued existence of gendered and racial inequality in society in general. As argued throughout the book, changes in social theory reflect changes in society. Although there have been significant changes in gendered and racial equality in society in general, in particular those sparked by the women's and civil rights movements, inequality in gender and race remains. The position of women and ethnic minorities within society in general, and academia in particular, obviously reflects and affects their position within social theory. Until radical changes take place regarding the positions of women and ethnic minorities within society, they will continue to be marginalized in their positions within sociological theory. However, this should not stop us from challenging the gendered and racial sidelining within social theory itself. By initiating changes such as those outlined above within the conceptual heart of social theory, we may in some small way inspire greater social change, which, in turn, may enable us to transform the positions of women and ethnic minorities and issues of gender and race more generally.

The penultimate section of the chapter moves on to explore the implications of attempts to develop a more inclusive social theory for the future of social theory. Despite the limitations of the change outlined above, if we do try to centralize issues of gender and race and theoretical outsiders, what will this mean for the future of social theory? For example, if the discipline has been opened up and outsiders are centralized within the discipline, will there still be a coherent sociological theory to speak of? Does the centralizing of concepts of race and gender imply a move away from sociology connected with substantive concerns to dissolution into postmodern *difference*? The chapter explores these concerns in the context of the future of social theory. The final two sections of the chapter provide an overview and conclusion to the book overall.

Rewriting Sociological Theory's Past

According to Stones (1998), the question of whether a discipline such as sociology should have a discernible and recognizable canon of works or thinkers that in some sense provide a core of that discipline is a vexed one. However, as explored within this book, whether vexed or not, in literature on the development of the sociological canon, there has appeared to be a canon. What we have explored are the various ways in which certain interpretations of the histories of the discipline of sociological theory have developed. We have looked at how some people are seen as canonical, classical and key social theorists whereas others have simply been cast out of the canon. Within this book we have focused in particular on those excluded because of their gender or race, because they are women or people from ethnic minorities (or both). As mentioned in the introduction of the book, the arguments about sociological exclusion can similarly be made in the context of sexuality or disability or regarding many other dimensions of identity. However, limited space and time in writing this book ensure that I must take part in a little process of exclusion myself in exploring only two dimensions of exclusion, that is, race and gender.

Within the book, I have explored how such exclusion can often be self-selected, as in the case of Anna Julia Cooper, discussed in Chapter 3. I have also, however, suggested that the gender- and race-blind views of some dominant social theorists have ensured the marginalization of other theorists from the canon, as was the case with Mills' exclusion of feminist theorist Simone de Beauvoir from sociological theory. However, what I have also focused on demonstrating in this book are the ways in which contemporary accounts written of sociology's past and present have often been guilty of such exclusion. As mentioned, those writing accounts of social theory have, until very recently, been white men who have focused their social theories on socioeconomic issues, ignoring issues of race and gender in the process. They have taken for granted the gender- and race-blind nature of sociological theories without challenging them or incorporating female or black social theorists into their accounts. In this way, reconstructions of social theory's past often reflect the positions and visions of white men. Accounts of social theory have been gender and race blind, constructing, in the process, a very white-male-biased history of social theory's past. As I have mentioned, this has changed more recently as those previously excluded are now tentatively being included into accounts of social theory's history.

Although this recent move to inclusion, when looking at sociology's past, is in its infancy, it can be seen to go hand in hand with a resurgence of interest more generally in reinterpreting sociology's past. With regard to classical theory, the most notable collection on this subject so far is that edited by Camic (1997), *Reclaiming the Sociological Classics*. Camic calls for a contextualization of classical theories and recognition of classical theory as a *field of research* in itself. According to him, research in the field brings to light some of the historical contingencies that led particular theories to be established at the expense of others. This calls into question what the discipline excluded as well as what it included. This has been the goal of this book: as argued before, to stop taking existing stories of past sociological theory for granted, but rather to critically examine that past. It is important, however, within social theory that this broadening out of the history of social theory does not stop with a reinterpretation of the classics. Social theorists who continue to write about social theory's past need to broaden their stories further to integrate accounts of Martineau with those of Marx, or DuBois with those of Weber. As shown throughout this book, the social theories of these excluded authors are just as interesting and valuable as those deemed to be classics and should therefore be included in our views of social theory's past. An incorporation of these theorists' work along with the work of the existing classics would mean that early sociology's engagement with inequality and power in a period of extraordinary upheaval would include an analysis of class along with the nineteenth-century and early-twentieth-century treatments of gendered and racialized inequalities.

The same points can be made with regard to accounts of social theories of the golden age. Those writing about social theory of this era must learn not to take the existing perceptions of social theory for granted. They must question the gender- and race-blind nature of the social theory of this time, including in their own accounts of social theory female and black authors whose work was sociological but who have been excluded from sociological theory because of their gender and race. This would take us beyond a focus purely on power and inequality in the form of social class, providing instead a more thorough account of the inequalities prevalent within the sociological theories of bygone eras.

Furthermore, as Parker (1997) argues, the canon can be constructed as being wider still if we move our gaze away from western modernity to explore other, non-western geographical and temporal contexts. As he rightly points out, the focus of existing accounts of social theory almost always relates to America and Europe (this book included). According to Parker (ibid.), we need to move beyond this. We also need to look at a wider span of history than that from 1600 (Goody 1996). Parker (1997) goes further still in his suggestions and asks: How many of the works in social theory that situate their theories in spatial and temporal context have consulted Taoist and Buddhist philosophies, or Asian conceptions of time? According to Stones (1998), there is now an intellectual space opened up for new classics, for new traditions to take hold and explore questions previously unasked in interpretations of sociological theory's past. What would be interesting would be for texts on social theory to start asking questions about why there are certain gaps in telling the story of sociological theory's history, while also addressing these gaps.

However, it is important to be clear here that what I am suggesting is not that we get rid of the existing classics and key figures. Rather we should recognize that they were not the only theorists writing at this time. Parker (1997) adds a further warning here. He argues that in the revision of social theory's history, it is important to counsel against a certain over-compensatory defensiveness of those previously classed as outsiders. Proponents of a reworking of sociology are, according to him, in danger of repeating older patterns of canonical judgement. For example, suggesting that DuBois' *The Souls of Black Folk* is superior to Durkheim's *The Rules of the Sociological Method* or that Fanon's *The Wretched of the Earth* is better than Gouldner's *The Two Marxisms* possibly undermines the project in hand. Parker (ibid. 140) asks on what grounds can such an argument be made. Furthermore, as Parker (ibid.) points out with regard to teaching sociological theory, it is insufficient to merely broaden the canon with 'decorative otherness' either at the beginning or end of a course on sociological theory. According to him, teaching Marx, Weber and Durkheim first and only then introducing the 'others' just reproduces the narrative we should be challenging (ibid. 141–2). Instead, sociology teaching should demonstrate how a wide range of perspectives entered into, debated with and constituted what sociology is, and it should point to a more inclusive future for the discipline. As Parker argues, as the sociological field expands and becomes more difficult to map, so the gateways into it must diversify. Accounts of social theory should reflect this diversity (ibid. 142).

Overall, theorists who continue to engage in writing about sociological theory's past must be clear in their project. They must first of all recognize that theirs is only one interpretation of the past, one among many. They must also learn to look beyond the taken for granted canonical writers found in most textbooks on the discipline. They must apply the social constructionist perspectives to themselves and their own work, asking why they choose certain authors in their texts while discarding others. Furthermore, theorists writing accounts of the history of social theory must learn not to ignore the gendered and racialized nature of sociology's past but rather more fully explore the role of gender and race in the work of past theorists. They must go back to social theorists of the past and look at their lesser-known works, for example by exploring Weber's or Parsons' work on ethnicity and nationalism or Mead's work on gender. They must not merely blame past social theorists themselves for gendered and racial exclusion but recognize that those writing social theory's past are largely white men and that they themselves provide accounts of the discipline's development that reflect this.

Through simultaneously broadening and reinterpreting sociology's past and recognizing the process of knowledge selection that takes place, we will be able to develop a more interesting canon and one that provides a more reflective and diverse entry into social theory's history. Having explored what we need to do when thinking about rewriting or interpreting sociological theory's past, I now want to move on to look at present and future social theory.

Writing Contemporary Social Theory

As discussed in the previous chapter, when we look at sociological theory's present and future, we can see that despite an opening up of social theory, there are still writers on the margins of the discipline, often women and theorists of colour. There are also several social theorists who have remained on the margins of social theory for other reasons. However, this book has focused in particular on theorists who have remained on the outside owing to gender and/or race. Therefore, again, suggestions for a less exclusionary social theory here are related in particular to race and gender, but they could also be applied to other areas of exclusion.

There are several suggestions I want to put forward in this section to enable us to move beyond a gender- and race-blind social theory. First, I argue that racial and gendered outsiders, and gender and race as subjects, must be centralized and viewed as equal within existing mainstream social theory. Several strategies are put forward in order to make this possible. Second, the chapter encourages a more publicly focused social theory, one that engages with and speaks publicly to issues of racial and gendered exclusion. Third, in dealing with the gender- and race-blind nature of social theory within this section, the chapter also suggests the adoption of a more empirically focused social theory, one that links theoretical issues to substantive concerns.

Race, Gender and the Centring of Outsiders

As argued above, although feminism and ethnic and racial studies and the advent of postmodernism have done much to challenge existing social theory and put race and gender on the agenda, the transformation of social theory from one based on exclusion of gendered and racial others to one that integrates them within social theory is far from complete. Further changes to social theory could be made. One such recommended change is the centralizing of racial and gendered outsiders within existing mainstream social theory. In this sense, I am recommending that existing white malestream social theorists face two tasks. They need to recognize that gender and race are important areas that need to be just as central to their social theories as any other. Second, it must also be recognized that female and black authors do not write social theories that are just about race or gender. These two issues taken together might go some way towards preventing the sidelining of issues of gender and race and of women and black theorists.

First, race and gender as theoretical concerns must be recognized as central within the work of existing mainstream (white male) social theorists. This would involve the recognition by white male theorists of their own gendered and racial positioning. Because of the dominant position of white men in history, existing mainstream social theorists see themselves as beyond gender, race or ethnicity. Although mainstream social theorists have recognized their own class position either as vanguard middle-class intellectuals providing a voice for a disabused working class or intellectuals of working-class origin speaking to their own class origins, they have mostly regarded themselves as beyond race or gender. As a result, these areas have been made secondary to the socioeconomic concerns in their work. In allocating a specialist position to female theorists or black theorists, mainstream white male theorists imply that they themselves are free from race and gender and therefore do not need to write about them. This, however, needs to change. Gender and race cross-cut all social theories no matter what race or gender the theorist is. As Knowles (2003) argues with regard to race, it is 'central to understanding the world in which we live, the troubles of our time and the individual lives composing it, and this qualifies it as a central object of social analysis' (ibid. 11). The same argument could also be applied to gender, which informs our everyday social practices and underpins our understanding of the social world; it therefore should be incorporated into the centre of social theory.

There are a number of ways in which malestream social theorists could further centralize race and gender within their social theories. First, instead of writing social theories only from their position of the white male perspective, white male social theorists should be encouraged to try to recognize the position of others – recognizing commonalities between themselves and others as well as differences. This would involve white male theorists writing their social theories from the partial perspective described earlier in the work of Donna Haraway (1988). Taking a partial perspective would mean not merely writing social theory from one's own position and generalizing that position for all, but also recognizing the position of the oppressed and marginalized and recognizing the differences and similarities in positions. If male social theorists were more willing to do this in their social theories, their theories perhaps would not be so gender and race blind.

Second, as well as opening their eyes to the position of others in their social theories, white malestream social theorists need to reflect critically on their own positions. For instance, they should no longer take their own position as 'white men' as given and should try to situate themselves in relation to their position of whiteness. In order to do this, social theorists need to engage with the literature on critical whiteness. According to Dyer (1997), whiteness occupies a central yet undeclared position. It is a position that makes claims to universality. In critical white studies, whiteness is named and identified as a position of privilege (Knowles 2003). It carries an admission of racial guilt and accountability, an acknowledgment of a history of exclusion and recognition that an anti-racist future would require white people to transcend their racial privilege (Cohen 1997). Social theorists should engage with this literature in order to situate their position of racial advantage within their social theories.

Furthermore, in recognizing their own position of privilege and its impact on social theory, white male theorists also perhaps need to engage more with the burgeoning literature on men and masculinity. According to Hearn (2004), men have been studying men for a long time and calling it 'history' (as discussed in the present volume). However, in more recent years there has been an increase in more critical studies on men, ranging from feminism to queer theory, that address men's position in the context of gendered power relations (ibid.). These have been important in questioning and exploring the position of men in society and 'men' as a social category. Although some male social theorists have engaged with this literature on masculinity (Seidler 1994), many do not. They still fail to recognize their own positions of male privilege. Social theorists could learn much by engaging more with this literature and recognizing the ways in which their social theories are produced through (not outside of) gendered power relations. White malestream social theorists could transform the gender- and race-blind nature of their social theories if they were to reflect critically on their own positions and to stop generalizing from their positions of privilege. As suggested here, this would involve recognition in their social theories of the centrality of gender and race and an acknowledgement that they are indeed not beyond gender or race.

This leads on to another, related point. While men should not be seen as outside gender or race, nor should women and theorists of colour just be recognized as specialists on the areas of gender and race. As things stand, women theorists are still seen primarily as 'doing gender', and black people are seen as primarily 'doing work on race' (Bordo 1997). As argued in Chapter 6, race and gender are still subsidiary areas of study, beyond the realms of existing mainstream social theory. Women and theorists of colour are often seen just to write their social theories about gender or about race and, in this way, are seen as peripheral to 'mainstream social theory' and are sidelined as a result. I have felt this myself in writing this book. The book is about social theory. My primary aim is to ask the key questions that many men writing social theory textbooks seldom ask, namely, how and why do we select sociological theorists to be core members of the social theoretical canon? Despite this, academic colleagues still refer to my book as a book about gender and social theory. When I tell stories of sociology's past and present, I am indeed telling stories of racial and gendered exclusion. However, I like to think the book provides a more integrated approach to social theories and is not just adding gender and race as appendages to general social theory. Mainstream social theorists need to acknowledge this when writing accounts of contemporary social theory.

Nowadays, of course, there are female and black social theorists whose work *is* being recognized in social theory as being not just about gender or race (although their number remains very small). One such theorist is Margaret Archer (1990, 1996, 2000), whose work has contributed extensively to the structure and agency debate. There are also black social theorists such as Paul Gilroy and Stuart Hall whose social theories command large amounts of attention across a range of academic sites. However, there are many other women and black theorists whose social theories cannot just be reduced to specialized critiques on race and gender, and this needs to be further recognized within social theory.

Gender, Race and Public Social Theory

As argued in the previous section, centring the areas of race and gender and recognizing that women and black social theorists do not just 'do' gender and race is one way of trying to challenge the marginalization of gender and race and women and black social theorists. Another way to a more inclusive social theory is to promote the role of the public social theorist. The role of the intellectual in academic and public life has long been a fascination of sociologists. Certainly, many have attempted to pitch their social theories beyond the discipline of professional sociology. For example, as discussed in Chapter 4, within his career as a sociologist, Mills wanted to reach wider audiences than the classroom. He wanted to create a 'public sociology' and attempted to do this through public lectures and by writing in magazines and newspapers. Mills was not the only theorist to do this; many others have also attempted to broaden the frameworks of social theory. Most public intellectuals did this in the past by discussing class issues and putting issues of economic inequality on public agendas. However, as B.S. Turner (1994) points out in discussing the English intelligentsia, historically radical academics who work within a university context have often had an ambiguous relationship with working-class politics, because their very success in academic terms necessarily cut them off from their working-class roots. This really places a question mark over the extent of their past involvement in public political debate.

In the current academic climate, authors such as Jacoby mourn the death in contemporary society of the public intellectual. Jacoby (1987) in his famous book *The Last Intellectuals* sees this as a consequence of the growth of the professional academic brought about by the expansion of higher education. Although this may be true in part, it is, as B.S. Turner (1994) points out, important to be context specific when talking about the role of the intelligentsia. I would argue that within both Britain and the United States there are a number of theorists who speak to a variety of audiences, not just professional sociologists. These are not just professional academics but contemporary social theorists immersed in public debate, in politics and the media. Lemert (1995) highlights the importance of such theorists and labels them 'extrasociological sociologists'. Many of them, according to him, are deeply situated in practical sociology but are able also to speak to the professionals.

Many of these contemporary public social theorists are women and/or black theorists who speak to the issues of race and gender academically and publicly. The engagement of these theorists with a wide range of audiences including the public must be encouraged. By linking debates on race and gender both publicly and academically, a heightening of their profiles is ensured. These theorists are able to connect with the politics of race and gender in a way perhaps that the bourgeois intellectuals of the past failed to connect to working-class politics. Although it may be possible to transcend class, it is not possible for most people (as yet) to transcend sex or skin colour. As a result, these theorists are uniquely able to speak to issues of race and gendered exclusion in the public realm from their positions of race and gendered exclusion.

As Said (2001) argues, one of the main functions of the public intellectual in contemporary society is to function as a kind of public memory and 'to recall what is forgotten or is ignored' (503). As argued throughout this book, race and gender and women and black social theorists have often been forgotten or ignored in the academic sphere and in society in general. These omissions can now be addressed by female and black public intellectuals and debated in the public sphere. Furthermore, public intellectuals in contemporary society are able to address a broader and more varied audience then those intellectuals of the past. They are able to reach a broader audience through a now globalized mediascape. An example of a theorist who transcends the academic sphere is Stuart Hall. He has done much to put race debates – conceptual, empirical and policy related – into the public realm for discussion and to foster interaction between these realms. Such public debates, particularly over race or gender, ensure that these issues of sexism and racism will continue to be challenged publicly, privately and sociologically. The public face of theorists such as Hall can, I think, only aid the incorporation of female and black theorists and race and gender as subjects into the realms of social theory. I hope this will result in the discipline lending more credence to race and gender at its centre rather than continuing to situate them in a subordinate position on the sidelines. This engagement and diversification of social theoretical dissemination is something that should be encouraged.

Empirically Orienting Social Theory

Finally, in addition to outsiders challenging social theory to become 'inside theorists', a shift towards social theorists who speak to a public audience and a general further drive to incorporate gender and race into a sociological core, there is also a need for more empirically informed social theory. A move towards a more empirically related approach to social theory could also enable a wider inclusion of outsiders. There are two strategies I want to advocate here. First, more social theories need to be applied empirically and theory-building needs to reflect empirical work. Second, there need to be more grand theorists and social theory textbook writers who conduct empirical work. Within this section of the chapter, I explore how this might help the inclusion of racial and gendered outsiders.

The call for a more empirically related social theory is far from new. Social theory has frequently been criticized for being too abstract, for not speaking to the lives of real people (Marshall 1997), and sociologists have for a long time called for a stronger link between theory and empirical work. However, rather than there being an increase in empirically driven theory, what has tended to happen is that the gap between social theory and the empirical world has grown wider, with social theory becoming seemingly more abstract and less relevant to social issues. This gap needs continually to be readdressed. While our society continues to be marked by racial inequality, violence, sexism, homophobia and deep social inequality, we must engage in empirical work to explore these issues, and social theory should be central to this. As Layder (1998) argues, the project of social theory is absolutely essential to social analysis in general and to social research in particular. He argues that the tie between general theory and theorizing about society, and the actual formulation and conduct of social research needs to be reaffirmed in the current context, particularly because a gap has emerged between them. According to him, social theory would be made more solid, and its explanatory capacity would be enhanced, by having its assumptions and presuppositions more closely explored through empirical research (ibid.).

In their work on grounded theory, Glaser and Strauss (1967) emphasize that the development of theories always begins with grounding in data a particular substantive area of sociology, such as racialization. After the development of substantive theory about the area, which results from researchers immersing themselves in empirical data, it is then possible to elaborate and extend this theory so that it may cover more general and formal areas of inquiry. Such an approach may, I think, enable the further incorporation of outside views into the sociological canon. For example, empirical work on gender or race may enable the generation of a more formalized general social theory that incorporates these issues more centrally into its remit. Furthermore, although authors may not wish to subscribe to a thoroughly grounded approach to theory, empirically testing theories and then reflecting back on them can only aid in the process of more inclusive theory building.

Empirically based social theory, therefore, should be encouraged. As argued in Chapter 3, for example, the members of the Chicago School incorporated empirical work into their sociological frameworks and, as a consequence, were a group who focused on issues such as race. Perhaps we can learn from this in order to develop a social theory that better reflects, and can be applied to, people's lives – a social theory that does not exclude. We can take this even further by encouraging those theorists who are well known for writing abstract theory and writing accounts of social theory to engage in empirical research or at least make their theories more empirically operable. Although the importance of the link between theory and empirical work has been frequently stated, it is still worth restating its importance. An engagement with real people and real problems in the empirical world enables those writing social theory to write it from a much more socially aware position than that of armchair theorists disengaged from the real world. There are, of course, some theorists who are starting to make their theoretical work more empirically relevant. However, this is something that needs to be further developed.

It is important to be clear here that I am not advocating empirical work with no social theory. As Anthias and Yuval-Davis (1993) point out with regard to work on race, empirical work on race, racism or racialized identities in a postmodern world is pointless without a clear idea of what these concepts mean. Craib (1992) gives a further warning. According to him, it is important not to fall into the trap of empirical sociology by itself. This may take the form of only collecting facts, of becoming absorbed in technical debates about methodology and statistical correlation or of relying on empirical sociology to 'expose' the reality behind popular mythology (ibid. 10–11). Without some attempt at overall theory, sociology remains an adjunct to other disciplines.

Furthermore, in advocating empirically related theoretical work we do not want to recreate that age-old dichotomy that I pointed out in Chapter 3 in discussing the Chicago School. This relates directly to the split in sociology between those who do abstract theory (i.e. men) and those who do substantive or policy work (i.e. women). This is a distinction that has been perpetuated (albeit subconsciously perhaps) in sociological theory and is mapped onto more general ideas about the status of social theory versus empirical/or policy-related work. An encouragement of empirically related theoretical work could lead again to this distinction and the maintenance yet again of women and ethnic minorities in areas of specialist critique. We need, therefore, to be careful here. We need to develop social theories that can be explored empirically by all theorists. If we do this, social theorists and theories will not be quite as exclusionary and will, I hope, speak to a broader audience.

Limitations to Gendered and Racial Inclusion

The suggested changes outlined above for social theory will, I hope, enable the development of a more inclusive social theory, one that does not exclude on the basis of gender and race. However, it must be recognized that there are limitations to making such changes in social theory based on the continued existence of gendered and racial inequality in society in general. Although there have been great advances in the position of women and ethnic minorities within society in general, western societies still exhibit significant inequalities, for example, between men and women, and between whites and other ethnic groups. For example, within the United Kingdom, Pilkington (2003) highlights the fact that all minority ethnic groups (e.g. Caribbean, Indian, African Asian, Pakistani, Bangladeshi, Chinese) have lower equivalent household incomes than whites.[1] These types of inequalities are also prevalent in the United States. Black Americans, for example, are less likely than white Americans to own their own homes, earn as much as whites, live as long or do as well in school, according to a report by the National Urban League (Ferguson 2004). What about the position of women? According to Walter (1998), women still lack equality and everything that comes with it. When we look at the economy, the general picture within the United Kingdom is one of significant growth in employment rates for women. However, for the majority, there is a continuity of their disadvantaged position in the labour market (Glover and Arber 1995), with the gender pay gap in the United Kingdom being the highest in the European Union. This is reinforced when we look at women's positions in the United States. According to Amott (2004), there is a crisis regarding women's relationship to the US economy. She argues that North American women have carried a heavy economic burden in recent decades. Attempts need to be made to reorganize this burden.

Furthermore, when we look in particular at the position of ethnic minorities and women within academia we can see a stark picture of inequality. For example, according to Delamont (2003), in the United States in 1991 women held 29 per cent of all tenured and tenure-tracked posts. In Britain in 2000, 11.9 per cent of the full professors in administrative, business and social studies were women. According to statistics obtained by the AUT (Association of University Teachers), there were only 29 black academics and 179 Asian academics with professorial grades in the 1999/2000 academic year, out of 11,000 university professors in the United Kingdom (Major 2002). Overall, we can see that although there have been huge transformations in the positions of women and ethnic minorities within society, stark gendered and racial inequalities still remain.

The position of women and people from ethnic minorities within society in general, and academia in particular, obviously reflects and affects their position within social theory. While they are marginalized within society in general, they will continue to be marginalized in academia and social theory. Until radical changes take place regarding the positions of women and ethnic minorities within society, they will continue to be marginalized. Changes at a broader societal level are required in order for effective change to be brought about – for example, better policies on childcare, challenges to unequal pay and tackling racism and sexism at an institutional level. We cannot explore these issues in the limited space of this book, nor can we change them purely within the context of social theory. However, this does not mean that we should give up on making changes to social theory. Although the extensive nature of gendered and racial inequalities in society at large place limitations on changes in social theory, they do not render them impossible. What we need to do is continue to challenge gendered and racial inequalities from within sociology itself. We need to maintain this challenge to gendered and racial marginality within social theory, implementing the suggestions made in this chapter. Ultimately, by initiating such efforts within social theory, centralizing issues of gender and race, publicizing academic issues in these areas and linking social theory with empirical work, we may inspire greater social change, which in turn may enable us to transform the positions of women and ethnic minorities and issues of gender and race more generally.

The Future of Social Theory

Within this chapter so far, we have explored the ways in which sociological theory can be opened up to include those previously viewed as outsiders. In terms of looking at past sociological theory this has entailed a reinterpretation and opening up of the canon. Regarding contemporary theory, however, there have been several recommendations, all of which, I hope, will result in a centring of those theorists previously seen as outsiders and a centring of gender and race within sociological theory. Although I have acknowledged the limitations on the extent of change possible within social theory, I do remain hopeful that social theory can and will over time become more inclusive. I want now to move on to ask, within this section, what would be the implications of a more inclusive social theory for the future of the discipline. If the discipline becomes opened up to include those previously classed as outsiders, and if so many topics are included into its remit, does this weaken what is sociological about social theory? Does it mean the end to sociological boundaries as such? And, if so, does this suggest an end to sociological theory?

Regarding the opening up of the canon of past sociological theory, I have already suggested that an incorporation of women theorists and theorists of colour or the subjects of gender and race does not mean that we debunk the existing classics or that we jettison the focus on social class. Rather, what I have suggested is that we integrate the accounts of authors such as Weber with those of DuBois and of Parsons with those of Arendt and de Beauvoir. I have recommended that we explore social theories of the nineteenth and twentieth centuries that focus not only on social class but also on gender and race. In doing so, we need to recognize that these factors interact and should be explored together, and we need to acknowledge, at the same time, that the entry into sociological theory of the past, and indeed the development of the discipline, is multifaceted. In this, I am not suggesting the irrelevance of canonical classical theorists or mainstream theories of the golden age. Rather, I am suggesting that we develop a less exclusionary interpretation of the past.

However, what about contemporary social theory? What kind of threat does a centralization of outside theorists and subjects of race and gender pose? There will be some existing malestream theorists who will aspire to keep sociological theory what it has always been – more or less a white boys club. The centralizing of sociological outsiders and subjects of gender and race will pose a threat to the existence of this club. As a result, many such theorists will continue to resist the need to put race and gender at the centre of social theory – those who continue to see themselves as existing beyond gender and race and those who view theorists of gender and race as subsidiary figures within the discipline. Such social theorists will continue to question the relevance of gender and race in social theory because they fail fully to appreciate the contributions made by feminists and race thinkers to the development of the discipline. Mouzelis, for example, states, 'I am unable to think of any important theoretical paradigm the parameters of which have been significantly transformed via the development of feminist theory' (1994: 175). There will be others who echo these views about both gender and race, social theorists who want to keep theory as exclusive as it always has been. Any threat, then, instigated by opening up the canon will be countered by a resistance to centralizing sociological outsiders and issues of race and gender in social theory.

This argument could be taken further by some theorists who may suggest that the opening up of the canon to include gendered and racial outsiders and gender and race as subjects encourages a free-for-all, a loss of disciplinary boundaries that will lead to a theoretical *impasse* and, worse, could result in the end of the discipline. In this sense, the changes I have suggested throughout this chapter may appear to some to indicate a diluting of sociological theory, advocating the loss of a coherent discipline and the introduction of overcomplexity in variables of analysis. In order to head off threats like these to social theory, authors such as Mouzelis (1991, 1994) have in the past suggested a move back to a more traditional style of sociological theory. This is a move that relies on the idea of a return to the notion of sociological 'craftsmanship' – including a retreat from speculative philosophizing and closer moves towards theorizing that incorporates substantive concerns. However, these solutions mirror those outlined in the paragraph above, as they appear to involve a return to sociological theory that constitute a boys club. As McLennan (1995) argues, there is something inherently patriarchal in suggesting a move back to sociological craftsmanship.

Any suggestion that sociology move back to such a traditional sense of sociological theory is not possible anyway. As argued by Stones (1998), social theory needs to understand that it cannot and should not want to create a discipline that is sealed off from outside influences, and this is, I hope, what I have shown throughout the book. Furthermore, what is suggested in this book is that the centralizing of theoretical outsiders does not mark the end of social theory as authors such as Mouzelis might suppose. The broadening out of social theory suggested here rather marks the birth of what Lemert (1995) calls 'sociologies', the emergence of which also brings recognition in social theory of those who talk in a language that speaks to many audiences: social theoretical, substantive and public.

Theorists such as Mouzelis (1991) may see the opening up of the canon as marking a transition from sociological theory related to substantive issues to a social theory based on speculative philosophizing. What I have recommended in this chapter is quite the opposite. If we open up social theory and further centralize areas such as gender and race, we are not slipping into a postmodern world of *difference*, nor are we divorcing social theory from substantive or socioeconomic concerns. Rather, we are actually linking social theory more deeply and more concretely to substantive issues, issues that can be theoretically developed and empirically explored. Thus, I would argue that the suggestions made here proffer a more diverse and multifaceted future for social theory. They do not mark the end of social theory as feared by some but rather mark the end of an exclusionary social theory.

Book Overview

The aim of this book has been to explore the ways in which as sociological theory has developed, certain theorists have come to be seen as sociological insiders whereas others have stayed on the peripheries or outside the discipline. The book has explored the ways in which insiders often may not see themselves as insiders; for example, the classical theorists hardly saw themselves as sociological, yet they have become the founding fathers of the discipline. The book has looked at why this has been the case. It has explored why some theorists have been excluded from the canon, relating this to issues of gender and race.

As has been shown throughout the book, from the outset of the discipline those writing from the position of the racial and gendered 'other' and those writing social theories around issues of race and gender were excluded from the canon. Although accounts of the development of sociology were concerned with inequality and power, this has been mostly in relation to social class not race or gender. Subsequently, many authors who wrote on these issues or who were gendered and racial outsiders have been excluded from the sociological canon. Within the book, we have explored the ways that this has changed over time. This can be seen, as argued in Chapter 4, in a recognition of the issue of race in the work of some theorists writing during the golden age and through the subsequent feminist and racial challenge to social theory brought about by the women's movement and the civil rights movement. It can also be seen through the development of postmodernism, which has led to a shift in focus from economic issues to culture. This has meant that class analysis has declined, and once-peripheral topics such as race and gender have now become recognized as important within social theory. However, as we concluded in the previous chapter, although those classed as outsiders have been included into the canon, this has been done in a partisan fashion. They still do not have equal status in the canon with white men. As I have suggested in this chapter, however, there are ways that we can continue to change this racial and gendered dynamic so that those previously seen as outsiders become more central.

In this final chapter a number of issues have been raised. We have looked at the possibility of expanding the telling of social theory's past. This can be done in part by integrating accounts and theorists of race and gender into textbook reconstructions and curricula on sociological theory's diverse history. We have also looked at what happens now with regard to the contemporary canon. Suggestions that were put forward were a further centralization of issues of gender and race, a move to encourage outside theorists to become public theorists and finally a need for a more substantive and empirically linked social theory that both conceptualizes and makes empirically operable social theories. Although there are limitations to these suggested changes, they nonetheless offer the opportunity of a more inclusive social theory, an opportunity that does not leads to an end to social theory but rather marks the beginnings of a less exclusionary, more substantively based social theory.

Conclusion

On a final note, it is important to acknowledge that we will always exclude and include theorists within our visions of the sociological past, present and future. These will reflect our own positions as women, men, Afro-Caribbeans, white Europeans, Asians, homosexuals, heterosexuals and so on. There is no such thing as one true history, only the interpretations that we have. What I hope, though, is that we can move beyond a social theory that excludes theorists and their work on the basis of race and gender. As argued by Lemert (1995), and indeed as argued throughout this book, some excellent social theories are those written by women or black theorists (or both). These must be engaged with and learned from and not just pigeon-holed into some specialized critique. Whether we are male or female, black or white, we all 'do' ethnicity, race and gender. Our social theories must engage with and reflect these positions.

More generally, though, in the telling of our discipline's past, we need to recognize that histories are selective. This is something that sociology has been very bad at doing. Many authors of accounts of social theory and many of those devising sociology curricula have relied on one key account of the discipline. As sociologists we are notoriously poor at applying the social constructionist approach to ourselves. I have been at pains to demonstrate that the existing histories of the discipline are valid in their own way – it is just that they are only one version among many. We need to situate our histories of sociological theory in social context. Telling these histories from a wide range of perspectives and positions is most important, crucial even, if the discipline is to survive. Sociology, as Stones (1998) points out, is a discipline that is uniquely equipped to focus on society and social life as such and, within that focus, to see society as more than a collection of individuals. This must not be lost. However, sociology must also be a discipline that does not restrict itself to a white male perspective. It must be regularly self-reflexive and evaluative, frequently questioning its own inclusions and exclusions. It is only when the discipline and those working in it learn to apply the social constructive approach to it, and to themselves, that progress can be made in developing the discipline's future.

Chapter Summary

- The aim of this chapter was to put forward new ways of developing an inclusive social theory.
- The chapter suggested a reinterpretation and broadening out of past social theory.
- It also suggested a number of ways forward for contemporary and future social theory. These included

  - A centralization of race and gender in social theory whereby it must be recognized that white male theorists are not without gender or race. Nor are the social theories of women and black theorists only about gender and race.
  - The role of the public social theorist must be encouraged, particularly among those who focus on issues of gender and race.
  - There must be a greater link between theory and empirical work.

- It was also recognized that there were limitations to the extent of the impact of these changes as a result of the extensive nature of gendered and racial inequality in society in general.
- However, as suggested, these changes are still able to make some impact within social theory itself.
- Furthermore, when implemented, these changes, rather then signifying the end of social theory as some may think, actually offer a more substantively linked, less exclusionary social theory.
- Finally, the overall argument of the book was summarized. Social theory has moved over time from theory based on gendered and racial exclusion, in early social theory, to the partial engagements of theories of the golden age, to marginal acceptance in contemporary theory and finally to my suggestions of a future non-exclusionary social theory.

Further Reading

For accounts of reinterpreting classical theory see J. Camic (ed.), *Reclaiming the Sociological Classics: The State of Scholarship* (Blackwell, 1997). For debates on whiteness see V. Ware and L. Back, *Out of Whiteness: Color, Politics and Culture* (University of Chicago Press, 2002). For debates on masculinity see R.W. Connell, *Masculinities* (Allen and Unwin, 1995). For debates on the role of the public intellectual see R. Jacoby, *The Last Intellectuals: American Culture in the Age of Academe* (Noonday Press, 1987). For an account of the links between social theory and empirical work see D. Layder, *Sociological Practice: Linking Theory and Social Research* (Sage, 1998).

Note

1. Pilkington is drawing here on data from the fourth Policy Studies Institute study *Ethnic Minorities in Britain* (Modood *et al.* 1997).

References

Abbott, A. (1999) *Department and Discipline: Chicago Sociology at One Hundred* Chicago: University of Chicago Press.

Abercrombie, N., Hill, S. and Turner, B.S. (1988) *Dictionary of Sociology* (2nd edition) London: Penguin.

Adorno, T.W. and Horkheimer, M. (1997) *The Dialectic of Enlightenment* (translated by John Cumming) London: Verso (first published 1947).

Adorno, T.W., Brunswik, E.F., Levinson, D.J. and Sanford, R.N. (1950) *The Authoritarian Personality* London and New York: Harper.

Adriaansens, H.P.M. (1980) *Talcott Parsons and the Conceptual Dilemma* London: Routledge and Kegan Paul.

Alessandrini, A. (ed.) (1999) *Frantz Fanon: Critical Perspectives* London: Routledge.

Alexander, C. and Alleyne, B. (2002) 'Introduction: framing difference: racial and ethnic studies in twenty-first-century Britain', *Ethnic and Racial Studies*, 25 (4): 541–51.

Alexander, J. (1988) *Durkheimian Sociology: Cultural Studies* Cambridge: Cambridge University Press.

Amott, T. (2004) *Caught in the Crisis: Women and the U.S. Economy Today* New York: Monthly Review Press.

Anthias, F. and Yuval-Davis, N. (1993) *Racialized Boundaries: Race, Gender, Colour and Class and the Anti-Racist Struggle* London: Routledge.

Archer, M. (1990) 'Human agency and social structure', in J. Clark, C. Modgil and S. Modgil (eds.), *Anthony Giddens* New York: Falmer Press. pp. 73–84.

Archer, M. (1996) *Culture and Agency: The Place of Culture in Social Theory* Cambridge: Cambridge University Press.

Archer, M. (2000) *Being Human: The Problem of Agency* Cambridge: Cambridge University Press.

Arendt, H. (1951) *The Origins of Totalitarianism* New York: Harcourt, Brace & Co.

Arendt, H. (1958) *The Human Condition* Chicago: University of Chicago Press.

Baker-Fletcher, K. (1994) *A Singing Something* New York: Crossroad.

Banton, M. (2001) 'Progress in ethnic and racial studies', *Ethnic and Racial Studies*, 24 (2): 173–94.

Barrett, M. (1988) *Women's Oppression Today* (2nd edition) London: Verso.

Barrett, M. (1998) 'Stuart Hall', in R. Stones (ed.), *Key Sociological Thinkers* Basingstoke: Palgrave Macmillan. pp. 266–78.

Becker, H.S. (n.d.) 'Professional sociology: the case of C. Wright Mills'; http://home.earthlink.net/~hsbecker/mills.html (accessed 14 September 2005).

Benhabib, S. (1992) *Situating the Self: Gender, Community and Postmodernism in Contemporary Ethics* Cambridge: Polity Press.

Bernard, J. (1989) 'The dissemination of feminist thought 1960–1988', in R.A. Wallace (ed.), *Feminism and Sociological Theory* London: Sage. pp. 23–33.

Bernstein, R.J. (1996) 'Did Hannah Arendt change her Mind? From radical evil to the banality of evil', in L. May and J. Kohn (eds.) *Hannah Arendt: Twenty Years Later* Cambridge, MA: MIT Press.

Bhabha, H. (1987) Contribution to 'Remembering Fanon', a special section remembering Frantz Fanon on the 25th anniversary of his death (other contributors S. Feuchtwang and B. Harlow), *New Formations*, 1 (Spring): 118–35.

Bordo, S. (1997) *Twilight Zones: The Hidden Life of Cultural Images from Plato to O.J.* Berkeley, CA: University of California Press.

Braverman, H. ([1974] 1998) *Labor and Monopoly Capital: The Degradation of Work in the Twentieth Century* New York: Monthly Review Press.

Brick, H. (2000) 'Talcott Parsons's "shift away from economics", 1937–1946', *Journal of American History*, 87 (2): 490–514; http://www.historycooperative.org/journals/jah/87.2/brick.html (accessed 14 September 2005).

Brodkin, K. (1998) *How Jews Became White Folks and What That Says about Race in America* New Brunswick, NJ: Rutgers University Press.

Brubaker, R. (1984) *The Limits of Rationality: An Essay on the Social and Moral Thought of Max Weber* London: George Allen and Unwin.

Bulmer, M. and Solomos, J. (eds.) (1999) *Ethnic and Racial Studies Today* London: Routledge.

Callinicos, A. (1999) *Social Theory: A Historical Introduction* Cambridge: Polity Press.

Camic, J. (ed.) (1997) *Reclaiming the Sociological Classics: The State of Scholarship* Oxford: Blackwell.

Carby, H. (1987) *Reconstructing Womanhood: The Emergence of the Afro-American Woman Novelist* Oxford: Oxford University Press.

Castells, M. (1983) *The City and the Grassroots* London: Edward Arnold.

Chicago Commission on Race Relations (1922) *The Negro in Chicago: A Study of Race Relations and a Race Riot in 1919* Chicago: University of Chicago Press.

Chriss, J. (2002) 'Gouldner's Tragic Vision', *Sociological Quarterly*, 43 (1): 81–96

Clough, P.T. and Schneider, J. (2001) 'Donna J. Haraway', in A. Elliott and B.S. Turner (eds.), *Profiles in Contemporary Theory* London: Sage. pp. 338–48.

Cohen, P. (1997) 'Labouring under Whiteness', in R. Frankenberg (ed.), *Displacing Whiteness* Durham, NC: Duke University Press.

Connell, R.W. (1995) *Masculinities* St Leonard's: Allen and Unwin.

Cooper, A.J. (1892) *A Voice from the South* Ohio: Aldine Printing House.

Cooper, A.J. (1988) *A Voice from the South* (with an introduction by Mary Helen Washington) Oxford: Oxford University Press.

Cooper, A.J. ([1925] 1988) *Slavery and the French Revolutionists* (1788–1805) (translated with forward and introductory essay by Frances Richardson Keller) Queenston, Ontario: Edwin Mellen Press.

Coser, L.A. (1979) 'American Trends', in T. Bottomore and R. Nisbet (eds.), *A History of Sociological Analysis* London: Heinemann. pp. 287–320.

Coser, L.A. (1991) 'Georg Simmel's style of work', in L.J. Ray (ed.), *Formal Sociology* Aldershot: Edward Elgar.

Craib, I. (1992) *Modern Social Theory: From Parsons to Habermas* Hemel Hempstead, Hertfordshire: Harvester Wheatsheaf.

Crompton, R. (1993) *Class and Stratification: An Introduction to Current Debates* Cambridge: Polity Press.

Crow, G. (2004) *The Art of Sociological Argument* Basingstoke: Palgrave Macmillan.

Cuzzort, R.P. and King, E.W. (1989) *Twentieth-Century Social Thought* London: Fort Worth.

De Beauvoir, S. (1943) *L'Invitée* Paris: Gallimard.

De Beauvoir, S. (1948) *Pour une morale de l'ambiguité* Paris: Gallimard.

De Beauvoir, S. ([1949] 1988) *The Second Sex* London: Pan Books.

De Beauvoir, S. (1959) *Memoirs of a Dutiful Daughter* (translated by James Kirkup) London: Andre Deutsch and Weidenfeld & Nicolson.

De Beauvoir, S. (1962) *The Prime of Life* (translated by Peter Green) Cleveland, OH: World Publishing Co.

De Beauvoir, S. (1965) *Force of Circumstance* (translated by Richard Howard) London: Andre Deutsch and Weidenfeld & Nicolson.

De Beauvoir, S. (1966) *A Very Easy Death* (translated by Patrick O'Brian) London: Andre Deutsch and Weidenfeld & Nicolson.

De Beauvoir, S. (1974) *All Said and Done* (translated by Patrick O'Brian) London: Andre Deutsch and Weidenfeld & Nicolson.

De Beauvoir, S. (1985) *Adieux: A Farewell to Sartre* (translated by Patrick O'Brian) Harmondsworth: Penguin.

Deegan, M.J. (1988) *Jane Addams and the Men of the Chicago School* New Brunswick, NJ: Transaction Press.

Delamont, S. (2003) *Feminist Sociology* London: Sage.

Douglas, J. (1966) *The Social Meanings of Suicide* Princeton, NJ: Princeton University Press.

Draper, H. (1977) *Karl Marx's Theory of Revolution: State and Bureaucracy* (Vol. 1) New York: Monthly Review.

DuBois, W.E.B. ([1899] 1996) *The Philadelphia Negro: A Social Study* Philadelphia, PA: University of Pennsylvania Press.

DuBois, W.E.B. ([1903] 1989) *The Souls of Black Folk* New York: Bantam.

DuBois, W.E.B. ([1920] 1999) *Darkwater: Voices from Within the Veil* New York: Dover.

DuBois, W.E.B. ([1935] 1998) *Black Reconstruction in America: 1860–1880* New York: Free Press.

DuBois, W.E.B. ([1940] 1968) *Dusk of Dawn: An Essay toward an Autobiography of a Race Concept* New York: Schocken Books.

Durkheim, E. ([1893] 1933) *The Division of Labour in Society* London: Collier Macmillan.

Durkheim, E. ([1895] 1964) *The Rules of the Sociological Method* New York: Free Press.

Durkheim, E. ([1897] 1970) *Suicide* London: Routledge.

Durkheim, E. ([1912] 1965) *The Elementary Forms of the Religious Life* New York: Free Press.

Dyer, R. (1997) *White* London: Routledge.

Elliott, A. (1994) *Psychoanalytic Theory: An Introduction* Oxford: Blackwell.

Elliott, A. (1996) *Subject to Ourselves* Cambridge: Polity Press.

Elliott, A. (2001) 'Anthony Giddens', in A. Elliott and B.S. Turner (eds.), *Profiles in Contemporary Theory* London: Sage. pp. 292–303.

Elliott, A. and Ray, L. (2003) *Key Contemporary Social Theorists* Oxford: Blackwell Publishers.

Elshtain, J.B. (1981) *Public Man, Private Woman* Princeton, NJ: Princeton University Press.

Engels, F. ([1884] 1968) 'Origins of family, private property and the state', in K. Marx and F. Engels, *Selected Works* London: Lawrence and Wishart.

Evans, M. (1996) *Simone de Beauvoir* London: Sage.

Evans, M. (2003) *Gender and Social Theory* Milton Keynes: Open University Press.

Fanon, F. ([1952] 1967) *Black Skin, White Masks* (translated by Charles Lam Markmann) New York: Grove Press.

Fanon, F. ([1961] 1963) *The Wretched of the Earth* (Preface by Jean-Paul Sartre; translated by Constance Farrington) London: MacGibbon and Kee.

Ferguson, C. (2004) 'Report: black, white disparities abound', *The Guardian*, 24 March; http://www.guardian.co.uk/worldlatest/story/0,1280,-3896664,00.html.

Fox-Genovese, E. (1986) 'The claims of common sense culture', *Salamangundi*, 72 (Fall): 134–51.

Friedan, B. (1963) *The Feminine Mystique* Harmondsworth: Penguin.

Fulcher, J. and Scott, J. (2003) *Sociology* (2nd edition) Oxford: Oxford University Press.

Game, A. (1991) *Undoing the Social: Towards a Deconstructive Sociology* Milton Keynes: Open University Press.

Giddens, A. (1976) *The New Rules of Sociological Method* London: Hutchinson; New York: Basic Books.

Giddens, A. (1984) *The Constitution of Society* Cambridge: Polity.

Giddens, A. (1987) *Social Theory and Modern Sociology* Cambridge: Polity Press in association with Blackwells.

Giddens, A. (1990) *The Consequences of Modernity* Cambridge: Polity Press.

Giddens, A. (1991) *Modernity and Self-Identity* Cambridge: Polity Press.

Giddens, A. (1992) *The Transformation of Intimacy* Cambridge: Polity Press.

Giddens, A. (1994) *Beyond Left and Right: The Future of Radical Politics* Cambridge: Polity Press.

Giddens, A. (1998) *The Third Way* Cambridge: Polity Press.

Gitlin, T. (n.d.) 'C. Wright Mills, free radical'; http://www.uni-muenster.de/PeaCon/dgs-mills/mills-texte/GitlinMills.htm (accessed 14 September 2005).

Glaser, B. and Strauss, A. (1967) *The Discovery of Grounded Theory* Chicago: Aldine.

Glover, J. and Arber, S. (1995) 'Polarization in mothers' employment' *Gender, Work and Organization*, 2 (4): 165–79.

Goldthorpe, J.H., Lockwood, D., Bechhofer, F. and Platt, J. (1968) *The Affluent Worker: Industrial Attitudes and Behaviour* Cambridge: Cambridge University Press.

Goody, J. (1996) *The East in the West* Cambridge: Cambridge University Press.

Gouldner, A. (1954) *Patterns of Industrial Bureaucracy* London: Routledge and Kegan Paul.

Gouldner, A. (1955) *Wildcat Strike* London: Routledge and Kegan Paul.

Gouldner, A. (1962) *Notes on Technology and the Moral Order* Indianapolis, IN: Bobbs-Merril.

Gouldner, A. (1965) *Enter Plato: Classical Greece and the Origins of Social Theory* New York: Basic Books.

Gouldner, A. (1971) *The Coming Crisis in Western Sociology* New York: Avon Books.

Gouldner, A. (1973) *For Sociology: Renewal and Critique in Sociology Today* London: Allen Lane.

Gouldner, A. (1980) *The Two Marxisms: Contradictions and Anomalies in the Development of Theory* (Critical Social Studies) Basingstoke: Palgrave Macmillan.

Hadden, R. (1997) *Sociological Theory: An Introduction to the Classical Tradition* Peterborough, ON: Broadview Press.

Hall, S. and Whannel, P. (1964) *The Popular Arts* London: Hutchinson

Hall, S. (1979) 'The great moving right show', in *Marxism Today*, January.

Hall, S. (ed.) (1997) *Representation: Cultural Representations and Signifying Practices* London: Sage.

Hall, S. and Jacques, M. (eds.) (1989) *New Times* London: Lawrence and Wishart.

Hall, S., Critcher, C., Jefferson, T., Clarke, J. and Robert, B. (1978) *Policing the Crisis: Mugging, the State and Law and Order* (Critical Social Studies) Basingstoke: Palgrave Macmillan.

Hamilton, R. (1978) *The Liberation of Women* London: Allen and Unwin.

Hammersley, M. (1999) 'Sociology, what's it for? A critique of Gouldner', *Sociological Research Online*, 4 (3); http://www.socresonline.org.uk/socresonline/4/3/hammersley.html.

Hansen, P. (2003) 'Hannah Arendt', in A. Elliott and L. Ray (eds.), *Key Contemporary Social Theorists* Oxford: Blackwell Publishers: 25–31

Haraway, D. (1985) 'Manifesto for cyborgs: science, technology and socialist feminism in the 1980s', *Socialist Review*, 80: 65–108.

Haraway, D. (1988) 'Situated knowledges: the science question in feminism and the privilege of the partial perspective', *Feminist Studies* 14 (3): 575–600.

Haraway, D. (1989) *Primate Visions: Gender, Race and Nature in the World of Modern Science* New York: Routledge.

Haraway, D. (1991) *Simians, Cyborgs, and Women: The Reinvention of Nature* New York: Routledge.

Hearn, G. (2004) 'From hegemonic masculinity to the hegemony of men', *Feminist Theory*, 5 (1): 49–72.

Held, D. (1980) *Introduction to Critical Theory: Horkheimer to Habermas* Cambridge: Polity Press.

Hill, M. and Hoecker-Drysdale, S. (eds) (2001) *Harriet Martineau: Theoretical and Methodological Perspectives* New York: Routledge.

Holmwood, J. (1996) *Founding Sociology? Talcott Parsons and the Idea of General Theory* London and New York: Longman.

hooks, b. (1990) 'Postmodern blackness', *Postmodern Culture*, 1 (1); http://jefferson.village.virginia.edu/pmc/text-only/issue.990/hooks.990 (accessed 15 September 2005).

Horowitz, I.L. (1983) *C. Wright Mills, American Utopian* New York: Free Press.

Hutcheon, P.D. (1996) *Leaving the Cave: Evolutionary Naturalism in Social Scientific Thought* Waterloo, ON: Wilfrid Laurier University Press.

Jacoby, R. (1987) *The Last Intellectuals: American Culture in the Age of Academe* New York: Noonday Press.

Johnson, M.M. (1989) 'Feminism and the theories of Talcott Parsons', in R. Wallace (ed.), *Feminism and Sociological Theory* London: Sage. pp. 101–18.

Kenny, M. (2003) 'Stuart Hall', in A. Elliott and L. Ray (eds.), *Key Contemporary Social Theorists* Oxford: Blackwell Publishing: 154–161

Kirby, V. (1997) *Telling Flesh: The Substance of the Corporeal* London: Routledge.

Knowles, K. (2003) *Race and Social Analysis* London: Sage.

Komarovsky, M. (1953) *Women in the Modern World: Their Education and Their Dilemmas* Boston: Little, Brown.

Kuhn, T. (1970) *The Structure of Scientific Revolutions* (2nd edition) Chicago: University of Chicago Press.

Kushner, T. (2002) 'Antisemitism', in D. Goldberg and J. Solomos (eds.), *A Companion to Ethnic and Racial Studies* Oxford: Blackwell Publishers. pp. 64–72.

Layder, D. (1994) *Understanding Social Theory* London: Sage.

Layder, D. (1998) *Sociological Practice: Linking Theory and Social Research* London: Sage.

Lemert, C. (1995) *Sociology after the Crisis* Boulder, CO: Westview Press.

Lemert, C. (ed.) (1999) *Social Theory: The Multicultural and Classic Readings* Boulder, CO: Westview Press..

Lemert, C. (2002) *Dark Thoughts: Race and the Eclipse of Society* London: Routledge.

Levine, D. (1971) 'Introduction'. in D. Levine (ed.), *Georg Simmel: Individuality and Social Forms* Chicago: University of Chicago Press.

Lockwood, D. (1964a) 'Social integration and system integration', in G.K. Zollschan and M. Hirsh (eds.), *Explanations in Social Change* London: Routledge and Kegan Paul: 244–57

Lockwood, D. (1964b) 'Some remarks on the social system', in N.J. Demereth and R.A. Peterson (eds.), *System, Change and Conflict: A Reader on Contemporary Sociological Theory and the Debate over Functionalism* New York: Free Press. pp. 281–92.

Logan, D.A. (2002) *The Hour and the Woman: Harriet Martineau's 'Somewhat Remarkable' Life* Dekalb, IL: Northern Illinois University Press.

Lukacs, G. (1971) *History and Class Consciousness: Studies in Marxist Dialectics* (translated by Rodner Livingstone) London: Merlin Press.

Macey, D. (2000) *Frantz Fanon: A Life* London: Granta.

Macionis, J.J. (2001) *Sociology* Upper Saddle River, NJ: Prentice Hall.

McLennan, G. (1995) 'After postmodernism – back to sociological theory?' *Sociology*, 29 (1): 117–32.

Major, L.E. (2002) '2% of professors from ethnic minority groups', *The Guardian*, 21 January; http://education.guardian.co.uk/racism/story/0,,636904,00.html (accessed 14 September 2005).

Marcuse, H. (1964) *One Dimensional Man: Studies in the Ideology of Advanced Industrial Society* London: Routledge and Kegan Paul.

Marsh, I. (ed.) (2000) *Sociology: Making Sense of Society* London: Prentice Hall.

Marshall, G. (1997) *Repositioning Class: Social Inequality in Industrial Societies* London: Sage.

Marshall, G. (ed.) (1998) *Dictionary of Sociology* Oxford: Oxford University Press.

Martineau, H. (1836) *Miscellanies* Boston: Hilliard Gray.

Martineau, H. (1836/7) *Society in America* (2 vols) New York: Sanders and Otley.

Martineau, H. (1838) *How to Observe Morals and Manners* London: Charles Knight.

Martineau, H. (1853) *The Positive Philosophy of Auguste Comte, Freely Translated and Condensed by Harriet Martineau* London: John Chapman.

Marx, K. (1844) 'On *The Jewish Question*', first published February 1844 in *Deutsch-Französische Jahrbücher* (proofed and corrected by Andy Blunden, February 2005); http://www.marxists.org/archive/marx/works/1844/jewish-question/ (accessed 15 September 2005).

Marx, K. ([1853] 1999) 'On imperialism in India', in C. Lemert (ed.), *Social Theory: The Multicultural and Classic Readings* Boulder, CO: Westview Press.

Marx, K. ([1867] 1976) *Capital: A Critique of Political Economy* (vol. 1) Moscow: Progress.

Marx, K. ([1875] 1968) 'Critique of the Gotha Programme', in K. Marx and F. Engels, *Selected Works* London: Lawrence and Wishart.

Mason, D. (2000) *Race and Ethnicity in Modern Britain* (2nd edition) Oxford: Oxford University Press.

May, L. and Kohn, J. (eds.) (1996) *Hannah Arendt: Twenty Years Later* Cambridge, MA: MIT Press.

Mead, G.H. (1934) *Mind, Self and Society from the Standpoint of a Social Behaviorist* (edited with an introduction by C.W. Morris) Chicago: University of Chicago Press

Mills, C. Wright ([1948] 2001) *The New Men of Power: America's Labor Leaders* Urbana: University of Illinois Press.

Mills, C. Wright ([1951] 1956) *White Collar: The American Middle Classes* New York: Oxford University Press.

Mills, C. Wright ([1956] 1970) *The Power Elite* New York: Oxford University Press.

Mills, C. Wright (1958) *The Causes of World War Three* London: Secker & Warburg.

Mills, C. Wright ([1959] 1976) *The Sociological Imagination* New York: Oxford University Press.

Mills, C. Wright (1960) *Listen, Yankee! The Revolution in Cuba* New York: Ballantine Books.

Mills, C. Wright (1963) 'Women: the darling little slaves', in I.L. Horowitz (ed.), *Power, Politics and People: The Collected Essays of C. Wright Mills* London and New York: Oxford University Press. pp. 339–346.

Mills, K. and Mills, P. (eds.) (2000) *C. Wright Mills: Letters and Autobiographical Writings* Berkeley, CA: University of California Press.

Modood, T., Berthoud, R. [with] Lakey, J. *et al.* (1997) *Ethnic Minorities in Britain* The Fourth National Survey of Ethnic Minorities, London: Policy Studies Institute.

Moi, T. (1994) *Simone de Beauvoir: The Making of an Intellectual Woman* Cambridge, MA: Blackwell.

Monteiro, A. (1995) 'W.E.B DuBois: scholar, scientist and activist'; http://members.tripod.com/~DuBois/mont.html (accessed 21 September 2005).

Morrow, R. and Brown, D.D. (1994) *Critical Theory and Methodology* London: Sage.

Mouzelis, N. (1991) *Back to Sociological Theory: The Construction of Social Orders* Basingstoke: Macmillan.

Mouzelis, N. (1994) *Sociological Theory: What Went Wrong? Diagnosis and Remedies* London: Routledge.

Oakley, A. (1974) *The Sociology of Housework* London: Pantheon Books.

Park, R. (1972) 'The crowd and the public, and other essays' (edited with an introduction by Henry Elsner, Jr) Chicago: University of Chicago Press.

Park, R. (1950) *Race and Culture* New York: The Free Press.

Parker, D. (1997) 'Viewpoint: why bother with Durkheim? Teaching sociology in the 1990s' *Sociological Review*, 45 (1): 122–46.

Parker, D. (2001) 'Good companions: decorative, informative or interrogative? The role of social theory textbooks', *Sociology*, 35 (1): 213–18.

Parsons, T. (1942), 'Democracy and social structure in pre-Nazi Germany', *Journal of Legal and Political Sociology*, 1, 96–114.

Parsons, T. (1949) *The Structure of Social Action* New York: The Free Press (originally published by McGraw-Hill, 1937).

Parsons, T. (1951) *The Social System* New York: The Free Press.

Parsons, T. (1966) *The Negro American* (edited and with introductions by T. Parsons and K.B. Clark, and with a foreword by Lyndon B. Johnson) Boston: Houghton, Mifflin.

Parsons, T. and Bales, R. in collaboration with Olds., J., Zelditch, M., Jr. and Slater, P.E. (1956) *Family, Socialization and Interaction Process* London: Routledge and Kegan Paul.

Piccone, P. (1986) 'Alvin W. Gouldner: outlaw sociologist'; http://www.worldandi.com/specialreport/1986/March/Sa11101.htm (accessed 2003).

Pieterse, J.N. (2002) 'Europe and its others', in D. Goldberg and J. Solomos (eds.), *A Companion to Ethnic and Racial Studies* Oxford: Blackwell Publishers. pp. 17–24.

Pilkington, A. (2003) *Racial Disadvantage and Ethnic Diversity in Britain* Basingstoke: Palgrave Macmillan.

Poulos, J. (1996) 'Frantz Fanon'; http://www.english.emory.edu/Bahri/Fanon.html (accessed 14 September 2005).

Ray, L. (1999) *Theorizing Classical Sociology* Milton Keynes: Open University Press.

Reed, K. (2003) *Worlds of Health* Westport, CT: Praeger.

Rex, J. (1970) *Race Relations in Sociological Theory* London: Weidenfeld & Nicolson.

Ritzer, G. (2000) *The McDonaldization of Society: New Century Edition* Thousand Oaks, CA: Pine Forge Press.

Ritzer, G. and Goodman, D. (2004a) *Classical Sociological Theory* (4th edition) New York: McGraw-Hill.

Ritzer, G., and Goodman, D. (2004b) *Modern Sociological Theory* (6th edition) New York: McGraw-Hill.

Ritzer, G. and Goodman, D. (2004c) *Sociological Theory* (6th edition) New York: McGraw-Hill.

Rojek, C. (2001) 'Stuart Hall', in A. Elliott and B.S. Turner (eds.), *Profiles in Contemporary Theory* London: Sage. pp. 360–70.

Rossi, A. (1973) *The Feminist Papers: From Addams to de Beauvoir* New York: Columbia University Press.

Said, E. (2001) *Reflections on Exile and Other Literary and Cultural Essays* London: Granta Books.

Seidler, V. (1994) *Unreasonable Men: Masculinity and Social Theory* London: Routledge.

Sharrock, W.A., Hughes, J.A. and Martin, P.J. (2003a) *Understanding Classical Sociology* London: Sage.

Sharrock, W.A., Hughes, J.A. and Martin, P.J. (2003b) *Understanding Modern Sociology*, London: Sage.

Shilling, C. and Mellor, P. (2001) *The Sociological Ambition: The Elementary Forms of Social Life* London: Sage.

Singh, N. Pal. (2002) 'Cold war redux: on the "new totalitarianism" ', *Radical History Review* 85 (1): 171–81.

Sivanandan, A. (2001) 'Poverty is the new black', *Race and Class*, 43 (2): 1–5.

Skeggs, B. (1997) *Formations of Class and Gender* London: TCS Sage.

Simmel, G. ([1900] 1990) *The Philosophy of Money* (edited by T. Bottomore and D. Frisby; translated by T. Bottomore and D. Frisby from a first draft by K. Mengelberg) London: Routledge.

Simmel, G. (1950) 'The stranger', in *The Sociology of Georg Simmel* (translated, edited and with an introduction by Kurt Wolff) New York: Free Press. pp. 402–8.

Smith, D. (1987) *The Everyday World As Problematic: A Feminist Sociology* Boston: Northeastern University Press.

Smith, D. (1999) *Writing the Social: Critique, Theory and Investigations* Toronto: University of Toronto Press.

Smith, S. (1993) 'Residential segregation and the politics of racialisation', in M. Cross and M. Keith (eds.), *Racism, the City and the State* London: Routledge.

Solomos, J. (1993) *Race and Racism in Britain* Basingstoke: Macmillan.

Solomos, J. and Back, L. (1996) *Racism and Society* Basingstoke: Macmillan Press.

Springer, C. (1996) *Electronic Eros: Bodies and Desire in the Postindustrial Age* Austin: University of Texas Press.

Stone, J. (1977) *Race, Ethnicity and Social Change: Readings in the Sociology of Race and Ethnic Relations* North Scituate, MA: Duxbury Press.

Stone, J. (1998) 'New paradigms for old? Ethnic and racial studies on the eve of the millennium', *Ethnic and Racial Studies*, 21 (1): 1–20.

Stones, R. (ed.) (1998) *Key Sociological Thinkers* Basingstoke: Macmillan Press.

Thomas, W.I. and Znaniecki, F. ([1918] 1958) *The Polish Peasant in Europe and America* New York: Dover Publications.

Tiryakian, E. (1994) 'Revisiting sociology's first classic: the division of labour in its actuality', *Sociological Forum*, 9: 3–16.

Tong, R. (1992) *Feminist Thought: A Comprehensive Introduction* London: Routledge.

Turner, B.S. (1994) *Orientalism, Postmodernism and Globalism* London: Routledge.

Wakefield, D. (2000) 'Introduction', in K. Mills and P. Mills (eds.), *C. Wright Mills: Letters and Autobiographical Writings* Berkeley, CA: University of California Press. pp. 1–18.

Walter, N. (1998) *The New Feminism* London: Little, Brown and Company.

Ware, V. and Back, L. (2002) *Out of Whiteness: Color, Politics and Culture* Chicago: University of Chicago Press.

Weber, M. ([1913] 1978) *Economy and Society* (2 vols; edited by G. Roth and C. Wittich) London: University of California Press.

Weber, M. (1976) *The Protestant Ethic and the Spirit of Capitalism* (2nd edition; previous edition of this translation 1930) London: Allen and Unwin.

Weinstein, D. and Weinstein, M. (1993) *Postmodern(ized) Simmel* London: Routledge.

Whitfield, S.J. (2002) 'Hannah Arendt', *Jewish Virtual Library*; http://www. jewishvirtuallibrary.org/jsource/biography/arendt.html (accessed 15 September 2005).

Wilkinson, I. (2004) *Suffering: A Sociological Introduction*, Cambridge: Polity.

Wood, B. (1998) 'Stuart Hall's cultural studies and the problem of hegemony', *British Journal of Sociology*, 49 (3): 399–414.

Wright, E.O. (1976) 'Class boundaries in advanced capitalist societies', *New Left Review*, 98: 3–41.

Wyrick, D. (1998) *Fanon for Beginners* New York: Writers and Readers Publishing Inc.

Index